Michelle Singletary has been writing the "Color of Money" column in *The Washington Post* since 1997. Over the years she has received hundreds of letters, telephone calls, and e-mails from readers all around the country and abroad praising the advice she dispenses each week. Here are just a few examples of some of those comments.

"Although there are many good columns out there, I find 'The Color of Money' so reader-friendly. It isn't over the heads of people without an MBA and isn't so pedestrian that you think you are back in elementary school. Michelle's advice is consistent—live within your means, don't try to keep up with the neighbors, educate yourself regarding your finances, and have a meaningful purpose for saving *and* living! Thanks for providing useful, appropriate, and entertaining financial advice for many levels of readers."

—Janis Allen, Carmarillo, California

"Your approach is a refreshing voice of reason in a world inundated with messages to 'buy, buy.' Your work really does make a difference."

—Betsy Anderson, Stockholm, Sweden

"You've made an enormous difference in my financial life. Your writing style makes reading about finances bearable."

—Krista Pacion, Casa Grande, Arizona

"I always read and enjoy your regular business articles in *The Washington Post*. I also like your articles that refer to your grandmother Big Mama. I save most of your articles and routinely send them to my grown children. One of the things that I like about Big Mama's wisdom is her attitude. Attitude is the most important quality that a person can have. I will take it over money or good looks all the time. Thanks again for all your help over the many years."

—Michael Tasevoli, Columbia, Maryland

"Michelle Singletary tackles personal finance from the trenches. By relating her own experiences and the lessons she's learned in life, she makes personal finance both approachable and human—something few other writers can manage."

—Ric Edelman, Fairfax, Virginia, author of the
national bestseller The Truth About Money

"I just had to let you know you've educated me about a lot of things that are extremely foreign to me, I'm a money virgin. I don't know squat about money. It's like another language. But your columns are really easy to understand, and I feel that they've been a great educational tool for me. As a thirty-something African American female, I feel you've made an impressive impact on how I look at money."

—Adriene Harris, Seattle, Washington

"Thank you for writing your column 'Saving and Giving' (August 24, 2003). It is a message that often gets neglected when people are talking about money. I think it's important for people to be reminded of the perspective that life isn't just supposed to be about accumulating more and more for oneself. I believe, as you do, that charitable giving should be an innate part of the family budget, not an afterthought; not something discretionary, but an essential. If we are lucky enough to have enough, I think it's our obligation to share. So thank you for talking about money in a way that isn't just a yuppie 'me-me-me' kind of way!"

—M. D. Manning, northern Virginia

"I love your column. You are the one who got me to look at the business page. Your advice and insight is so timely. I also appreciate your humanness and ability to share personal situations."

—Kriss DeBaca, Pittsburg, California

"As a regular reader of Michelle Singletary's column, I find her advice to be thoroughly researched, excellently written, and extremely practical for anyone seeking sound financial advice."

—Michael LeBoeuf, Paradise Valley, Arizona,
author of The Millionaire in You

"I always look immediately for your column when I get to the business section! I have been a reader of your articles for several years. Often I cut them out and toy with sending them to my adult children. Your advice and philosophy are common sense personified!"

—Jeannette Kidd, Harrisonburg, Virginia

"I started reading your column . . . and now I'm on a debt-reduction plan."

—Gail Amen, Greenwich, Connecticut

"Your column is the friend we take to coffee when we have a financial question. Your no-nonsense, down-to-earth advice is a breath of fresh air when facing the complicated (and, occasionally, intimidating) financial concerns of the twenty-first-century family."

—Patrick Schultz and Robin Adler, Seattle, Washington

"I never fail to read 'The Color of Money.' Keep up your sensible, enjoyable column, and I will continue to read it, quote it, and, sometimes, snip it and hand it out to those who could use the advice."

—Rose Drew, Norwalk, Connecticut

7 MONEY MANTRAS FOR A RICHER LIFE

7 MONEY MANTRAS FOR A RICHER LIFE

How to Live Well with the Money You Have

MICHELLE SINGLETARY

RANDOM HOUSE NEW YORK

7 Money Mantras is a commonsense guide to personal finance. In practical advice books, as in life, there are no guarantees, and readers are cautioned to rely on their own judgments or seek advice from legal or financial professionals about their individual circumstances and act accordingly. In addition, please note that certain information, products, telephone numbers as well as postal and e-mail addresses will change by the time you read this book.

Copyright © 2004 by Michelle Singletary

Portions of this work appeared previously in full or in part in *The Washington Post* and are reprinted with permission.

Library of Congress Cataloging-in-Publication Data

Singletary, Michelle.
7 money mantras for a richer life: how to live well with the money you have/
by Michelle Singletary.
p. cm.
Includes index.
ISBN 0-375-50753-1
1. Finance, Personal.   I. Title: Seven money mantras for a richer life.   II. Title.
HG179.S514 2004
332.024—dc21   2003046805

Printed in the United States of America on acid-free paper
Random House website address: www.atrandom.com

987654321

First Edition

Designed by Joseph Rutt

For Big Mama.
I was listening.

Contents

—

INTRODUCTION: BIG MAMA'S SAVING GRACE   ix

**PART ONE: SEVEN MONEY MANTRAS TO
GUIDE YOU TO FINANCIAL SERENITY**

CHAPTER 1: MANTRA #1: "IF IT'S ON YOUR ASS, IT'S NOT AN ASSET"   3

CHAPTER 2: MANTRA #2: "IS THIS A NEED OR IS IT A WANT?"   12

CHAPTER 3: MANTRA #3: "SWEAT THE SMALL STUFF"   21

CHAPTER 4: MANTRA #4: "CASH IS BETTER THAN CREDIT"   26

CHAPTER 5: MANTRA #5: "KEEP IT SIMPLE"   33

CHAPTER 6: MANTRA #6: "PRIORITIES LEAD TO PROSPERITY"   36

CHAPTER 7: MANTRA #7: "ENOUGH IS ENOUGH"   40

PART TWO: THE BASICS OF SAVING, SPENDING, AND INVESTING YOUR MONEY

CHAPTER 8: PARAGONS OF PARSIMONY: PENNY-PINCHERS
SHARE THEIR MONEY-SAVING STRATEGIES   47

CHAPTER 9: ANOTHER DAY OLDER AND DEEPER IN DEBT   71

CHAPTER 10: FINANCIAL BOOT CAMP   109

CHAPTER 11: BROTHER, CAN YOU SPARE A DIME?   125

CHAPTER 12: HEART CURRENCY   151

CHAPTER 13: IT'S NOT PLAY MONEY   161

CHAPTER 14: WHEN LIFE AND DEATH HAPPEN   171

CHAPTER 15: THERE'S A SWINDLER BORN EVERY MINUTE   208

CHAPTER 16: BUILDING A NEST EGG? START WITH ONE TWIG
AT A TIME   219

ACKNOWLEDGMENTS   249

INDEX   253

Introduction

—

BIG MAMA'S SAVING GRACE

The best financial planner I've ever known was my grandmother. Big Mama raised me, my two sisters, and my two brothers on a salary that never reached more than $13,000 a year.

Big Mama knew the difference between buying things that improve your net worth and stuff that just makes you look wealthy. "Child, it don't make no sense to pay more money for a pair of jeans just because somebody's name is on it," she would preach. "The only one who's going to get rich is the person whose name is on your behind. And that makes you the ass."

Every paycheck, Big Mama would pay herself first. Each week, come hell or high water, she would deposit some money in her credit union before paying any of her bills. She never stopped contributing to her rainy-day fund no matter how tight money got. The reason you need a rainy-day fund, she said, is because there's always rain. Sometimes it's a drizzling rain, such as when the washing machine breaks and you have to replace it. Sometimes it rains so hard you feel as if you're in the middle of a monsoon, such as when you lose a job.

In our case, the storm was my grandfather.

Papa, rest his soul, was a drunk. He wasn't an abusive alcoholic. When Papa was sober he was quiet and gentle. When he drank he became expressive and funny. But it wasn't funny when he drank up his paycheck. Papa would frequently make stops at his favorite bars on Friday—payday. By the time he stumbled home, his clothes were filthy and smelled of cigarette smoke and urine. And much of his paycheck was gone.

There were numerous times when Big Mama would pile me and my brothers and sisters into the station wagon to search for Papa before he got drunk. We would drive around Baltimore for hours. If we found him in time, there would be more money that week to help with the household bills. If we didn't, I would spend the night with a pillow pushed down on my head to drown out Big Mama's yelling when Papa finally came home.

Sometimes things got desperate. That's when Big Mama would make one of us crawl on our hands and knees along her bedroom floor to try to slip money out of my grandfather's pants, which he would drop on the floor before passing out. My brothers and sisters and I would argue over whose turn it was to get the money. We would shove one another forward until one of us just gave in and agreed to go into the bedroom.

Once I got stuck under my grandparents' four-poster bed trying to pull cash out of Papa's pants. Papa had begun tossing and turning up above. I nearly wet my pants. I was ready to bolt, but through the darkness I could see my oldest sister, who was standing in the hallway as the lookout. She held up her hand to warn me to just stay put until my grandfather fell back to sleep. It seemed like hours before he stopped moving around and I could crawl out of the room with the money.

Despite Papa's drinking problem, Big Mama managed to make ends meet. But she worried about having enough money all the time.

So you see, I understand why, if you grew up not having enough, you want so much now—even if it means going into debt. I understand the urge to give your children what you feel you were deprived of as a child. I know how it feels to want to buy stuff to fill up the sadness and emptiness you feel because of your childhood traumas.

Or maybe you were the often-talked-about quintessential Jones family and thus the trendsetters. Perhaps yours was the family that had a new car every four or five years, took nice vacations every summer, or bought brand-name clothes and the latest electronic equipment. Maybe yours was the family everyone envied. If so, I'm willing to bet your parents nearly went broke trying to keep up that image. There may have been many arguments about money in your family even though from the outside it appeared you were doing just fine. And now you are repeating the pattern, trying to keep up the appearance of prosperity at any cost.

But I'm here to tell you that living high is costing you too much. You are a sucker if you continue to lead an inflated lifestyle by borrowing other people's money. Most of us are living the American dream on credit. We're stressed because we spend too much. We spend too much because we're stressed.

The way my grandmother handled her money taught me that most of us, whatever our situation, can get by on what we make. I know Big Mama's commonsense lessons about money can help you spend less and save more. My grandmother believed in the principle that it's not how much you make that matters, but how you make do with what you have.

So if you don't have much money, you have to scrimp and save to make sure it stretches far enough. If you're fortunate enough to have some money, you have to scrimp and save to make sure it lasts long enough.

In this book you will find insights from me, my grandmother, and financial experts to help you hold on to your money, and if you're wise and lucky, you'll be able to make it grow. What I bring to this personal-finance genre is no-nonsense, commonsense advice about money.

I know from being brought up by my grandmother that if you want to achieve financial security, you have to develop a certain attitude. You have to stop whining about not having enough money and do better with what you have. Truth be told, everything I ever needed to know about money I learned from Big Mama, who never invested a dime in a certificate of deposit, bond, or stock. And yet by using simple wisdom she was able to save enough to provide financial security for herself. Big Mama was by no means rich. But she made enough and saved enough to pay her basic bills. She had enough to indulge her one passion—buying fancy church hats. She was fine financially because she didn't want much.

Today, folks are taking all kinds of risk with their money because they are scared to death of not having enough. However, if you manage what you have better, even if you never make a dime in the stock market, you can get by—even in retirement. Big Mama lived well in retirement because she had no credit card debt. She bought reasonably priced cars, which she paid off early. Most important, she paid off her home before she retired.

To start, I've broken my book down into two parts. In the first section I'll introduce you to a list of commonsense money mantras. A mantra is a chant, phrase, or prayer that you repeat to yourself. The following mantras are ingrained in my psyche. I repeat them often. I use them to put a stop to my spending or to inspire me to save more. I always fall back on them when I'm not sure what financial decision to make. Here they are:

Mantra #1: "If it's on your ass, it's not an asset."

Mantra #2: "Is this a need or is it a want?"

Mantra #3: "Sweat the small stuff."

Mantra #4: "Cash is better than credit."

Mantra #5: "Keep it simple."

Mantra #6: "Priorities lead to prosperity."

Mantra #7: "Enough is enough."

Each of these mantras will help set you straight on the path to financial security. I start with "If it's on your ass, it's not an asset" because many people spend too much of their money acquiring things that don't appreciate in value. We are a nation that loves to look good, but at what expense?

Think about the money you waste on clothes, cars, and the latest electronic toys. In the end that kind of spending will not help you reach the goals you say you want—a college education for your children, a down payment on a home, a nice retirement nest egg.

The second mantra, "Is this a need or is it a want?" is in the form of a question for a reason. If you want to use your income wisely to put yourself on the road to wealth, you have to question every purchase you make. When you begin to distinguish between things you need and stuff you want, you'll find you can quit using credit to inflate your lifestyle. You can begin to tune out the advertising that makes you think you need certain things.

Once you become good at questioning every purchase, the next step is to pay attention to every penny you spend to acquire the things you need. Once you become economical with your cash you will begin to rethink how you use credit. Using cash will free you from your plastic bondage.

Big Mama inspired the "Keep it simple" mantra. I think we underestimate the wisdom of folks who like to keep things simple. If more of us relied on this commonsense rule, we might not be conned into buying stuff we don't need or making investments that are downright fraudulent.

The last two mantras are in no way the least important. They are last because I want you to end this section of the book on a positive and inspirational note. When you believe that your priorities will lead to prosperity, you will stop doing stupid things with your money, such as leasing a car or going on shopping sprees to fill a house you really couldn't afford with stuff you hardly use. "Enough is enough" should be the linchpin in your entire financial plan. Look at your life. Determine what is the most important thing to you. Is it your family, your faith, your financial security? If it's any one of those things, you probably have enough already. Whatever your priorities, you must realize you can't have it all unless you have Bill Gates's billions, and even then that may not be enough. If you stop pursuing more, you will find you have more money than you think to do the things you say matter most.

I hope you will use these mantras as a mental exercise to help transform your unconscious spending into conscious saving. So write them down on note cards and stick them on the refrigerator or bathroom mirror. Tape them to the dashboard of that luxury car you can't afford. Carry them in that Coach bag that cost a fortune. Input them in that expensive PalmPilot that you really didn't need. (When did just plain old inexpensive date books become passé?) I assure you that if you begin to meditate about these mantras, you'll achieve financial serenity.

The second half of the book deals with the day-to-day money decisions we all have to make. I'll give you commonsense advice on basic financial issues such as filling out your W-4 form, avoiding credit card debt, buying life insurance, and basic information about investing. Most important, I'll offer guidance on how to handle the many financial issues that come up in your life. I'll answer questions such as should you lend money to friends and relatives (only if you never, ever need the money again); should you cosign (No!); and whether you should have separate bank accounts when you get married (absolutely not).

I hope you didn't buy this book looking for easy directions to Easy Street. If you did, I'm sorry for you. For everyday folk there is rarely an easy way to become rich. Even though the ranks of the rich are increasing, the majority of the nation has always fit into the middle-income category. However, I know from watching my grandmother handle her money that it is possible, if you use your God-given common sense, to spend less, save more, and have a secure financial future. Big Mama never aspired to be rich, but she always said, "I may be poor, but I ain't going to die broke."

Part One

—

SEVEN MONEY MANTRAS TO GUIDE YOU TO FINANCIAL SERENITY

I
—

MANTRA #1:
"IF IT'S ON YOUR ASS,
IT'S NOT AN ASSET"

Think about the word *asset*. What exactly does it mean? An asset is an item of property, a person, thing, or quality, regarded as useful or valuable.

That definition is broad enough to allow most people to justify most of what they buy as an asset. You convince yourself to buy a big, expensive car because it will "hold" its value in case you want to sell it later. But selling this asset usually means acquiring debt to obtain another car. Doesn't that defeat the purpose? Does a banker consider your Lexus an asset? Does it improve your chances of getting a home loan? Not if you still owe money on it.

We amass a great deal of things, but how much of that stuff maintains its value? Did you know that there are more than thirty-five thousand self-storage facilities in this country? Americans' houses and garages are overflowing with so much stuff that we have to rent extra space to keep it in. I know someone who rented space in a self-storage facility for her clothes because she ran out of room in her closet. Crazy!

I want you to think about all the stuff you have because, ultimately, I want you to determine whether too much of your income is being devoted to servicing debt to pay for personal property that depreciates every year.

There are four types of assets that make up your net worth. Three

you to rent self-storage space and are more likely to put
h to financial security. They are called appreciating assets.

> **Common definition of appreciating assets:** Assets that have
> the potential to increase in value and/or produce income.
>
> **Commonsense definition:** Assets that you don't wear or drive
> and that will help keep you from asking at age seventy-five,
> "Would you like a shake with those fries?"

Appreciating assets include the following:

- *Liquid assets.* Cash or other financial assets that can easily and quickly be converted into cash with little or no loss in value. Liquid assets include checking, savings, and money-market accounts and certificates of deposit.

- *Investment assets.* Assets held for their potential to appreciate, or increase in value. They include stocks, bonds, and money in a mutual fund.

- *Real property.* Land and things attached to it (house, garage). This is by far the greatest source of wealth for American families.

The second asset category is personal property. This includes your automobiles, furniture, clothing, and electronic equipment. Technically, personal property is counted on the asset side of your personal balance sheet. However, once you walk out of the store or drive off the car lot with this type of asset, it immediately loses a great deal of its value. These assets are otherwise known as depreciating assets.

> **Common definition of depreciating assets:** Assets that lose
> their value over time.
>
> **Commonsense definition:** Assets that may make you look good
> but don't do a darn thing to make you rich.

Want to see how much of your income is spent to acquire assets that aren't likely to make you wealthy? It's not a perfect formula, but figuring out your debt-to-income ratio will give you some idea of where your money is going. This is a number, expressed as a percentage, that compares the amount of your debt (excluding mortgage or rent payment) with your monthly gross income.

Mortgage lenders look at the debt-to-income ratio all the time. When you apply for a mortgage, a lender will first determine the percentage of your gross monthly income that goes toward housing expenses.

Common definition of gross pay: Income before taxes, deductions, and allowances have been subtracted.

Commonsense definition: Income you wish you brought home before everybody and their mama, including Uncle Sam, gets their cut.

Typically, your monthly housing expense should not be greater than 28 percent of your gross monthly income. Mortgage lenders will then look at your total-debt-to-income ratio (all your debt obligations including your mortgage payment) to determine whether you are able to handle a home loan. The maximum ratio they typically like to see is 36 percent, although increasingly lenders have allowed borrowers to have a total-debt-to-income ratio as high as 50 percent. Still, your basic debt-to-income ratio compares your debt load with your income. The lower your ratio, the better off you are financially.

"Maintaining a good debt-to-income ratio will keep vital financial doors open," said Rudy Cavazos, director of corporate and media relations for Money Management International, one of the nation's largest nonprofit credit-counseling agencies. "Owning a home and a car is just the beginning. A home requires improvements, and cars must be replaced."

To calculate your debt-to-income ratio, use your gross monthly income. Include any bonuses, tips, commissions, alimony, child support, dividends, interest earnings, and government benefits. Next, figure out your monthly debt obligations (excluding mortgage or rent payment). Include payments for your car, installment loans on furniture and appliances, bank loans, student loans, and credit cards (use the minimum amount due).

Now divide your monthly minimum-debt payments by your monthly gross income. For example, if you have a gross monthly income of $2,000 and minimum payments of $400 on a car loan and your credit cards, you have a debt-to-income ratio of 20 percent ($400 divided by $2,000 equals 0.2).

According to debt-counseling experts, if your debt-to-income ratio (excluding mortgage or rent) is

- *15 percent or less.* You are doing a good job keeping your debt at a manageable level.

- *15–20 percent.* You're still a good candidate for credit by most lenders.

- *21–39 percent.* "This range definitely raises a red flag," Cavazos said. At this level, start looking at your spending habits and eliminate credit card balances that carry high interest rates.

- *40 percent and above.* "This is a serious situation," Cavazos said. The average client seen by Money Management has outstanding debt (not including mortgage or rent) of $19,000 and annual income of $27,100. If your debt-to-income ratio is this high, Cavazos said, you probably should seek credit counseling. To find a consumer credit-counseling agency near you, contact the National Foundation for Credit Counseling at (800) 388-2227 or go to www.debtadvice.org.

About one in twelve American families had a negative net worth in 1998. About one in eight families had a net worth of less than $5,000.

"Wealth creation rarely happens by chance," said Theodore R. Daniels, president of the Society for Financial Education and Professional Development. "It is generally the result of informed choices about spending, savings, and investment."

How do you begin to accumulate appreciating assets?

Reduce the amount of your personal property. And that begins with curtailing your love of consuming. Think about what it means to consume. Here's how the Merriam-Webster dictionary defines the word:

- To do away with completely.

- To spend wastefully.

- To waste or burn away.

Many of us—actually you because I'm a reformed shopaholic—shop as a form of entertainment. Americans go shopping on average 1.9 times a week, according to retail consulting firm WSL Strategic Retail.

"I shop therefore I am" is the credo of the new American consumer, the firm announced when it released its "How America Shops 2000" survey, which tracks how, where, and why Americans shop. "The role of shopping in American life has changed dramatically since 1990," said Wendy Liebmann, WSL president. "No longer is shopping solely about practicalities alone. Today, shopping is about who we are, how we live. Shopping is life."

Have people lost their minds? How on earth did shopping become our way of life?

Does the tenet "I shop therefore I am" define who you are? If it does, you'd better get used to saying, "I shop therefore I don't own a pot to pee in or a window to throw it out of."

> **The most important fact about our shopping malls, as distinct from the ordinary shopping centers where we go for our groceries, is that we do not need most of what they sell, not even for our pleasure or entertainment, not really even for a sensation of luxury. Little in them is essential to our survival, our work, or our play, and the same is true of the boutiques that multiply on our streets.**
>
> **—Henry Fairlie, British author**

Our obsession with shopping is standing in the way of our financial security. We should be treating shopping as a chore, not a social outing.

Stop participating in an activity that requires spending money you don't have. In many respects, men have it right when it comes to shopping. Many men abhor shopping. As a result, they minimize the time spent in malls.

Let's look at how a lot of men shop. They decide what they want.

They pick a day to go to the store. They go to the store. If they can, they park right outside the store to avoid having to trek through the mall. They buy only what they planned to purchase and leave immediately afterward. Their shopping trip is short and sweet.

Malls should be for shopping. Don't hang out at the mall. Don't meet your girlfriends there. Avoid, if you can, eating at the mall. Don't window-shop. Tell yourself you are on a mission.

I actually don't enjoy shopping anymore, but I'll be honest: This hasn't always been the case. I once wrote a weekly column for the *Baltimore Evening Sun* called "Born to Shop." I lived to find bargains. Shopping gave me a high. I once spent a solid month going back and forth to a store nearly every day waiting for a $200 sweater to go on sale. During each trip, I would take the sweater in my size and hide it among clothes on another rack so it couldn't be sold. The sweater finally was reduced by 70 percent. Do you know I've worn that sweater all of three times in the fifteen years I've had it?

At one time in my life I thought bargain shopping was my God-given gift. I would actually have withdrawal pains if I went one weekend without shopping. However, I realized that every time I set foot in a mall, I came away with things I didn't need and had no intention of buying. I often bought something just to make the trip worthwhile.

If you want to accumulate appreciating assets and not sweaters, you have to stop thinking you have discretionary income.

> *Common definition of discretionary income:* **The amount of income left over after essentials such as housing and food have been paid for.**
>
> *Commonsense definition:* **The money you spend without having any idea where it went.**

The key to cutting your spending is tuning out the marketing machine that tells us we need to buy, buy, and buy. How can you avoid the advertising hype? Here's how:

- *Remove yourself from temptation.* Recovering alcoholics shouldn't frequent bars, nor should spendthrifts frequent malls.

- *Keep a spending journal.* Whenever you're tempted to go shopping, write down why before you go. Write down how it will make you feel to add more debt to your credit card. Write down what's motivating you to spend the money. Are you stressed about something at work? Are your children getting on your last nerve? Has your spouse ticked you off? Putting your thoughts to paper has a way of making you think about your actions.

- *Tape your latest credit card statement to the inside of your journal.* Maybe this will help you remember what it feels like to open that bill and see that bloated balance. Use this journal also to keep track of the money you spend for everyday purchases.

- *Ask why before you buy.* Are you really going to use that bread maker? Look around your kitchen. Is that Crock-Pot you bought still in the box? (Mine is.) Be honest with yourself. Sure, it looks easy on the infomercial to prepare banana-nut bread, but are you likely to become Martha Stewart? Are you really going to slice and dice a bunch of vegetables for your children? I know. You worry that your children live on cheese curls. You want them to eat healthier. But start first by buying fresh vegetables and fruits before you spend three easy payments of $19.99 to buy some machine to slice and dice them.

- *Give yourself a time-out.* Make it a habit to wait at least twenty-four hours before making a purchase, no matter how small. This is especially true for items you see on infomercials. This is going to take discipline. I've been there before. You're sick or bored or depressed, and you turn on cable. You see the commercial for Dean Martin's Celebrity Roasts. It's funny. The deal sounds so reasonable. You can start your collection today with the roast of Frank Sinatra for only $9.95 (plus $3.95 shipping and handling), the voice-over says.

  About every other month, you will receive two individual full-length roasts on videotape for $19.95 each plus shipping and handling. You can cancel anytime! But you know what always happens. You don't cancel the order, and now you've spent another $40 or $50 on something you don't need. How funny is that? Not very.

- *Remember that when you use your credit card you are getting a loan.* Each time you reach for your credit card, ask yourself if you would go into a bank branch and ask for a loan for whatever it is that you're about to buy. Really, do it. When you pick up a shirt, ask yourself, would I sit down with a bank-loan officer and ask her to finance a shirt and pair of pants? Would you fill out a loan application for bath beads? For your tenth pair of pumps would you run down to the local bank and fill out those long forms, listing your former address, current employment, salary, and all the other information needed to get a loan? Of course you wouldn't, and yet that is fundamentally what you are doing when you charge purchases on your credit card.

- *Go cold turkey with your credit card.* For two months at a time try to avoid using credit (even if you pay the bill off every month). You will be surprised at how much you save.

- *Find yourself a "saving sponsor."* In Alcoholics Anonymous and other Twelve Step programs, people are encouraged to find a sponsor to guide them along their road of recovery. I encourage you to do the same if you need to save. My sponsor happens to be my husband. Together we keep each other on the saving path. A saving sponsor helps keep you on track. Think of this person as the angel on your shoulder who will help you become a saver, not a spender. This person's main job is to talk you out of buying stuff. Take your sponsor shopping with you. Call her when you are tempted to go to that midnight shopping sale. By the way, ask yourself what it is that you have to buy that can't wait until daylight hours.

- *Step away from the spendthrift.* Many people have a friend or relative who loves shopping. Their mantras are "Born to shop" and "Shop till you drop." This friend or family member can't wait to tell you about some sale or the latest discount-store opening. When it comes to shopping, separate yourself from the spendthrifts in your life because the high they get from spending can be infectious and dangerous to your financial health. This is the person who says to you when you go shopping, "Go ahead, treat yourself." "You only live once." "Don't be so cheap. You work too hard to deny yourself." "You can't take it with you." These platitudes will not help you prosper. You can love spendthrifts, but don't go shopping with them.

- *Clean house.* If you want the best incentive to stop spending, clean your house. Go through every closet and cabinet and set everything out on the counter. Take an inventory. I don't know about you, but I have the habit of buying things I already have at home. You know what I mean. You think you're out of something because there's so much clutter in your house that you can't find anything. Whenever I do an inventory, it immediately kills any urge to splurge. I realize that I already have too much stuff.

- *Implement the two-year throw-away rule.* If you haven't used it or worn it in two years, throw it away, give it to charity, or take it down to the consignment shop, where you might make some money on it. If you do this, you are becoming serious about keeping assets that have value. You need to make room in your life for the things that really matter. And just because you have freed up some closet space doesn't mean you should run out and shop. It's a nice feeling to open the closet door and not have things falling down.

- *Learn to say no to your kids, relatives, spouse, sales clerks, and marketers—and mean it.* Nobody can make you spend your money.

Now that you know where you stand financially and you have put in place some anticonsuming measures, stop accumulating stuff. Ask yourself this question: Are my assets crammed into my house or is a self-storage facility costing me money?

If you answered yes keep chanting, "If it's on your ass, it's not an asset."

2

MANTRA #2:
"IS THIS A NEED OR
IS IT A WANT?"

If you want to get a handle on your finances, you have to begin to distinguish between wants and needs. If you're not careful, your wants soon become necessities. Understanding the difference between a need and a want is the first step toward eliminating wasteful spending and putting yourself on the path to successful saving.

For example, take Kymberli and Chris, a couple I met during a taping of *The Oprah Winfrey Show*. A producer asked me to look at this couple's monthly expenses and see if there was anything they could cut.

Chris worked for an engineering company and earned about $65,000 a year. His wife, Kymberli, earned $20,000 as a waitress. They lived in a nice three-story home with their three small children.

They also had nearly $50,000 in debt, most of it from charges on more than fifteen credit cards. The couple's home was stuffed. One basement wall resembled the children's movie section at Blockbuster. An upstairs bedroom looked like an entire section at a toy store.

Chris and Kymberli had just about everything an upper-income family could want, but not financial security. A disruption in their income could send them into deep financial trouble. Chris was investing in his company's 401(k) plan, but they had borrowed from it. At one point the couple had just $200 in their savings account.

"We have gone from a cultural ethos of saving for a rainy day to a boomer generation of 'just do it' consumption," said Robert D. Manning, author of *Credit Card Nation: The Consequences of America's Addiction to Credit*. "Americans have consumed far more than could be paid with their household income. People have shifted from using credit cards for convenience to financing an inflated standard of living."

It was challenging to get Chris and Kymberli to see the excesses in their life because, like many consumers today, they have blurred the difference between necessities and luxuries.

I recommended the couple cut out cable television.

"What?" Kymberli said. "No way, we can't do without that."

I told them to get rid of the cell phone.

"I have a real problem with that," the husband quickly responded. "That's something we really need. What if the van breaks down?"

It's true that a cell phone can be helpful if your car breaks down. Even so, it is a luxury you may not be able to afford.

In an emergency, any cell phone, even one in which you no longer have a cell-phone contract, is required by the FTC to be able to make a 911 call.

Your family and children can go without cable if you are overwhelmed with debt.

"I couldn't see getting rid of cable because I just kept thinking it's just forty dollars a month," Chris said. "But that comes to almost five hundred dollars a year for something you can get for free. I think we got accustomed to a certain style of living. We thought all the things that were luxuries were necessities. . . . You just throw all of it on your credit card and forget about it."

While you're out shopping, what can you do to ensure you won't overspend? I repeat the mantra I learned from my grandmother. She taught me to always ask myself: "Is this a need or is it a want?" It's such a simple question, and yet so many of us fail to ask it. Sometimes I get as far as the checkout counter and then stop, turn my shopping cart around, and put back half the things I picked up. I ask myself, "Girl, do you really need another pair of black shoes? Do you really need a grill that tilts your food so the grease drips down? How many sheet sets do you really need for your bed? What did the kids do with the last cartful of toys?"

When my son was a baby I unpacked all the onesies my oldest daughter wore. Admittedly, some of them were "girlish," with cute little bears or flowers on them. Even so, I went right ahead and put them on my son. If you're like most people, you're probably shaking your head right now. I don't care. (I did draw the line with the solid-pink onesies.) Anyway, some of my family members were fit to be tied.

"You can't put those onesies on that boy," my sister said.

"Why not?" I asked.

"Because he's a boy," she shot back.

"Please, I'm not spending good money to replace perfectly good onesies. Anyway, he's a baby. What does he care? He can't distinguish colors. He can barely see me."

One of the rules I learned in Big Mama's financial boot camp is to tune out what other people think I should do with my money.

When my oldest daughter, Olivia, was very little she had just two pairs of shoes, a pair of sneakers and a pair of black shoes for church. Again some of my family members accused me of being too cheap because I wouldn't buy her more shoes to match her outfits. To them I was depriving my child. You could afford to buy her more shoes, my relatives teased.

But how many pairs of shoes does a three-year-old really *need*? She's only got one pair of feet. It's not like the other toddlers at her school were going to taunt and tease her for wearing the same shoes every day. Her little friends had better things to do, like learning to use the potty.

We stuff our kids' closets not because they *need* all those clothes but because we *want* them to look nice and as cool as the other children. We want them to fit in, and I understand that. There's nothing wrong with your children looking nice. However, ask yourself if that's something you value over sending them to college. They can look nice with half of the clothing and shoes you now buy.

I'm not expecting you to live like a pauper, but you can't have everything. Financial success is a lot about making choices. If you absolutely have to have that expensive cup of coffee every day, then you have to cut out that $1.89 soda you buy at lunch. You can't lavish your children with things, accumulating massive amounts of credit card debt to do it, and expect to have enough money to send them to college.

> **A shortcut to riches is to subtract from our desires.**
> **—Francesco Petrarch**

The first step in getting back to the basics of handling your money is examining your spending. You have to separate your needs from your wants. You may want a new car, but you don't need a new car if all your ten-year-old car needs is a set of new brakes and a paint job.

Do you really need a DVD player, or does your VCR play movies just fine?

When a friend showed my husband his DVD player, I watched as my husband's eyes grew as large as those of a kid bounding down the stairs to look at the loot under the Christmas tree. He had to have one. Thus began the great DVD debate in our household. The conversation went like this.

"Honey," my husband said, "a DVD has better sound and picture quality than our VCR. You don't have to rewind. You get all these special features, like cuts by the director that didn't make it into the movie."

"Give me a break," I told him. "Not once while watching a tape on our VCR have you said, 'Darn, I sure wish that sky was bluer,' or 'I wish I could hear that car crash like I was right there.' Not once have I heard you complain about missing scenes the director cut out. Most of the time we both fall asleep before the movie is even over."

To be fair to my husband, I'm not one to embrace new technology. He had to pry my fingers off the keyboard of my 286 computer just a few years ago. Even as he packed up my old computer to give away to charity, I mourned. It was a perfectly good computer. All I used it for was word processing. I didn't mind that I couldn't connect to the Internet.

To combat the urge to spend on things you don't really need, it's important to develop a routine of examining buying decisions. That's actually the benefit of the long, drawn-out talks my husband and I have about any major purchase (and $200 is a major purchase to us). This is especially useful for electronics. By the time my husband persuades me to come into the twenty-first century, the technology has usually improved and costs less. Each and every time we want to make a purchase, such as buying a DVD player, my husband and I have a lengthy discussion about whether we should spend the money.

Every day we are bombarded with messages from Madison Avenue to upgrade the old stuff we have or buy new stuff we really don't need. As Canadian humorist Stephen Leacock said, "Advertising may be described as the science of arresting the human intelligence long enough to get money from it."

In fact, the increase in DVD-player sales is an interesting study in the subliminal sales tactics many consumers succumb to. Why are so many people convinced they need a DVD player? Who cares about Tom Cruise's motivation in making *Mission Impossible 3*? Years down the road when it comes time to send your child to college, will you have to say to your kid, "Sorry, honey, we don't have the money to pay for your tuition because we needed to see how Jackie Chan managed that stunt in *Rush Hour 3*"? Sounds silly, doesn't it?

"People have to stop chasing the dream of having bigger and better," said Steve Rhode, president and cofounder of Myvesta, a non-profit consumer education organization.

The problem is, you don't stop at the DVD player. It just begins there. It goes without saying that a DVD player is useless without DVD movies to play—scads of them. Next, you need special new speakers and a digital amplifier to create the "surround sound," lest you not "fully appreciate" the moviegoing experience. And the experience wouldn't be complete without an even bigger and wider-screen TV.

Get the picture?

Another day older and deeper in debt.

A study by Tahira K. Hira, professor of consumer economics and personal finance at Iowa State University, found that many people buy based on their desires, not their needs.

This is particularly true of women. Hira's study found that women shoppers were far more likely to buy something without needing it compared with men (36 percent versus 18 percent). They often bought something because it was on sale (24 percent versus 5 percent). They shopped impulsively (36 percent versus 18 percent) or shopped to celebrate (31 percent versus 19 percent).

A quarter of American families have net financial assets of less than $10,000 and have lost wealth because of rising consumer and home-equity debt, according to a study by the Consumer Federation of America. The study also found that 53 percent of those surveyed said they live from paycheck to paycheck. In our consumption-obsessed society, we have developed an amazing ability to rationalize whatever we desire as "essential." We need a computer, high-speed Internet service, a cellular phone, a beeper, a PalmPilot, a big-screen television, an answering machine, a VCR, a DVD player, a portable CD player, a video recorder, a digital camera, a special bread machine, a tabletop grill, scads of shoes, and closets stuffed with clothes—plus an SUV to take us to the mall.

Is the growing list of so-called necessities keeping you from having what you value the most?

Here's a radical but effective way to cut your spending around the holidays. Join the "Hundred-Dollar Holiday" movement. The mission of this movement is simple. Each family tries to spend just $100 on gifts for Christmas. You don't have to reread that sentence. Your eyes didn't fail you. I said spend just $100. And, yes, that includes presents for your children.

When I sprang this concept on my husband, his face took on the same expression he always gets when he thinks I've suggested something ridiculous but he doesn't want to say so.

"You mean only one hundred dollars? For everybody?"

"Yes, honey," I said. "Just a hundred bucks."

"Our family will think we're just being cheap."

"My family already knows I'm cheap," I said.

But the Hundred-Dollar Holiday isn't about being a Grinch. When this movement was begun by New York writer Bill McKibben and a few of his friends, it was out of concern about all the stuff that we buy—much of which ends up in a landfill. The campaign was started out of concern for the poor who could be helped if we donated even a fraction of the money spent during Christmas. The creators of this movement wanted to inspire families to find an alternative to the commercialism of Christmas.

In a 2001 poll by the Center for a New American Dream, a third of all parents interviewed reported that they worked more hours during the holidays to earn more money. How does that make sense? Think about it. Many parents take a second job during the holiday season to pay for more presents for their children. They take precious time away from their family to buy more stuff. The best gift we can give our friends and family is our time.

In truth, you know why we have trouble thinking of gifts to buy for our friends or family members? Because they already have everything they really need. That's why we end up buying a Chia Pet, garish ties, a fake mounted fish that sings, and kitchen gadgets and appliances that will just clutter up another counter. One study by a credit card company found that 40 percent of Americans said they planned to buy for fifteen people or more during the holiday season.

Okay, so a $100 Christmas may be too extreme for you. Each family should set a realistic goal based on their finances. But the point is to stop *saying* you want to scale back and actually *do* it. Try to think of things to give people that they really *need*. Here are a few ideas:

- Working parents could use coupons for baby-sitting services much more than another coffee machine.

- A single friend, who eats out a lot, might enjoy a certificate for a home-cooked meal rather than a weird-colored sweater.

- Make a tape of your children singing for out-of-town grandparents.

- Speaking of grandparents, why not make a tape of yourself reading your grandkids' favorite bedtime stories? Send them the book and have their parents pop in the tape. I can't think of a better way for a child to get ready for bed.

- Use that video recorder you have and tape your oldest relatives talking about the family history. Now send that tape to family members for Christmas. You'll save money and preserve your family history at the same time.

- Collect your favorite recipes. Input them in that new high-speed computer you have, and give your friends and family a personal cookbook.

- Take those boxes of photos you have (the ones stuffed in a drawer or closet or shopping bag), scan some into the new computer, and make a photo album for family and friends. Not only would you have created a wonderful gift, but you could use the time with your kids or spouse to reminisce.

The point is to be more creative during the holidays, and that will result in your not just spending less but giving people things they might actually value. However, here's a warning. Scaling back for Christmas won't be easy. You'll feel guilty about not spending. You'll get resistance from some family and friends. Some of them may even talk about you behind your back. Be prepared for the "I can't believe they gave me some cheap handmade gift" comments.

Most important, don't make the mistake my husband and I made. We didn't warn people about our plan to join the Hundred-Dollar Holiday movement. You need to tell folks way ahead of time. They may still moan and groan, but at least you've given them fair warning. Some might even use the opportunity not to buy you something either in retaliation or out of relief. It doesn't matter. Remember this: Some studies show that it takes six months before many people pay off their holiday shopping bills.

Now, let's see if you are confusing wants with needs. Take out your credit card statements and look at the total amount you owe. I've prepared a sample worksheet you can use:

	DESCRIBE CHARGED ITEMS	AMOUNT CHARGED	DATE CHARGED
Visa card #1			
Visa card #2			
MasterCard #1			
MasterCard #2			
Discover card			
American Express			
Department-store credit cards			

Now, without looking at the detailed list of charges from the previous year, try to remember specifically where you spent the money and on what. Take the total you owe on each card and subtract out every expense you can recall right down to the penny. Do this exercise even if you pay off your credit cards every month. Record what you recollect. Now match your memory with the actual credit card statement.

Can you even remember how much you spent on specific items? You wouldn't forget a mechanic's bill to fix your car. Most of us need a car to get to work or take our kids to school. But can you remember all the dinners, movies, clothes, and miscellaneous items that you just casually put on your credit card? If every expense was a need, as you so often say, then this should have been an easy exercise. However, if you couldn't remember exactly what you bought with your credit card, you have needlessly charged away your wealth on stuff you can't remember a year or even six months later.

When I tried this exercise with the couple from the *Oprah* show, the wife couldn't even remember what she had purchased on her credit card the week before. "I know it was for clothes and stuff, but I can't remember exactly what," she said.

If you can't remember what you put on your credit card, that's a huge indicator that you are overspending on stuff to fulfill wants.

Be honest with yourself, especially if you are deep in debt. Stop confusing wants with needs. If you want to save more, stop buying so many toys for yourself and your kids. Don't charge that vacation trip even if you are overworked, tired, and need to get away. Think about how stressed you will be when you return and have to face the credit card bill. By eliminating spending on luxuries, you can find money to achieve the things you say you value, such as saving for your retirement, a home, or college education for your children.

When you are tempted to confuse your wants with needs, think of what Benjamin Franklin said: "The more a man has, the more he wants. Instead of it filling a vacuum, it makes one."

3

—

MANTRA #3:
"SWEAT THE SMALL STUFF"

Ben Franklin wrote, "Beware of little expenses; a small leak will sink a great ship." I know you've heard that you shouldn't sweat the small stuff. It was even a bestselling book. In some cases that expression is true and applicable, but not when it comes to money. Many people are nickel-and-diming themselves into debt. If you want to create wealth, you have to sweat the small stuff.

For example, how much could you accumulate by saving just $1 a day? Well, if from birth to age sixty-five, you invested a $1 a day ($365 every year compounded monthly in a tax-deferred account) at an annual 8 percent rate of return, you could have $1.1 million at retirement.

I bet that got your attention.

So many seemingly small expenditures keep people from accumulating assets.

Try this next exercise. Look around your house. Make a list of all the things you have bought for under $50. Start with the kitchen, then move to the dining room, den, family room, basement, and bedrooms. Especially include the kid's playroom or the big bin where you keep all their toys. How often do you find yourself saying, "Oh, it's just $9.99 or $19.99," or "What harm will it do to buy this little toy for Johnny, it only costs $5?"

Now think. How often do you really use those items? I'll bet there are plenty of Ronco "set it and forget it" rotisserie and roaster ovens sitting unused. I know a lot of them, like many inventions sold on infomercials, have been stored away and forgotten.

To get a handle on your finances and reduce your debts, you have to begin questioning *all* your purchases, especially the small ones. This is an essential point to grasp if you want to live within your means.

If you cut your spending, you will increase your bottom line. Not convinced? Look at how small savings add up over the years.

- *When your coworkers say "Let's do lunch," your response should be "Let's not."* Assume you buy your lunch every day, spending $5. That's $1,300 a year. If you invest that money every month over the next fifteen years at an annual 5 percent rate of return, you could boost your savings by more than $28,000.

- *Can we talk?* If you're Joan Rivers, you can afford to talk long-distance. But if you're not, cut out the chitchat. Stop trying to find the cheapest long-distance plan and write a letter. That will cost you just 37 cents. If you spend $50 a month on long-distance calls, try to cut that in half. For example, let's say your child is now five years old and will go to college in thirteen years. By investing that $25 saving every month at an annual return of 5 percent, you could have $5,400 for your child's education. Not much, you say. Well, 38 percent of students attend four-year colleges that charge less than $4,000 a year for tuition and fees (see Table 1, opposite page).

- *Stop eating.* Out, that is. Eating out is one of the biggest busters of average people's budgets. Eliminate one restaurant meal a month for a family of four, and you can save $720 a year. Now take that $60 a month and invest it for twenty years at 11 percent, and you have $48,500 at retirement.

> **One who restrains his appetites avoids debt.**
> **—Chinese proverb**

- *Cut the calories and increase your bottom line.* The Schwab Center for Investment Research, a division of Charles Schwab &

TABLE 1. AVERAGE FIXED CHARGES FOR UNDERGRADUATES, 2002–2003 (ENROLLMENT-WEIGHTED)

SECTOR	Tuition and Fees			Room and Board		
	2002–2003	2001–2002	% CHANGE	2002–2003	2001–2002	% CHANGE
Two-Year Public	1,735	1,608	7.9	*	*	*
Two-Year Private	9,890	9,200	7.5	5,327	5,245	1.6
Four-Year Public	4,081	3,725	9.6	5,582	5,266	6.0
Four-Year Private	18,273	17,272	5.8	6,779	6,479	4.6

*Sample too small to provide meaningful information.

These are *enrollment-weighted averages,* intended to reflect the average costs that students face in various types of institutions.

Source: Trends in College Pricing 2002. Copyright © 2002 by College Entrance Examination Board. Reproduced with permission. All rights reserved. www.collegeboard.com.

Company, found that you could save about $117 and 54,000 calories a year just by leaving the cream cheese off your bagel (assuming you eat a bagel a day and pay 75 cents to add cream cheese). That $117 invested at 10 percent for twenty years can yield more than $7,000.

- *When you go out to dinner, pass on the appetizer and dessert.* In a year you can save 44,622 calories and $676. Invest that savings for twenty years at a 10 percent rate of return, and you can have $40,800.

- *Don't burn money.* Cigarettes are a highly expensive habit and one that will only get more expensive as deficit-laden states increase taxes on tobacco products. In 2002 some New Yorkers began paying more than $7 a pack for many major cigarette brands, more than double the national average for cigarettes. Quitting smoking can save you a bundle. If you light up from age eighteen to age sixty-five (at $3 a pack), you'll send more than $51,000 up in smoke.

- *Don't pay to take your own money out.* On average, most bank customers make four trips to the ATM per week. That's $3 for each visit ($1.50 charged by your own bank and $1.50 charged by the bank that owns the ATM). Use your own bank and you could save $48 a month. Over three years, if you invested this amount at an annual 5 percent rate of return, you could boost your savings by $1,800.

- *Save by saying, "I love you."* Cut back the number of greeting cards you buy. Have you seen the price of cards lately? Greeting cards retail between $2 and $4, according to the Greeting Card Association. The average U.S. household purchases thirty-five individual cards per year. At $4 a card, that's $140 a year. Over five years, if you invested that $140 at the end of the year with an annual 5 percent rate of return, you could boost your savings

TABLE 2. AVERAGE EXPENSES IN NONFIXED BUDGET COMPONENTS, 2002–2003 (ENROLLMENT-WEIGHTED)

	All Students	Resident Students		Commuter Students		
SECTOR	BOOKS/ SUPPLIES	TRANS.	OTHER	ROOM AND BOARD**	TRANS.	OTHER
Two-Year Public	727	*	*	5,430	1,104	1,462
Two-Year Private	766	633	1,221	*	1,086	1,478
Four-Year Public	786	749	1,643	5,730	1,013	1,853
Four-Year Private	807	645	1,173	6,239	957	1,419

*Sample too small to provide meaningful information.

**Room and board costs for commuter students are average expenses for students living off-campus but not with parents. These are not fixed institutional charges as reflected in Table 1, but rather estimated local living expenses for off-campus students.

These are *enrollment-weighted averages,* intended to reflect the average costs that students face in various types of institutions.

Source: Trends in College Pricing 2002. Copyright © 2002 by College Entrance Examination Board. Reproduced with permission. All rights reserved. www.collegeboard.com.

by $775. One winner of my annual penny-pincher contest got together with friends and decided they would recycle greeting cards. So, instead of signing the cards they signed their names to a small yellow Post-it note and stuck it inside the card. The Post-it note can be removed and the card reused. Personally, I stopped buying birthday cards for preschoolers. They can't read!

"Every seemingly small step you take using the practical tools of thrifty living to save money is buying your freedom from worrying about financial security," says Sarah Crim, who teaches a community-college course about secondhand shopping. "This doesn't mean you have to deny yourself everything. Funnel your money toward what is important to you or your family and what makes you happy, and hold down the costs on the stuff that doesn't matter as much."

Look at it another way. Say you spend $2 a day during the work-week on sodas. It's just $2, right? What difference can that make? It can make a big difference. Just put that money in the bank. In a year you would have $500 (assuming you get a two-week vacation). That $500 certainly isn't enough to pay for four years of college, but it will pay for many expenses, such as textbooks (see Table 2, previous page). Ask any college student if she could use $500 in cash. Before you can finish the question, she'll rip the money out of your hand.

As Big Mama used to say: "You can't have a dollar without a penny." Sweat the small stuff!

4

—

MANTRA #4:
"CASH IS BETTER THAN CREDIT"

Nothing seems expensive on credit.
—Czech proverb

I find it interesting how having a credit card will make us act like we have no good sense. Take, for example, an experiment by MIT marketing professor Drazen Prelec and University of Chicago Business School professor Duncan Simester. In a sealed-bid auction for basketball tickets, half of the participants in the experiment were told they had to pay for the tickets with cash. The other half were told they could use a credit card. The researchers found that the average credit card bid was about twice the average cash bid.

For many people credit cards aren't real money, at least until the bill arrives. I call this phenomenon the CCC (credit card craziness) syndrome. If you are like the average cardholder, you have nearly $9,000 in charges on your credit cards, maybe more. ($8,940 in 2002, to be exact.) Let's suppose you're making only the 2 percent minimum monthly payment of $180. At 18 percent, it will take you 670 months to be rid of the debt—almost 56 years. If it took you that long you would pay almost $26,000 in interest.

We buy things on credit that we would think twice about purchasing if we had to use cash. Would you buy a $69.95 Flowbee Haircutting System that sucks your hair into a vacuum if you had to pay cash for it? No way would you hand some retail clerk good money for a hair trimmer with a hose attached.

Credit has become the modern-day shackles that enslave many people from Beverly Hills to Boca Raton. Our debt level and our lack of savings make the nine-to-five job mandatory. Between our mortgages, car payments, and credit card debts, we can't afford to quit. We are minimizing our lives and financial potential by making minimum credit card payments.

Americans estimated that they would spend an average of $9,300 annually on discretionary (there's that dreaded word again) items, according to a 2001 survey by American Express. This figure includes an average $1,188 for dining out; $948 for birthday, anniversary, and holiday gifts; $852 for entertaining; $732 on fast food and takeout; and $384 on cellular-phone service. And much of these goods and services are paid for with a credit card. People think of credit cards as an extension of their income.

Let me walk you through some mind-numbing numbers:

- Over half of families that earn less than $10,000 a year have over $1,000 in credit card debt.

- About 40 percent of people ages twelve to nineteen have access to a credit card; 36 percent of high school seniors have an ATM or debit card of their own.

- One study found that 22 percent of college students got their first credit cards in high school. Not surprisingly, over the past ten years there has been a 50 percent rise in the number of people under twenty-five filing for bankruptcy.

- NFO WorldGroup, a marketing-research company, found that consumers under age thirty-five carry an average credit card balance of more than $3,500; that translates to 10 percent of their annual gross income, according to NFO. Finance charges for the under-thirty-five group average $456 per year, NFO found when it surveyed 4,100 U.S. consumers between September and November 2002.

- According to Consolidated Credit, consumers usually spend up to 30 percent more when paying with plastic instead of cash.

- The average credit card balance among college students in 2002 was about $2,300.

- From 1970 to 2000, mortgage debt for the average family has risen from 36 percent of annual income to 70 percent. Since 1985, mortgage debt has quadrupled, growing faster than income in all but one of those years. This would be fine if property values were keeping pace with this rising debt, but they aren't. For many families, their home has become their piggy bank. Too many families are depleting the equity in their homes through refinancing and using that money to pay off credit card debt.

Frankly, I'm astounded at the growing number of teens and college students with credit cards. Just why are we giving credit cards to teens?

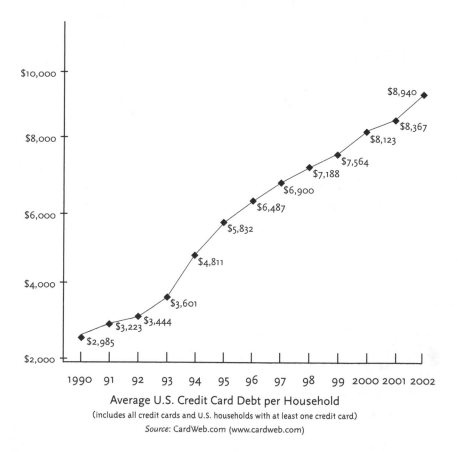

Average U.S. Credit Card Debt per Household
(includes all credit cards and U.S. households with at least one credit card)
Source: CardWeb.com (www.cardweb.com)

Why does an undergraduate college student with no full-time job need a credit card?

"They might need it in case of an emergency" is the answer I always get. Okay, I would believe that argument if the charges on the card were always—every single one—the result of an emergency. So, are they? I thought not. Not even close. If it were true that credit cards in the hands of teens and young adults were used only in an emergency, every day I would drive down the road and see miles upon miles of teenage and college kids standing by their broken-down, smoking cars.

Here's another touted reason to hand a young person a credit card: "They need a credit card to establish good credit." And where does that little gem come from? The banking industry, of course.

Money is a poor man's credit card.
                        —Marshall McLuhan

Better eight hundred in cash than a thousand on credit.
                        —Chinese proverb

The world is a puzzling place today. All these banks sending us credit cards, with our names on them. Well, we didn't order any credit cards! We don't spend what we don't have. So we just cut them in half and throw them out, just as soon as we open them in the mail. Imagine a bank sending credit cards to two ladies over a hundred years old! What are those folks thinking?

                        —Sarah Louise Delany, speaking
                        for herself and her sister Annie
                        Elizabeth, who, at 101, was two
                        years her junior

I hate this shallow Americanism which hopes to get rich by credit.
                        —Ralph Waldo Emerson

> Life was a lot simpler when what we honored was father and mother rather than all major credit cards.
>
> —Robert Orben, U.S. journalist and humorist
>
> Be assured that it gives much more pain to the mind to be in debt, than to do without any article whatever which we may seem to want.
>
> —Thomas Jefferson to his daughter Martha

Credit cards teach you to be a debtor. The experts (that is, credit card issuers and financial professionals) will say that the proper use of credit teaches people to manage their money.

How? Correct me if I'm wrong, but when you use a credit card, whose money are you using? Because it sure ain't (excuse me, but this just cries out for an *ain't*) your money. What you are learning to manage is debt.

Why do teens and college students need to know how to manage debt?

There is only one purchase that they really have to buy on credit—a home. I would say that's as close as it gets to "good" credit.

> A debt is a debt, whether it's margins or mortgages; and debts are all the same, no matter how you try to camouflage 'em. You never get much out of 'em except trouble. On the farm or in Wall Street, if you use the other fellow's money, it costs you a lot more than it's worth.
>
> —Sue Sanders, U.S. oil producer

I'm certainly not naïve. I know that credit has become a key measure by which we are judged. This is the price of credit today. Everyone from employers to landlords to car-insurance companies can now use your credit history against you. Pay your credit card bills late, and somehow that is an indicator that you are likely to file an auto-accident claim?

We are living a crazy credit card life. Realistically, lenders do have to have some proof that you are capable of paying your debts. One way to measure that is to look at how you've paid your debts in the past.

But since it will be years before your teen or college student needs to buy a home or even a car, she doesn't need to spend the first years of her working life paying off credit card debt to prove she is worthy to be a home or car owner. You only need a credit history if you plan on accumulating debt.

If you are doing your job right as a parent and instilling in your children the need to be debt-free, then their summer-job money is being saved to buy their car outright. The used-car market has never been better. It is possible to buy a safe, reliable car these days for $5,000 or less thanks to businesses like CarMax and the knuckleheads who lease cars. Both cars I own now were "preowned," which is a fancy word for used.

If your teen or college-bound student must get a credit card, encourage them to get an American Express card, which has to be paid off every month. They can use the card sparingly to show that they know how to responsibly pay off debt each month. That's really all they need to establish that they are creditworthy.

But it's not just young people who get into credit trouble. Consumers filed for bankruptcy protection in record numbers during the twelve-month period that ended March 31, 2003. Personal-bankruptcy filings totaled 157 million—up 7.4 percent from the same period in 2002.

According to the Florida-based Consolidated Credit Counseling Services, 56 percent of the 850 people in its buying-and-spending survey for 2002 said they had planned to spend less during the holiday season because they were still paying off debt from the previous holiday season.

Spending less? They shouldn't be spending at all!

Consumers continue to pile up more debt every year, forcing many to use an ever-increasing share of their income to make credit payments. Irresponsible credit card use can turn you into a deadbeat.

Common definition of deadbeat: One who persistently fails to pay personal debts or expenses.

Commonsense definition: This isn't someone who robs Peter to pay Paul. This person can't even rob Peter.

Never forget that credit is other people's money. There is always a high price to pay when you use other people's money. We have taken a shortcut to prosperity by way of credit cards. We keep up with the Joneses by borrowing. But if you were to get a glimpse of the Joneses' finances, you'd find they are deep in debt themselves. Besides, you know one of the problems with keeping up with the Joneses? "Just as you catch up to them, they refinance," said motivational speaker Bonny Wilson.

Think about the advertising slogans for credit cards. Visa says it's everywhere you want to be. The MasterCard slogan is "There are some things money can't buy; for everything else there's MasterCard." But if you use your Visa card to inflate your lifestyle with money you haven't earned, you could be getting a passport to credit card hell. Watch out, or MasterCard will become your master. As Anton Chekhov said, "When you live on cash, you understand the limits of the world around which you navigate each day. Credit leads into a desert with invisible boundaries."

5

—

MANTRA #5:
"KEEP IT SIMPLE"

A little simplification would be the first step
toward rational living.
—Eleanor Roosevelt

Knowledge is a process of piling up facts;
wisdom lies in their simplification.
—Martin Fischer, German-born physician and author

"There is always a danger of simplifying too much."

That statement was made to me in an e-mail after I wrote about a simple way to calculate what you need in retirement. I wholeheartedly disagree.

Never underestimate the power of simplicity. It is the everyday person's protection. My grandmother was a simple woman, but she handled her affairs like a professional money manager. She was never taken advantage of because she always kept things straightforward. She had a passbook savings account. She had a term life-insurance policy. She had a plain, old-fashioned, thirty-year mortgage. Perhaps she didn't earn all the money she could have on her savings. Maybe she did miss some good deals. But if Big Mama couldn't understand something or the salesperson couldn't explain it to her so that it made sense in her mind, she just left it alone.

I take after Big Mama, so I have one basic rule about my money:

Keep it simple. Keeping it simple can be the most sophisticated thing you do with your money.

This is perhaps the one mantra that will keep you from being bamboozled, hoodwinked, and suckered. It's not just greed that ends up making so many people the victims of con artists. It's not taking heed of this mantra. Con artists are masters at talking over your head. They try to confuse you with a lot of facts and figures. They dazzle you with details. Complication is their friend.

Let me give you an example. Thousands of investors are conned every year in a growing scam involving "prime banks." Losses from prime-bank scams amounted to well over $1.5 billion in 2001, according to the North American Securities Administrators Association (NASAA).

The recession and the topsy-turvy stock market make these sham investments all the more appealing. So many investors are looking for better returns than the local bank's CD rate. Promoters pushing this scam promise high double-digit returns with little or no risk. Investors are told they can take advantage of secret high-yield debt instruments offered by "prime" banks that only the very rich know about. Promoters use the term "prime" to describe the world's top domestic or international banks. They falsely claim that the investments are guaranteed or secured by some sort of collateral or insurance.

Make anything sound sophisticated, and you can fool otherwise reasonable people. And that is just what the crooks in this scheme do. They use sophisticated-sounding language telling investors they can get in on a "prime-bank debenture-trading program." It's pure hogwash. No such instrument exists. But it does sound impressive, doesn't it?

"A veneer of sophistication is often all that's needed to sell a prime bank scam," said assistant U.S. attorney Benjamin Wagner. Wagner and other law-enforcement officials joined the NASAA in issuing warnings about this scam. "The con artists use a lot of financial jargon, and the investors don't question them because they don't want to appear naïve. But there are no dumb questions when it comes to your money."

One reason prime-bank scam artists are able to mislead people is because the instruments they claim to be using—standby letters of credit, bank debentures, and bank-secured trading programs—sound so fancy and legitimate. In Illinois, for example, state securities regulators shut down an Internet-based scam that promised to pool investor money to obtain an "irrevocable line of credit from a fiduciary bank." Investors were told the line of credit would be used to purchase negotiable receivable invoices and raise capital funds against these invoices and other secondary market-debt instruments for par values higher than the actual face value of the original irrevocable letters of credit. The fiduciary bank would then exchange the receivable invoices for a certificate of deposit from a Prime Western Bank. The certificate of deposit would then be used to pay back investors with interest.

Did you get that? My eyes glazed over after the "irrevocable line of credit" part. Prime-bank scams could be the fraud of the twenty-first century, according to the International Chamber of Commerce.

When it comes to things like this, listen to your gut, your intuition, or that little voice in your head that is saying: "I don't know what the hell this person is talking about." The moment your head starts spinning, take your money and run. If you feel someone is talking over your head, pass on the deal. If you can't understand a loan document, don't sign it. If you're not sure about a certain type of investment, don't invest in it. It's better to do nothing until you can understand what you're doing than to lose your money trying to act like you know.

Use your ignorance as a weapon against getting involved in loans or investment deals that could rob you blind. Don't let your greed and desire for high returns cloud your better judgment. There are just too many simple, legitimate ways to make money.

As French writer François Duc de la Rochefoucauld said, "There are a great many simpletons who know themselves to be so, and who make a very cunning use of their own simplicity."

6

—

MANTRA #6: "PRIORITIES LEAD TO PROSPERITY"

**Where your treasure is, there your heart will be also.
—Matt., 6:21 New King James Bible**

I truly believe that if you put your values first, you will get in life what you value the most. This is doable at most income levels. However, you must have a set of priorities because that sets the stage for how you spend your money.

Make a list of your values, and then attach a goal to it. This list will become your spending-and-saving blueprint. I know you hear all the time that you should set goals, and you claim you do. But when pressed all you can say is "I want to be rich" or "I don't want to have to worry about money" or "I want to retire early" or "I want to send my children to college." Those are just empty statements if you don't have a financial road map that you've committed to following. As I've told you, my grandmother didn't have much money, but she had a list of goals. She wanted to pay off her home by the time she retired. And she wanted to have some money saved for her retirement. She accomplished both even though in her mid-fifties she took in five grandchildren to raise.

If, for example, you value a good education for your child and you set that as a priority, then you won't go on shopping binges to deck them out in the latest brand-name clothes. You would rather have someone hit you in the head with a hammer than pay $200 for a pair of sneakers. You won't shop all the time because that money is spoken for already. It's being directed to some account for college. You won't use your credit card all the time because you know next month you have to make that automatic payment to a mutual fund or savings account for your kids.

This is about making choices. You don't have to live like a pauper, but you can't have it all either.

So, is it important to you that your children have brand-name clothes or that they graduate from a brand-name college without student-loan debt? It's really your choice. Maybe you are shallow and vain and you want your kids to be the best-dressed in the neighborhood. Perhaps it's important to you that little Rebecca or Anthony have over-priced birthday parties at some kid's theme restaurant every year. Fine with me. They'll also be the college graduates with enough debt to choke a horse at their big fancy graduation party.

If you truly value a good, paid-for college education for your children, then you can tune out their whining that their friends have a PlayStation 2, Xbox, Game Boy, or whatever. They'll say, "Why can't we go to McDonald's?" You'll say, "Can't—college fund." They'll say, "Why can't I have a Tommy Hilfiger sweatshirt?" You'll say, "Are you crazy? I'm not paying ninety dollars for a sweatshirt. Besides—college fund." You see, if you put your priorities first, all the pressure from your kids, their peers, and your peers to spend instead of save becomes background noise.

You think I care that my little girl, Olivia, wants to spend money every time we walk into a store? I don't even hear her. Think I care if she throws herself on the floor, kicking and screaming? Nope, doesn't even faze me. I just walk over her little butt and head for the car. I know that eventually she'll get up and follow me or the store security guard will bring her out. When we go to the movies, do I care that she whines because I won't buy her any of the overpriced candy? I don't hear her. She ought to be glad she's seeing a movie.

As the Book of Matthew says, "Where your treasure is, there your heart will be also." To break it down for you, this passage of Scripture is saying talk is cheap. You want to know what you treasure? Take a good long look inside your checkbook. How many checks have you written to Domino's in the last three months? How many checks to retail stores? How large and how many checks do you write to various credit card companies? Now, compare this spending to the money you're putting in your kid's college education fund. How much is diverted out of your paycheck for your retirement savings? Where your treasure is, there your heart will be also.

What is a treasure? A treasure is something you value most, something on which you place the greatest importance, something you hoard, something you will try to get whatever the cost.

So, if you want to retire early, then save now. If you don't want your child to pile on student debt to get through college, then save now. If you don't want creditors hounding you, then stop charging.

If you care about a secure financial future for your family, ask yourself, "Am I putting my resources toward what I say is important to me?"

Look at where you are investing your money for an indication of what you value. You'll discover who or what has your heart. As John Calvin said, "It is a major plague, which we find rampant amongst mankind, that they have a mad and insatiable desire for possessions."

Stop blowing your money. There is no such thing as disposable income.

Common definition of disposable income: **The amount of income left to an individual after taxes have been paid and that is available for spending and saving. Disposable income may either be spent on consumption or saved.**

Commonsense definition: **Money you burn and later regret.**

Take "disposable income" out of your vocabulary. Could you burn any of the money you make? If not, why do you treat so much of your income as disposable? Just because it's not targeted for anything, it has no purpose other than to be spent at your whim.

You say you can't afford to throw away money, and yet every time you pay interest to a credit card company, that is exactly what you are doing. Every time you trade in a perfectly good car because you just gotta have the latest model of whatever, you are throwing away good money. Don't even get me started on the foolishness of leasing a car. (I'll deal with that later in the book.)

There are many decisions everyday folk have to make about their finances. But key to those choices is being in control of how we consume. People's values are often pushed to the side because of irresponsible consumption or pressure from peers or people who aren't earning a dime of your money. Who cares what they think? Much of what we do with our money comes down to making the right choices based on what we "say" we value.

The American Savings Education Council (ASEC) and the Employee Benefit Research Institute (EBRI) have established the Choose to Save Education Program to help people plan for their future financial needs. They say the program is necessary when you look at these facts:

- Only about one third of workers have any idea how much they need to save for retirement.

- The average Social Security benefit for retired workers in 2002 was $895 per month.

- Social Security benefits represent about 38 percent of income of the elderly.

These organizations have it right on the money. You have to make a conscious decision to save. Money isn't just going to magically appear in your savings account. It's a choice. But you also have to save so that you have choices. When the tires on my car become worn, I don't have to drive on them a few hundred more miles because I don't have the money to replace them. I can get new tires without incurring more debt because I choose to save money for expenses like that.

When it comes time for our children to go to college, we won't have to choose between letting them incur mounds of student-loan debt or taking out a home-equity loan or raiding our tax-deferred retirement accounts. We are choosing to save now so we won't have to make bad decisions later.

7

—

MANTRA #7:
"ENOUGH IS ENOUGH"

A man is rich in proportion to the number
of things which he can afford to let alone.
—Henry David Thoreau

There is enough in the world for everyone's need,
but not enough for everyone's greed.
—Frank Buchman, U.S. evangelist

Honey, you have to stop stressing about having
enough money. When is enough enough?
—Kevin L. McIntyre, my husband

One night I couldn't get to sleep because I was complaining about my work schedule. I was trying to figure out how to do several television appearances, make it to a couple of speaking engagements, and meet the deadlines for my syndicated column. My husband suggested that I needed to start saying no to some of the requests. After all, he pointed out, we have three small children and I was just trying to do too much.

A bit annoyed, I snapped back that I was doing all this—writing a book, contributing to a radio show, delivering speeches, and writing a twice-a-week column—because we needed the money. We needed the money, I reminded him, so that we can pay for our children's college education.

"Look at you," he said. "You're cranky because you're tired. You're tired because you're working too hard. You aren't making enough time for the kids or me." (He meant I wasn't giving him enough sex, and he was right.) "When is enough enough? One of us could stop working right now and we would have enough money to meet our needs. We would be fine financially. The kids would get to college, even if they have to take out student loans."

My husband's question—"When is enough enough?"—stopped me cold. I didn't have a pithy comeback. I sat on the edge of the bed and cried. I had been trying to reach for so much that I was missing the gems I had right in front of me. The thought that I had lost touch with that made me weep.

Shoot, I hate it when my husband's right.

But he was so right. We have enough.

I'm obsessed with saving enough money for our retirement, for emergencies, and for our children's education. If I go over a budgeted item, I mope for days. I overwork. At times I am too focused on our future financial goals at the expense of what we already have now.

I certainly have more than my grandmother ever had. The house I live in now is twice as big as the one I grew up in.

During the course of writing my syndicated column I decided to start a feature called "A Higher Value." On occasion I profile people who have decided money isn't everything. I'll be talking a lot about money in this book, but I also want you to pause and consider the higher value of your pursuits as opposed to just the dollar value.

For example, when Bob Thompson sold his Michigan-based asphalt-and-paving business in 1999, he could have pocketed all of the $422 million he made on the deal. Instead, he decided to share nearly $130 million of the proceeds with his 550 employees. Some of the workers became instant millionaires. Thompson's decision was news because it doesn't usually happen this way. If he had kept all the money from the sale, nobody would have blinked an eye. It's the American way. Take the money and run. Nobody would have faulted him. It was his business, his money.

But Thompson and his wife, Ellen—who had to agree on this—exemplify a higher, greater value.

I write about money all the time. I quote experts advising people how to make money, how to invest, save, or spend money, or how to keep what little money they've got. What the Thompsons did humbled me.

Thompson, founder of Thompson-McCully Company, said he wanted to take some of the $422 million he received for his Belleville, Michigan, business and reward his employees for working hard for the company he and his wife started and ran for more than forty years. "What was I going to do with all that money anyway?" said Thompson. "Besides, I'm in a business where my employees have to work all day and half the night. They have to work in tough weather like the ninety-degree days . . . This is hard work. It's not like I invented some software that made me a lot of money. My people are really dedicated, and I know I couldn't be successful without them."

And who can forget the baseball fans who graciously handed Mark McGwire back several of his record-breaking balls after he smashed them into the stands? I especially remember Michael Davidson, a fan who said he would rather give McGwire his sixty-first home-run ball back than to take the millions he might have gotten for it. "It would mean more to Mark McGwire and baseball than a million dollars or whatever would to me," Davidson said after grabbing ball #61, which McGwire hit into the stands at St. Louis's Busch Stadium to tie Roger Maris's single-season home-run record.

It would have been so easy, and even understandable, if Davidson had cashed in on his luck. Frankly, I'm not too sure I would have returned the baseball to McGwire. The prospect of a million bucks just for snagging a $10 ball is mighty tempting.

"There is need and then there is greed," Thompson said. "We all need certain basic comforts, and beyond that it becomes ridiculous."

So, how much is enough?

Are you working so hard to acquire the luxuries in life that you don't have time for the things you value the most?

Is what you're doing aligned with your values? Are the things you are doing worth your time? If you calculate your "real hourly wage," you may realize that you could live on less, said Vicki Robin, coauthor of *Your Money or Your Life: Transforming Your Relationship with Money and Achieving Financial Independence.*

For example, suppose you make $100,000 a year ($50 an hour). By the time you eliminate all the expenses associated with maintaining that $100,000 job and lifestyle—trendy clothes, fancy car, lavish vacations taken to get away from the stress of the job—your real hourly wage might actually be $12.50 an hour. "People don't realize how much they sacrifice for their standard of living," Robin said to me in an interview.

Think about this when you're out on yet another weekend shopping spree, towing along tired, cranky kids who probably don't need whatever it is you're buying. Think about that the next time you agree to overtime at the expense of spending time with your family.

This book is meant to help you achieve financial security, but you can't let the pursuit of prosperity steal away the most precious thing you have—time.

> **The things that will destroy America are prosperity-at-any-price . . . the love of soft living, and the get-rich-quick theory of life.**
> **—Theodore Roosevelt**

How many hours are you putting in at the office? How often does your job take you away from your family? Are you working so hard to pay a hefty house-mortgage note that you're barely at home?

> **Of prosperity mortals can never have enough.**
> **—Aeschylus**

At this time in this century there is so much emphasis on becoming rich. People are made to feel that they are failures if they don't retire with millions in their stock portfolio. At the height of the stock market, *Newsweek* had a cover story titled "Everyone's Getting Rich but Me."

"The economy's booming," the article said under the headline "They're Rich and You're Not." "So why do so many of us feel we're missing out on the party? More than ever, achieving the American Dream is a game of chance—and picking the right stock."

Look at all the hype that surrounded the ABC game show *Who Wants to Be a Millionaire.* The creators didn't even bother with a question mark. Who wouldn't want to be a millionaire?

Make your millions by playing on a TV game show. Play the market. Play the lottery. Wait for a relative to die. It's all about money. It's as though striking it rich is the only thing people are thinking about.

Saying to yourself "Enough is enough" is important because so many of us are working so hard and worrying so much about getting enough money that we can't appreciate what money can't buy—family, friends, spiritual peace.

I think all of us need to be reminded to put money and the pursuit of it in perspective. Try as we might, most of us are not going to be millionaires. So, decide what you value the most and spend your energy and money trying to achieve those goals. I promise you, if you set priorities for your time and money, you will have a prosperous future and you will have enough.

Part Two

—

THE BASICS OF SAVING, SPENDING, AND INVESTING YOUR MONEY

8

PARAGONS OF PARSIMONY: PENNY-PINCHERS SHARE THEIR MONEY-SAVING STRATEGIES

PARAGONS OF PARSIMONY

I've been called a cheapskate, a penny-pincher, and a Grinch (this last one because of the Hundred-Dollar Holiday idea I espoused earlier). A fellow columnist once described me as fiscally hyperresponsible. I'm not like normal consumers, she implied. Normal consumers are too easily influenced to buy what they don't need. I had to think. Do I consider myself the poster woman for the penny-pinchers of the world? Am I a savings saint?

I'm not a martyr when it comes to avoiding all wasteful spending, but I sure know how to hold on to a dollar.

For example, my husband and I were traveling to Orlando once and we were running late. So we checked our one bag at the curb. My husband gave me $2 to tip the skycap. Then we bolted to the gate to catch our flight. But as we began to board, my husband noticed I had my fist clenched. "What's that in your hand?" he asked.

I looked down, and there were the two dollars he had given me to pay the skycap. I had clutched the money so tightly I forgot to pay the man.

"Woman, we'll be lucky if our bag doesn't end up in Alaska," my husband said.

I once bought a stick-shift car because it was $1,000 cheaper than the automatic in the same model. There was just one little problem. I couldn't drive a stick shift. But I had a friend at the time who could, so he drove the car for a week until I could learn how to drive the darn thing. On the way home from work one evening I got stuck on a hill for fifteen minutes because I couldn't shift out of first gear.

I breast-fed all three of my kids because the milk was free. In fact, I breast-fed my first two kids until they were two years old. I get giddy just thinking of all the money I saved on infant formula.

My goal is to put aside at least 20 percent of my income every year. I could save more than that, but my children insist on being fed and clothed.

I'm not overly influenced by subliminal sales messages because I've set priorities for my money. I want my children to go to college and graduate—debt-free. I want to retire early so my hardworking husband and I can spend our golden years traveling and volunteering. I don't care what my used car looks like as long as it gets me where I need to be. I don't care what labels are on my clothes.

I enjoy being thrifty. Despite the teasing from friends and family, I routinely ask for doggie bags from just about every restaurant lunch or dinner meal I have. To me, it's perfectly normal to grab every morsel of food from the restaurant table no matter how small, including the bread from the basket. I carefully unwrap gifts so that I can reuse the paper and save money. I think it's fine to give as presents books and items I've managed to get free. I'm the master at regifting. Is this tacky? No. It's called being money-smart. I'm not embarrassed to tell anyone that I save little pieces of soap and mash them together in an effort to use every bit of the bar. I hate spending money.

Once I decided to use my daughter's fluorescent-green coin holder with a picture of Winnie the Pooh on the front because I didn't want to buy a change purse. I figured my daughter didn't really need it—she was only three at the time. But every time I pulled out the purse to pay for something, Olivia would throw a fit because she thought I was spending her money. I finally had to break down and buy my own change purse after I found my daughter on the floor playing with the one I had taken from her. She was passing out $20 bills and some change to one of her playmates.

But as cheap as I am, there are others who would consider me a spendthrift. So, every year, in tribute to the truly thrifty, I hold a "Penny-pincher of the Year" contest.

One of my favorite penny-pinching entries was about Beatrice Staunton, who had to raise the last three of her five children alone after her husband died in 1960. Staunton charged her next-door neighbors to use her telephone. Not only that, but she charged them more than they would have paid to use the public phone. One of her daughters asked her why she charged them at all. Her response was that there were three grown men in that house and they were just too cheap to pay for phone service. She felt that if she didn't charge them, then they would want to use her phone all the time.

Okay, but why the surcharge?

"She said she saved them a two-block walk to the nearest pay phone; they didn't have to have exact change; she provided them a warm, comfortable place to sit down, and if they didn't want to pay, then they didn't have to use her phone," said her daughter Patricia.

In this chapter I profile some practical and just plain crazy penny-pinching ideas. Some of these strategies will surely save you money, and others will just leave you shaking your head. No matter. At least all the ideas will have you thinking about pinching pennies.

Savings from Above

The first-ever winner of my Penny-pincher of the Year contest was Louise Meyer of Washington, who saves money by solar-cooking her food. Louise has solar cookers on her rooftop and uses them for practically every meal. Meyer is a member of Solar Cookers International, a Sacramento-based nonprofit organization that is trying to promote cooking with sunlight. Meyer said she saves about $40 a month on her electric bill during the winter and $140 in the summer months by solar cooking her food and by avoiding using her clothes dryer and air-conditioning. According to Meyer, solar cooking is easy and saves a lot of time. No need to stir a pot or watch your food—which, of course, never burns. All it takes is a sunny day, water-resistant, aluminum-laminated cardboard, a clear plastic oven-roasting bag to create a mini–greenhouse effect, and a dark pot with a tight-fitting lid for maximum heat absorption. "This is free energy, and it is one of the best-kept secrets," Meyer said. "Besides, it's like a challenge to get something for free. It's a real exciting high."

Some Whine with That Wine

One reader sent in an entry about a relative who was obsessed with diluting every possible food product. "You never had to worry about people getting tipsy at her home because she would dilute the wine for dinner," the woman wrote. "The [catsup] looked more like runny tomato soup. The kids still remember spreading peanut butter on their saltines and watching it run through the little holes. When she got home from the grocery store, she looked like an alchemist at work with all of her bottles and bowls, wire whisks and measuring cups. Needless to say, her house was not the kids' favorite place for dinner, but it sure left everyone with some good memories."

Half Smoked, Big Savings?

One woman admitted that her husband has a habit of picking up half-smoked cigars. "He cuts the end that was lit off and relights and smokes the cigars," she said.

Don't Try This at Home

I was amused at one grandmother's determination to save by refusing to buy potholders. This woman was so outraged to find that stores charge up to $4 per pair that she decided to make them herself—from shoulder pads she had salvaged from clothing. She would take two shoulder pads and sew them together, creating potholders that she then declared were just as functional and far more attractive than any store-bought item. Unfortunately, the practice was short-lived. The homemade holders were prone to catching fire.

Salvaging Stamps

Here's a way to save a few pennies, wrote one reader. "I receive quite a few charitable requests in the mail that contain return envelopes with postage stamps that for one reason or another, I don't want to honor." When this happens I immerse the envelopes in hot water for a few minutes until the stamps peel off easily." He then dries them and uses a glue stick to apply the recycled stamps to envelopes as needed.

Pieces of Paper

You don't have to be an environmentalist to know that trees take time to grow and that paper should be recycled. Many penny-pinchers will tell you not to throw away junk mail, printer goofs, and miscellaneous notes. Turn the paper over and reuse it in the printer, or cut up junk mail and use it for notes to yourself, shopping lists, or bookmarks.

The Envelope, Please

Don't throw away those junk-mail envelopes either. If the envelopes have electronic markings on the bottom, just cover them up with first-class labels that you can order cheap from a catalogue. Small tears in the back flap of old envelopes can be camouflaged with Wal-Mart yellow smiley-face stickers.

Shower Yourself with Savings

It happens more times than we would like to admit. You slip in the shower, and in an attempt to keep from falling, you grab the shower curtain. Over time the shower curtain begins to rip. One possible solution is to use a hole puncher to punch a hole near the damaged hole and put the shower curtain hook through that hole.

Cold Water = Cold Cash

Here's a winning penny-pincher idea. One thrifty person said he takes a cut-off plastic one-gallon milk jug into the shower. According to this frugal fellow, it takes approximately two minutes for the hot water to reach the shower. So, he captures the potentially wasted cold water in the jug and fills the tank of his toilet, thus saving the cost of the water that would be used to fill the toilet tank.

Bathroom Bargain

Here's how one winner racked up a bathroom bargain. She got the idea to use the tissue paper from fruit as toilet paper. You know those colored (usually purple or green) tissue squares you see in the produce department of the supermarket, the ones in which pears and kiwis and the like are wrapped? Well, this woman collects them to use instead of toilet paper! "Sure, they're colorful and sometimes impart a nice fruity aroma, but c'mon, if that's not penny-pinching, what is?" her husband wrote.

Squeeze Your Way to Savings

One winner in the penny-pincher contest was Barbara R. Davies of Brookeville, Maryland. She nominated her father, Walter Davies, who demonstrated many penny-pinching strategies raising twelve children. But one incident stood out in her memory. "He thought the toothpaste manufacturers were making the tube opening bigger so that customers would use the toothpaste quicker," Davies wrote. "So he took the cap, drilled a hole in it, and put it back on the tube. That worked two ways: less time spent removing and replacing the cap, and less toothpaste used due to the thinner ribbon."

Squeezing Savings Part 2

Squeezing out the right amount of toothpaste can be difficult when the tube is running low. One reader found a way to get all that he paid for. "After you have squeezed all the toothpaste from the toothpaste tube, you cut the tube open in the middle. Inserting your toothbrush into the tube you can easily get another 2 to 4 days of brushing."

2 Ply = 1 Ply × 2

It takes an extra-devoted penny-pincher with a lot of free time to undertake this penny-pinching idea. "How about buying 2-ply toilet paper and using the cardboard roll to roll off one ply and having two rolls of 1 ply toilet paper," one industrious reader wrote.

Panty-Hose Penny-pinching

Over the years a number of women have sent in ideas on how to salvage a pair of panty hose that has a run. They recommend buying the same brand of panty hose and following this drill: When one pair gets a run, cut off that leg but leave the panty part. When another pair gets a run in an opposite leg, cut that one off. Then wear the two pair together. The dual panties also give a bit more support. "It may take a little getting used to, but I remind myself that I'm saving $5 every time I wear them," one saver said.

Coast Your Way to Savings

Here's a new-economy cheapskate idea. Use those CD-ROMs that come unsolicited from Internet providers for drink coasters. There's a never-ending supply, and they are a real conversation piece at parties.

Preview Savings

Purchase previewed movies from a video store. You can save as much as half the cost of a new video. For example, one reader bought a previewed movie, *Dinosaur,* for $6.99. The original cost: $19.99.

Cereal-Costs Cutter

Do your kids refuse to eat generic cereal? Well, buy the brand-name cereal and save the box. When they aren't looking, pop in the bag from a no-name brand of similar cereal. I bet they won't be able to tell the difference.

Bread 101

You can save money by turning your stale bread into croutons. Save bread slices in a Ziploc bag in the freezer until you have ten or more.

Defrost the bread and place it on a baking sheet that has been sprayed with cooking oil. Sprinkle the bread with dried herbs such as oregano, marjoram, sage, salt, and pepper. Bake at 300 degrees F. until crisp. Cut up the croutons or crush for bread crumbs.

Microwave On? Maybe It Shouldn't Be

For those who don't cook at home, keeping the microwave unplugged may help save a few dollars a month in electrical charges. Appliances use electricity even when they are not in service. When your VCR or microwave displays the time, that's electricity at work. Simply unplugging unused appliances may reduce your electricity bill. A note of warning, however: keep your refrigerator plugged in; no power means spoiled food.

Fruit Price Fix

Overripe fruit may not appeal to everyone, especially kids. One penny-pinching mother wrote in with an excellent idea on how to use every last bit of fruit in your house. "If there is a piece of fruit left over that doesn't look good, throw it in the blender and make a slurpee with ice, juice, and frozen bananas."

Cheapskates' Lemonade

Why spend $2 for soda at a restaurant? Instead of buying a drink with a meal, ask for a glass of water with wedges of lemon. Squeeze the lemon and add some sugar or a sugar substitute. I call this "cheapskates' lemonade."

A Bag of Savings

Every penny-pincher worth a dime does this. The basic scenario: you go to the grocery store and return home with lots of grocery bags. But what to do with the bags? Well, use them as trash bags. Ideally, this penny-pinching idea is best used in smaller trash cans.

Money in the Bag

Some supermarkets around the country may give customers a few pennies for each grocery bag they bring in to reuse. It's both good economics and environmentalism. "In my state, the supermarkets pay you 5 cents per bag," reported T. S. Dwyer of Aurora, Colorado. "Since I go grocery shopping at least three times a week and always take in at least three of my own bags, that comes to 45 cents per week, $23.40 a year. Since this program was initiated about 10 years ago, I've probably saved at least $234. I did absolutely no work except grab some plastic bags from the floor of the backseat of my car!" But even if there is no cash rebate, instead of trashing the bags return them to the store to be recycled.

Time Is Money

Ever been surprised at the end of the month when the phone bill arrives? All those minutes do seem to have a tendency to add up without you realizing it. Here's an idea: Keep a timer by your telephone to time your long-distance calls.

Nickel-and-Dime Yourself Some Savings

For those who like clear round figures, here's a money-saving tip. One reader said when he records checks in his checkbook, he always rounds up the amount. For example, if he writes a check for $9.10, he writes down that the check was written for $10. That creates a 90-cent surplus in his bank account. "Depending upon how many checks you write during the course of a year, you have a built-in holiday savings account," he wrote.

Penny Postcards

It seems like such a waste to receive a greeting card and then throw it away. To one person, however, greeting cards are postcards waiting to be created. "I have learned to save money by reusing my old greeting cards and turning them into recycled postcards. You can reuse the front of the cards (when the reverse side is blank)." Just cut away the side with the sappy greeting.

Year-Round Savings

John P. Tiernan of Bedford, New York, sent along this penny-pinching tip. "Although I like big full-color wall calendars with mountaineering photos, I'm not fond of throwing them away," he wrote. "New ones cost money I'd rather not spend, but the photos remain fascinating. What I've discovered is that I can print the new months out each year on Microsoft Word's calendar template. Then I use an adhesive stick to mount the new months over the old ones."

Dryer-Sheet Double Duty

You can get double duty from your dryer sheets by taking a used one and using it to dust or wipe up spills from your floor. I do this myself.

A Mind and a Magazine Are Terrible Things to Waste

The first-place penny-pincher winner for 2001 was Mary Sue Geib of Richmond, Virginia. She won with her husband, Donald. "At Christmas, I opened a coupon informing me that I would be receiving subscriptions to *Vegetarian Gourmet, Bon Appetit, Condé Nast Traveler,* and *Vegetarian Times,*" Geib wrote. "I was delighted. Of course, when the first round of magazines showed up I was quite surprised to discover that I had received a *Gourmet* dated January 1992 and a *Bon Appetit* dated January 1994!" Turns out Geib's husband went searching for the magazines at recycling and book-exchange centers. "After five months of these special subscriptions, I had to admit that the views from around the world and the recipes featured in the old issues probably haven't changed that much," Geib wrote. "After all, they are new to me." Geib did draw the line when her husband tried giving her old issues of *Newsweek.* "He discovered I didn't like dated news and discontinued that gift subscription."

Cashing In on Kitty Litter

Warning! This is extreme penny-pinching at work. An eighty-year-old grandmother from South Korea could put some penny-pinchers to shame. She washes and reuses kitty litter!" Yes, that's right—kitty litter. Instead of throwing it away after a few days' use, she washes it and dries it in the sun.

Fast Food for Less

Ever gone into a fast-food establishment when you weren't all that hungry, but bought a combo meal because you rationalized that it was cheaper? If the answer is yes, you need to pay attention to what this thrifty person recommended. "My wife learned this trick driving across the country. When stopping at a fast-food restaurant, instead of ordering two combo meals we order one 'super size' meal plus a sandwich, then share the fries and drink. You get the same amount of food, but usually save at least $2."

Printer-Toner Touch-up

There's nothing worse than seeing the copier flashing the "add toner" sign. Some people at this point would give up and buy another toner. But one reader doesn't. She wrote, "I put [the toner cartridge] in a box in the trunk of the car and take it on my next two or three errands. Inevitably, I get a month or two more use out of the same cartridge simply by the vibrations that redistribute the toner as it jiggles merrily down the road. I would guess that I save at least 25 percent to 33 percent by not replacing a cartridge immediately and giving it a chance to rejuvenate itself!"

Driving All the Way to the Bank

Connie Jones of Virginia found a way to save money after paying off her car. After her last payment on her 1989 Honda Accord, she kept making a "car" payment, only the money went into her bank account.

Cutting Car Insurance

One senior penny-pincher wrote, "If you are over fifty-five, take the 55-Alive Mature Driving Course. Most insurance companies will give a discount to those who take the course."

A Shower Cap of Savings

Maybe the research-and-development division at Saran was paying attention to what people around the country were getting wise to—

using shower caps to cover various food items. One penny-pincher wrote me to recommend using shower caps to cover cooked meals. "Just wash them out and reuse them over and over." This sure beats the expensive store version that recently came on the market. QuickCovers from Saran retail at about $3 for fourteen plastic covers.

Shower Cap Part 2

Now you know how useful hotel shower caps can be in the kitchen, but they can cover other things besides your head and your food. They can cover your feet too. When you have muddy/wet shoes on and you need to walk through the house, place a plastic shower cap over the bottom of each shoe—your rugs and floors will stay clean! Yet another example of why you shouldn't throw away those hotel shower caps from your vacation or business trips.

Don't Leave Home Without It

I've practiced the next piece of advice many times. "Always carry your receipt with you after buying something," advises Penny Dackis of Maryland. "Check back in the store. If the item you bought has been reduced further, the store will (often) issue a price adjustment and re-fund the difference between what you paid and the new sales price. All you need is your receipt. I have saved a bundle this way."

Popcorn Packaging

Next time you move, pack a bowl or two of popcorn with your belongings. Popcorn can work like packing peanuts except it's biodegradable and comes in handy if you get hungry while packing. You might want to use unsalted plain popcorn.

Penny-Jar Treat

At the end of the day put all your change in a jar. You will be amazed at how much you can save at the end of the week, month, or year.

PENNY-WISE, POUND-FOOLISH

Every year as I sort through the entries for my Penny-pincher of the Year contest it occurs to me that some of my frugal ways are a bit crazy.

As one reader wrote, "I think in many people's cases, an extreme focus on penny-pinching or avoiding the spending of money for money's sake is just as bad or unhealthy as being the extravagant spender who spends beyond his/her means."

This reader raised an interesting point. When does penny-pinching become "penny-wise, pound-foolish"?

I once ran out of gasoline trying to reach a station where the fuel was two cents a gallon less than at the ten or so gas stations I had passed on the way home (with the needle way past *E*). My husband later asked, "Honey, why didn't you stop and get just enough gas at one of the more expensive stations to get you to the cheaper station?"

"D'oh!" I said, slapping myself on the forehead.

I didn't stop because I was too focused on saving those two cents a gallon. I was, without a doubt, being penny-wise and pound-foolish.

Trying to save a buck isn't always smart money or an effective use of your time. Sometimes penny-pinching does result in an excessive concern about spending too much, which in turn can cost you money. Ever just bought stuff you don't need because you *had* to take advantage of the discount bargains?

What about all the free stuff we penny-pinchers love to collect? I have so many free coffee mugs that I've had to devote an entire kitchen cabinet to storing them. I don't even drink coffee.

Have you ever driven from store to store most of the day trying to find the lowest price on an item?

"If shopping around takes time away from your kids or family—which are the really important products in your life—you haven't saved a thing," a fellow penny-pincher pointed out. "I have found myself traveling around to different stores to get the best deal, and then in the middle of this realized I spent hours in traffic trying to save a few bucks while my kids are at home doing nothing. So I think we need to evaluate these penny-pinching ideas to see if they really are beneficial."

Penny-pinching is basically a defensive strategy. People who are frugal tend to think first before spending. By keeping track of your money, you eventually give yourself more choices, such as the option to retire early.

I started the Penny-pincher of the Year contest because I wanted to have a little fun highlighting people's frugal ways. But I also wanted to point out that, for many of us, it's not how much money we make but how we make do with the pennies, nickels, dimes, and dollars we earn. That can make the difference between building wealth and living paycheck to paycheck.

Ultimately, your goal should be to minimize your costs by maximizing what you get for your money.

A GIFT THAT KEEPS ON GIVING

As I've told you, I regift. And I'm not ashamed of this practice.

When I receive gifts for my kids or myself that are too small, too big, out of season, inappropriate, duplicates, or not quite right, I often rewrap them and give them away to others.

Don't let anyone guilt-trip you into thinking that regifting is a cheap, tacky thing to do. It saves money because you don't have to go out and buy a gift when a baby shower or birthday comes around. It also keeps my closets from being cluttered with unwanted presents. Most important, it allows me to give away something that someone else might enjoy.

For example, my son received a large truck for his fourth birthday. It was a lovely gift, but my son doesn't really play with trucks. He would rather play educational games on our home computer. I didn't want to offend the gift giver by asking for a receipt to return the truck, so I decided to put it in my regifting closet. Several months later, my seven-year-old daughter was invited to attend a birthday party and I found out that the birthday boy loved trucks. We gave him the truck my son had received.

A 2002 holiday-spending survey conducted by Money Management International, a consumer credit-counseling agency, found that 36 percent of respondents earning $100,000 to $150,000 had regifted to cut holiday costs. In fact, the higher the income bracket, the more the likelihood of regifting. See, wealthy people know how to save a buck.

Still, I know there is a stigma about regifting. In fact, here are some typical arguments against the practice posted on an online discussion board.

One person wrote: "I think that gift-giving requires sacrifice on the part of the giver. It can be time, money, or effort, but I just don't see any self-sacrifice in regifting because it doesn't cost the giver anything."

Another opponent said: "Personally this sort of thing feels like you're saying, 'You're not good enough.' "

Good enough for what? Good enough to spend money on? Nonsense.

Many of the objections to regifting make me wonder how many people really know what the word *gift* means.

A gift is defined as something voluntarily transferred by one person to another without compensation. I didn't find a single definition that said the giver had to make a sacrifice.

Once I did an online discussion about budgeting for the holidays. About half of the questions were from people worried that they would give what would be perceived as a cheap gift. I'm amazed at how people are willing to put themselves into debt for fear that they'll be scorned for not spending enough.

I've heard people say that they wouldn't want a gift that's been recycled. Why? If the gift is something you might need or want, why should someone have to purchase the item if they already have one in their possession?

I'll tell you why: because we really don't believe that it's the thought that counts. Too many people believe the purchasing of material goods is evidence of love or appreciation. Therefore, the more you spend, the greater your love. If this weren't true, then why would you care whether a gift was inexpensive, free to the giver, or recycled? Isn't it good enough that they even thought to give you something in the first place?

In truth, we all miss the gift-giving mark sometimes. So why not turn those mistakes into presents for others?

To that end, here are a few of my own regifting rules:

- Don't ask, don't tell. Don't ask if your gift is recycled. Just be grateful someone thought enough of you to give you something in the first place. And don't tell someone that you are regifting out of some misplaced guilt. If you are giving what you feel is an appropriate gift, you don't need to reveal its origin.

- When you receive something you don't want and suspect you'll recycle it, label it with the name of the giver. You don't want the present to end up with the person who gave it to you.

- Rewrap any item you're regifting. Be sure to remove any evidence of a previous giver (especially those little gift cards on gift bags).

- The gift should be in good shape. Regifting doesn't mean getting rid of junk to clear closet space.

- Don't try to pretend your gift was expensive by purposely putting it in a box or bag from a pricey store. That is deceptive and could prove embarrassing to the receiver should he try to return the item to the store.

- If the person receiving your regifted item insists on exchanging the item for whatever reason (it's too small, they don't like the color, they already have it, et cetera), come clean and offer to replace the gift with something more to their liking. If she is a true friend and a kind person, she will laugh with you about the situation. If she gets mad, be nice but don't take it personally. She is an ingrate.

Now, let me be clear: I do not advocate passing along some hideous item your dog wouldn't even want to chew on. Personally, I think the only criterion for a gift is that you think the person will appreciate it.

Most important, keep in mind that any gift you get—whether it was bought, homemade, or regifted—should be accepted with grace. As Ralph Waldo Emerson said, "He is a good man who can receive a gift well."

GIVE THOUGHT TO CHOOSING GREAT GIFTS

While I'm on the subject of giving gifts, let me give you something more to think about. The late British author Pamela Glenconner said: "Giving presents is a talent; to know what a person wants, to know when and how to get it, to give it lovingly and well. Unless a character possesses this talent there is no moment more annihilating to ease than that in which a present is received and given."

Giving gifts can be like arranging a vase of long-stemmed roses. If you do the job right, you are pleasantly rewarded. But if you aren't careful, you may get a nasty nick and ruin the experience. Let me address some typical questions about selecting gifts well.

Q: Is there a rule of thumb as to how much one should spend on a gift?

A: No. "Keep in mind your own budget," said Ruth L. Kern, an international etiquette consultant from Barrington, Illinois. "Don't go broke just to make an impression. How much you spend on the gift should depend on how well you know the person." These days you know a year ahead of time when someone is getting married. So, figure out how much you can afford on gifts every year and plan accordingly. And remember what a gift is: a way to show you care. The price tag on a gift is not a yardstick of your affection.

Q: If how much you spend isn't important, then how do you determine the right gift?

A: Perhaps the biggest reason so many gifts are gaffes is that we don't take the time to find out what people like, says Giovinella Gonthier, a Chicago etiquette consultant. "People often give other people what they would like to receive. That's their first mistake. Their second mistake is that they don't do any research." Gonthier, a former diplomat who advises executives on their business gift-buying, says it takes skill and not just a rushed trip to the mall to find the appropriate gift. "A lot of time we view gifts as an afterthought. We get an invitation. We reply to it, and then weeks go by before we think of what to get." Gonthier advises that if you are unsure of what to buy, ask someone close to the person receiving the gift. Most of all, put some imagination into your gift giving.

Q: If I attend a wedding or graduation, do I have to buy a gift?

A: "Guests invited to the wedding ceremony and reception have an obligation to send a gift, whether they are attending or not," said Peggy Post, the author of numerous etiquette books and the great-granddaughter-in-law of Emily Post. There are some exceptions— for instance, if you live far away from where the wedding is taking place or you have been out of touch with the couple for several years. The receipt of a wedding announcement after the wedding carries no gift obligation. If you are invited to a graduation ceremony, you're expected to bring a gift, Post added.

Q: Is it okay to tell guests what gifts to get?
A: Ask and you shall be rude, according to the experts. "I'm just appalled that so many people feel it's okay to ask for money or certain gifts," Kern said. "I understand that in many cultures there may be a tradition of giving money for a wedding, for example. But to actually ask for money or anything else is improper." Gonthier was equally offended at the commonplace practice of asking guests to contribute toward a certain gift. "I don't think guests should be asked to help pay for a honeymoon. It's terribly ungracious and smacks of avarice. If you don't have the money for a big wedding, then keep it simple." Just so you know, a graduation, birthday party, anniversary, or wedding is not an opportunity to fund-raise.

Q: What should you do if you find out someone thinks your gift is cheap?
A: Nothing. You don't need to respond to such rudeness. Giving the right gift isn't always easy. But keep this in mind: Your generosity lies less in how much you spend and more in how much thought you put into your giving.

FEEL GOOD ABOUT GIVING ALL THAT YOU CAN GIVE

I've talked about giving gifts; now let me focus on why so many people fret about giving gifts that appear cheap, especially during the holidays. Here are two typical reader questions: "How does one live in the real world and still stay on a budget without looking miserly?" And "How does one be generous without breaking the budget? I've chosen a target of $20 (plus or minus) for each gift to my extended family and friends, excluding shipping. It seems that $20 doesn't go as far as it used to; however, it quickly adds up to a large sum."

Another reader's worries were described this way: "Some of my friends have more money than me and as a consequence buy more expensive gifts. I usually give a small gift—around $10 for friends, $20 to $30 for family. So how do you handle the inevitable guilt?"

Really, why all the angst? Since when are you being a cheapskate to give what you can afford? Why feel guilty about receiving a nice gift and not being able to reciprocate with an equally priced present?

Of course, I know why. We may say it's important to spend time with our friends and family, but then we spend ourselves into debt during the holidays and other times during the year buying gifts out of guilt for time not spent with them. Or we buy on credit because we don't want to appear too cheap.

"People are often trying to buy the feelings of the holidays, and you can't do that," said Kathryn Amenta, a certified financial counselor based in San Francisco. "A lot of emotional stuff is attached to the holiday season. If people are willing to go into great debt or more debt because they have this feeling of cheapness, they have to address that feeling."

So, let's address why so many people worry about being perceived as cheap if they stick to a budget. Going back to the reader's question above, what does it mean to be miserly?

Is it being greedy and stingy to be prudent with your money? If you are choosing to spend less on Christmas gifts because you have to pay down your debts, save for your kid's college education, or fund your retirement, the answer is absolutely not. And if the person receiving your inexpensive gift—whether homemade or store-bought—chooses to complain, then just keep in mind what my grandmother said about such people: "They ain't your friend anyway."

As Amenta advises, "You can take the criticism that you're being cheap and own it, or know that what you are doing is offering gifts from the heart. You are giving yourself a gift by spending in a way that allows you to be financially successful in the upcoming year. Scaling back can be scary, but it can also be empowering."

Now, let's deal with this feeling of guilt because you can't match what others give.

"People get a surprise Christmas gift and feel like they have to run out and get something for that person in return," said Alex White, a family and financial-management specialist at Virginia Tech in Blacksburg. "But don't do it if they aren't on your list. Just say thank you and treat them nice." Otherwise, you could end up in an unwanted gift-giving cycle. Someone buys you a gift. You feel obligated to get him one in return. Then he gets added to your list the next year, and vice versa.

"People don't know how to allow others to give. This shouldn't be a game of tit for tat," Amenta said. "Have some integrity when it comes to your finances. It's really important for people to examine their own values and not cave in to buying something for everybody."

I don't want to discourage anyone from being generous. But be honest about how generous you can be. Get rid of the angst and guilt and give what you can afford.

GREEDILY EVER AFTER

Finally, I can't leave this subject of gift giving without addressing what I consider a growing and disturbing trend of genteel panhandling.

On her wedding day, tradition says, a bride should have something old, something new, something borrowed, and something blue. Well, increasingly brides and grooms have been adding to that list something green—as in cash.

Many couples are asking that their wedding guests forgo buying them toasters, blenders, or china. Instead they are shamelessly asking for money to pay for the wedding or a lavish honeymoon. To these couples I say, if you want to cruise the world on your honeymoon, more power to you, but do it on your own dime.

When I wrote about this topic, a number of readers supported this polite panhandling. Many criticized wedding guests who ignored their requests for cash, stock, or other nontraditional gifts in favor of giving unwanted toasters, towels, or what one reader called "useless twaddle."

Here is a letter I received from a couple with student-loan debt of more than a quarter of a million dollars:

> Our wedding was not lavish. [We] had about 140 people. Still, it cost $30,000. Add that plus the ring and the honeymoon and other credit card debt and we're now looking at $50,000 in short-term high-interest credit card debt. We registered at several stores and let our parents know that if people asked whether it was okay to give money that we would welcome that. In the end, friends and family gave a total of about $10,000 in checks, which we used to pay expenses. Lots of other people bought gifts, some thoughtful, others bizarre

> **and useless. You might like to paint the picture of today's brides and grooms as money-grubbing yuppies with cash to spare, but in reality, most of us are struggling to pay our current bills and are throwing weddings for our friends and families far beyond our means. It is simply what is expected.**

I find it disturbing that a couple with $250,000 in student-loan debt felt obligated to have an expensive wedding. And, since when is a $30,000 wedding a modest affair?

Contrary to popular belief, you do not have to live beyond your means. If potential guests expect you to go into debt so they can have an open bar and a grand dinner buffet at your wedding reception, they aren't worth inviting.

What sense does it make to pile on more debt for a wedding and then moan and groan that someone was being thoughtless by giving you a "useless" gift instead of cash to help you settle your debts?

Modern newlyweds argue that their needs should override the perceived tackiness of pleading for people to just give them what they want. Shoot, why not just set up a cash register at the reception and charge admission to recoup costs?

Have we really degenerated so far in this culture that couples feel entitled to be compensated when they get married? A gift is an expression of affection, not a business transaction. So what if a wedding present is ugly, unusual, or useless? Are we really past "it's the thought that counts?"

I refuse to embrace this trend of newlyweds asking for what they "really" want, need, or crave.

Asking directly or indirectly for wedding guests to help build up your investment portfolio, or help pay for a car, home, or honeymoon, is just being avaricious. Weddings shouldn't be used as an opportunity to hit up your relatives and friends.

A CHEERFUL GIVER

I once paid $130 for two tickets to attend a charity dinner and auction held by my church. As my husband and I were cruising around the lobby of the banquet hall, feverishly jotting down our bids for various donated items, my pastor spotted us and came over.

"I'm surprised to see you bidding on stuff, Michelle," he joked.

I also noticed a few of my fellow congregants staring in amazement as I tried to outbid people during the silent auction. I guess they were shocked because I certainly don't keep my cheapness a secret. I'm not embarrassed to ask for a gift bag to be returned to me if I see that the recipient is about to throw it away.

I know how to hold on to a dollar.

But I also know the value of charitable giving. I'm frugal, but I'm not a miser. I was more than happy to bid on the items at the charity dinner because the money was going to support a good cause. As my husband often says, "To whom much is given, much is required."

In my family, charitable giving is not an afterthought. We build it into our annual budget.

"By definition, budgeting means you are concentrating on making sure any type of outlay is something you can afford to do," said Tim D. Stone, executive vice president of NewTithing Group, a nonprofit philanthropic research organization. "We encourage people to think about charitable giving and what they can comfortably afford in relationship to their income, investment assets, living expenses, and tax consequences."

How much you give is a personal choice. But whatever percentage of your annual income you choose to give, make it a conscious decision.

It's also important to have rules for your charitable donations. When you establish guidelines for how your money is to be spent, you spend it wisely. For example, my husband and I don't give money to for-profit companies hired to solicit charitable donations. Far too often, professional fund-raisers keep an extraordinarily high percentage of donated dollars. One Florida-based police athletic charity ended its relationship with a for-profit fund-raiser because the charity received only 5 percent of the money. Out of the $4.2 million raised, the charity netted just $200,000. This type of split is not an anomaly. It happens all the time.

One of the first questions I ask someone soliciting for a charity is how much of my money will be used to pay fund-raising costs. The Better Business Bureau's Wise Giving Alliance says charities should not spend more than 35 percent of what they raise on fund-raising.

Also included under my family's giving guidelines is a ban on school fund-raising. It's not that I don't believe it's worthy to support school projects. I just loathe trying to get other parents, coworkers, friends, and family to buy overpriced wrapping paper, calendars, or candy.

I also object to having my children or myself used as unpaid salespeople for professional fund-raising companies. Believe me, I understand the psychology behind all this selling. It's not easy to get folks to fork over money, even for a good cause. I also realize this type of fund-raising is successful in providing money for needed school supplies and activities.

But seriously, how many of us—without the guilt—would spend $11 for a five-ounce Coca-Cola mailbox tin filled with mixed candy? I know I would never pay $7 for several sheets of wrapping paper, which most of the time aren't long or wide enough to cover anything I want to wrap. How about paying $11.50 for a tin of animal cookies? Personally, I think we parents should agree to stop peddling to one another. If you want to give money to a school, fine. But this routine of "I buy from your kid, you buy from mine" is maddening.

As a result, my husband and I just write a check directly to the school or parent association. That way they get to keep 100 percent of the money.

My husband and I also discuss which causes are important to our family. For instance, we give to our church because of all the community work it does. We support the local public radio and television stations. We especially love the commercial-free TV programming. It keeps our children from badgering us to buy them stuff.

There are at least two advantages to establishing your own charitable-giving guidelines. First, if it is a rule in your family to make charitable giving a priority, that expenditure won't get dropped because something else unexpectedly has to be paid.

Second, it becomes easier not to be guilt-tripped into giving. So when a telemarketer calls to ask for a donation for an unfamiliar police or firefighter fund that will see precious little of the money, you can truthfully say your charity dollars have already been allocated.

Because so many people don't have a plan for giving, charitable donations become something that has to be wrenched from them. Or they think that everybody has his or her hand out begging for money. Worse, they may end up giving money to a fraudulent charity.

If you take control of your giving and make it an essential part of your budget, you get to feel good about yourself—and good causes receive the most you can afford. Just as important, you can comfortably say no to other charitable appeals because you've already given generously and thoughtfully.

9

—

ANOTHER DAY OLDER AND DEEPER IN DEBT

A good debt is not as good as no debt.
—Chinese proverb

Let's face it, only the most disciplined among us is going to live a life without debt. Frankly, I despise debt—even my home mortgage. I can't wait until my house is paid off. I hate owing anybody anything. I think credit is evil because consumers' overreliance on credit cards has corrupted our common sense.

Debt allows people to buy what they don't need when they want it regardless of whether they have the money for it. It's reliance on credit cards that has resulted in many families overspending. Spending money you haven't earned leads to ruined marriages, spoiled kids, and a broken spirit.

As a reporter, I used to cover bankruptcy court. That assignment cemented what I had already learned from my frugal grandmother. For the most part, many individuals who file for bankruptcy do so because some crisis—job loss, major medical illness, and divorce—pushes them into insolvency. Yet many of those people would admit that if they had saved more, they probably could have weathered their crisis. The disruption in their income would have been easier to handle if they hadn't had so much consumer debt.

I understand that for most Americans debt is the only way to acquire certain assets, chiefly a home or a car. But even good debt should be managed properly. Good debt is money borrowed to buy or pay for something that has the potential to appreciate over time. Borrowing to buy a home is good debt. Borrowing to pay for a college education is good debt.

In the following sections I'll explore the financial attitude adjustment you will need to make to cut the credit card habit and effectively use debt to buy a home and car.

I OWE MY SOUL TO THE COMPANY STORE

You load sixteen tons, what do you get?
Another day older and deeper in debt
                    "Sixteen Tons," Merle Travis, 1946

"Sixteen Tons" was the theme song for the American miner, but it could just as easily apply to today's workers. Many owe their soul to MasterCard and Visa.

Perhaps a little history lesson is in order. Typically, miners were paid monthly in what was called scrip currency that was only good at the company store. By the end of the month, a miner would owe the company for the house he and his family lived in, the tools and supplies he used, and groceries and other items, all provided at gouging prices by the mining company. Miners and their families had to pay a high price for that credit. Because of this life on credit, no matter how hard and how long they worked, they just got deeper in debt. But given the times, the miners had no choice.

You have a choice.

The deep dependence on debt by so many families is jeopardizing people's ability to provide all the things their family really needs. Part of the reason you don't have the money for your insurance needs or retirement savings or a college fund is because you owe your soul to the company store. Credit cards are the modern-day scrip.

Here's an experiment to see how dependent you are on credit. First, go get your credit cards and an envelope. Go ahead. Put the book down right now.

Got your cards? Look at all of them carefully. Count them. Now seal them up in an envelope. Your mission is to spend the next two months without using a single credit card.

> **No man's credit is ever as good as his money.**
> **—Edgar Watson Howe,**
> **U.S. editor and author**

What's that I sense? Fear. Doubt. Panic. Here's the point of this exercise:

- To practice paying for what you want with cash or a check.

- To show you how much you can save when you stop using credit to live beyond your means.

- To prove to you that with a credit card you spend more.

Earlier in the book I told you about an experiment by two professors, Drazen Prelec and Duncan Simester. Their study was called "Always Leave Home Without It: A Further Investigation of the Credit-Card Effect on Willingness to Pay." The professors found that when people were paying with a credit card, they were more likely to pay more (as much as 100 percent more). In this experiment, MBA students were offered the chance to bid on a pair of tickets to a sold-out, last regular-season game between the Boston Celtics and the Miami Heat. The Celtics needed to win to capture the division title. So these were hot, I-got-to-have-one tickets. One group of students was told their bid had to be paid for with cash. A second group was told their bid could be paid for with a credit card.

Not surprisingly, the group that had to come up with the cash bid significantly lower than those who could pay for their tickets with a credit card. The average cash bid was about $28. The average credit card bid was 113 percent higher at more than $60. To further their point and counter arguments that perhaps the people with the credit card earned more or had more money, the study also showed that had the students who bid with cash been allowed to pay with a credit card, they would have paid more.

"This is the first study that demonstrates that willingness-to-pay is increased when customers are instructed to use a credit card rather than cash," the study authors wrote.

I have no doubt that there exists a "credit card premium," as coined by the researchers. Think about it. We pile up stuff in a cart in the store without regard to the cash we have on hand (either in our wallet, purse, or bank account).

For example, take a typical trip to the mall. You've only got about $45 in cash. But that's okay because you only plan on buying a pair of $30 sneakers for your three-year-old son. That will leave you with $15 for lunch with the kids.

But then you see a buy-one-get-the-second-item-half-off sale. You figure you would be crazy not to get a second item. So, instead of one pair of shoes you pick up a second $30 pair of sandals ($15 on sale) for yourself. You don't need the shoes, but why waste a good sale, right? You look in your wallet and realize that if you pay for both pairs of shoes with cash, you won't have any money left over for lunch (there isn't an ATM nearby). Despite a promise to yourself to reduce your use of credit, you charge the shoes anyway. You walk out of the store pleased with your savings.

But wait. What just happened?

You only planned to spend $30 for one pair of shoes. You haven't saved $15. You've spent an additional $15. Using cash would have saved you money because you would have stuck to your budget. Yes, you got a great bargain on the second pair of shoes, but you didn't need them in the first place.

When you buy a $30 pair of shoes for $15, how much are you saving? Seems like a simple math question, right? You probably answered $15.

Wrong.

You didn't save a dime. You spent $15, and on credit.

Want to save yourself some real money? Stop "bargain shopping."

WHAT CREDIT COSTS

I'm not going to spend precious time telling you how to get a credit card or how to find a credit card with the best rates. There's no need for that. Just about anybody who wants a credit card can get one these days. Even people who have just walked out of bankruptcy court can get a credit card. That's because the credit card companies know that you can't file again for bankruptcy for another six years. That means any new debt can't be erased.

Instead, I want to discuss what your current credit card is costing you, emotionally and financially.

Just as an example, let me tell you the story of a young man I interviewed a few years ago. He was a twenty-seven-year-old mortgage broker earning nearly $100,000 annually. He was doing fine. He was living large—fancy car, nice home, eating out often. He had it all—until his company closed down. Less than four months after losing his job, the young man, who had amassed more than $30,000 in debt on almost a dozen credit cards, filed for bankruptcy. He gave up his car because he could not afford the $420 monthly payment. He no longer could spend $2,000 a month to eat in restaurants. He had to sell his belongings, except his clothes, and move back home with his parents. "I was wiped out almost instantly," he said.

The unemployed bankrupt broker represents a new breed of debtor: individuals earning decent salaries whose credit card debt is overwhelming them. Many end up filing for bankruptcy or going to a credit-counseling agency for help.

A survey by Visa found that of those individuals who had filed for bankruptcy during a twelve-month period in 1995 and 1996, nearly 29 percent said the precipitating factor was excessive spending, rather than family or professional emergencies.

With easy access to credit, many consumers are able to live longer on debt before a major crisis, such as a job loss, divorce, or medical problems, causes severe financial trauma. Often those borrowers continue to make minimum payments, keeping themselves afloat as long as they can until they can't carry the debt any longer.

Ann, a substitute teacher, didn't view herself as a deadbeat debtor.

Her bankruptcy wasn't an effort to shirk her financial responsibilities. She just didn't know what else to do. "I've had sleepless nights from this," she said. "I wonder who will know or who will find out." Ann said she tried to pay her debts, which at one point climbed to $129,000—more than three times her annual salary. In all, she had thirty credit cards with a total credit line of about $150,000. I know that's shocking, but it's a situation that's becoming all too common.

Ann acknowledged that she charged like there was no tomorrow. In addition to buying herself some things with credit cards, when friends needed money she took out advances on the cards or drew down her lines of credit at her bank. When her parents needed improvements on their home or new appliances, she charged it. When family or friends needed a down payment for a home or car, she lent them money. Her rationale for all this spending over twenty years: "I just felt guilty for what I had and what my family and friends didn't," she said soberly. "It was stupid."

For a while Ann tried to pay back her creditors. At first she paid just the minimum balances, but that wasn't making a big-enough dent in the debt. At one point she visited a counselor at Consumer Credit Counseling Service, which helps financially overwhelmed debtors work out a repayment plan with creditors. On the eighteenth of each month, she dropped off a check for $2,500.

But that whopping payment—more than most people's monthly mortgage—became impossible to make when her annual income dropped from $50,000 to about $30,000. She finally went to see a bankruptcy lawyer. "I just needed to get a little bit of relief," she said.

You might not be as bad off as Ann was, but many people are doing what Ann did. She kept accepting credit cards and using them because she kept getting seductive offers.

In the end Ann may have charged herself into bankruptcy, but the banks were there bankrolling her all the way. Just because you can get credit doesn't mean you should accept it.

If you want shock therapy, go sit in on a bankruptcy hearing. I've witnessed dozens of them. You won't find people gleefully sprinting from the courtroom, pleased to be able to wipe out all those bills. Instead, you will see women, men, elderly couples, single mothers, and out-of-work people trembling, teary-eyed, and terrified about someone finding out that they couldn't handle their finances.

You may not be headed for bankruptcy court, but many of you are nonetheless living on borrowed money at high interest rates. It's so easy to get caught in the credit card cyclone. You want for so much, and credit is so easy even if it is expensive.

And what you don't know about your credit card could cost you. Here are some common terms that you need to understand:

- *APR.* The annual percentage rate is the yearly interest rate you pay on any outstanding balance.

- *Cash advance.* Avoid borrowing cash on your card if you can. Cash advances usually carry a higher interest rate than purchases, incur an extra fee (often 2 to 5 percent), and come with no grace period. The interest on a cash advance begins accruing immediately. According to a credit card survey by Consumer Action, the average cash-advance APR in 2002 was 19.27 percent, compared with the 11.73 percent on purchases.

- *Credit available.* The amount still available after the lender deducts the amount you already owe on the card.

- *Credit limit.* The maximum amount you can owe at any time. If you go over your credit limit, you can be charged a fee and it might trigger a higher interest on the card.

- *Grace period.* This is the time during which you may pay for your purchases in full without being charged interest. Usually this is twenty-five days, but it's getting shorter—in some cases twenty days. For example, if the billing date on your credit card is September 1, you have until September 21 to pay your entire bill. That does not mean mailing it on September 20. Your payment has to reach the credit card company by the due date.

- *Late-payment charge.* If your payment arrives after the grace period, you may be charged a late fee. The majority of issuers in the Consumer Action survey charged a $29 late fee, but some issuers are charging up to $35. If you don't pay on time, late fees are not the only punishment you face: Almost three quarters of issuers impose a higher interest rate (also known as a default or delinquency rate) on customers who make one or more late payments. For example, if you make two late payments within six months, you could see your rate jump from 15 percent to almost 30 percent.

- *Minimum payment.* This is the percentage of your balance that must be paid monthly in order to not be in arrears. For many cards, that rate is as low as 2 percent of the unpaid balance.

On the back of the bill you should find which method is used to calculate the interest rate you are charged:

- *Fixed rate.* The interest rate remains constant until the credit card issuer gives written notice of a change. By federal law, issuers must notify consumers before changing the fixed-interest rate. Do you know you could reject the new rate? If the card issuer is based in Delaware, you can opt not to sign off on the changes, according to Robert McKinley, chief executive of CardWeb.com. You have to let the issuer know in writing before any due date specified in your notification. Doing so effectively closes the account, but you can continue to pay off the balance under the old terms. Signing off like this doesn't work with a variable-rate card, McKinley said.

- *Tiered rate.* Different rates are applied to different levels of your outstanding balance. For example, you may be charged 15 percent interest on the balance up to $1,000 and 18 percent on the amount over $1,000.

- *Variable rate.* The interest rate is subject to change depending on the index used by the issuer. Some of the common indexes are the prime rate or Treasury-bill rates (one, three, or six months).

Most important, realize that when you use a credit card you are getting a loan. If your credit card is not paid off in full each month, you incur a finance charge. The following are four methods used to calculate finance charges:

- *Average daily balance.* This is the most commonly used figure for determining interest charges. Your average daily balance is determined by adding each day's balance and then dividing that total by the number of days in the billing cycle. The daily balance includes the current outstanding balance plus any new charges and minus any payments or credits.

- *Adjusted balance.* This is figured by subtracting the payments you've made from the previous month's balance.

- *Two-cycle average daily balance.* The balance is calculated by averaging the daily balances for two consecutive months.

- *Previous balance.* The finance charge is based on the amount owed at the end of the previous billing period.

According to Consumer Action, a consumer group based in San Francisco, even though interest rates sank to a forty-year low in 2003, credit card rates still remained high. But you knew that.

Have you kept track of the other costs of using a credit card? Here's what Consumer Action found out in a 2003 survey of 143 credit cards from 47 lenders:

- Late fees continue to rise. They range from $10 to $35 at many issuers. The average late fee is $27. The majority of surveyed card companies charge a $29 late fee.

- More than one third of the issuers surveyed said they would raise a cardholder's rate because of poor credit with other creditors, even if that cardholder has a good record with them.

- Sixty-two percent of issuers surveyed hit cardholders with a late fee if their payment is not received by the due date. If you don't pay on time, late fees are not the only punishment you face. Seventy-six percent of all surveyed card issuers penalize customers who make one or more late payments. The penalty rates range from 12 to 29.99 percent.

Listen, if you choose to continue playing in this credit card game, make sure you know the rules. And the most important rule to remember: Paying the minimum every month is financial suicide.

WHERE DOES ALL THE GOOD AND BAD CREDIT INFORMATION GO?

Whether you like it or not, there is a credit file on you that contains information on how you pay your bills. This file exists primarily to give employers, lenders, landlords, utilities, and now insurance companies an ongoing account of how you pay your bills and repay loans. Think of it as your credit report card. Included in your file are the following:

- Personal information such as your full name, any previous names you may have used, current and previous addresses, Social Security number, current and past employers, and, if applicable, similar information about your spouse.

- Details about your loans and retail and credit card accounts, including account numbers. The report will identify your accounts by type, such as a mortgage, student loan, and revolving credit or installment loan. You will see the date you opened any accounts; your credit limit or the loan amount; any loan cosigners; and, most important, your payment history.

- A listing of any court action such as a bankruptcy filed by you, tax liens, or monetary judgments against you.

- A listing of all parties that have requested your credit report, including any inquiries you've made.

Your creditors supply the information in your file. The bureaus compile the information and sell it to businesses authorized to get a look at your file. Information in your credit report is used to evaluate your applications for credit, insurance, employment, and other purposes, such as leasing an apartment.

How do you get a copy of your credit report? All you have to do is contact the three major credit bureaus either by telephone, in writing, or via the Internet. The three major credit bureaus are:

- Equifax (www.equifax.com); P.O. Box 740241, Atlanta, GA 30374; (800) 685-1111

- Experian (www.experian.com); P.O. Box 2002, Allen, TX 75013; (888) 397-3742

- TransUnion (www.transunion.com); P.O. Box 2000, Chester, PA 19022; (800) 888-4213

Is there a charge for your credit report? Yes, if you order it from the bureaus. You will pay up to $9. However, you can get a free credit report if:

- You are a resident of Colorado, Massachusetts, Maryland, New Jersey, or Vermont. Residents of those states may receive one free credit report per year from each credit bureau. If you are a resident of Georgia, you may receive two free copies of your credit report each year from the credit bureaus.

- You have been denied credit, insurance, or employment within the past sixty days as a result of your credit history.

- You can certify in writing that you are unemployed and intend to apply for employment in the sixty-day period beginning on the date in which you made the certification.

- You are a recipient of public-welfare assistance or you have reason to believe that your file at the agency contains inaccurate information due to fraud.

There are a number of services that offer a three-in-one report with information from all three credit bureaus. The bureaus' websites offer these services, and these consolidated reports cost between $30 and $40. Let me do the math for you. If you order your report separately from each bureau at $9 each, that comes to $27 and a savings of about $13. However, it is nice to have an easy-to-read report with side-by-side information from all three bureaus. These all-in-one reports also eliminate the need for you to supply all your personal information three different times. For that, it may be worth the extra money. And the consolidated report often includes your credit score, which is a three-digit number used to determine your creditworthiness.

How long do the credit bureaus keep credit information in your file? Positive information can remain on your credit report indefinitely. So can a credit transaction involving a principal amount of $150,000 or more. However, negative information has to be removed after a certain time, depending on what it is. Here's how long:

- Bankruptcies: ten years from the settlement date.

- Civil suits and civil judgments: seven years from the filing date.

- Late payments: seven years from the date of the original delinquency.

- Accounts turned over to a collection agency: seven years.

- Paid tax liens: seven years.

Please keep in mind that your credit report is always changing. Information is being added all the time. That's why you should review yours for inaccuracies or omissions at least once a year. This is particularly important if you are considering making a major purchase, such as a car or home.

BEWARE OF THOSE WHO WOULD "FIX" YOUR DEBT

Almost every day I get e-mail from some company peddling a get-out-of-debt plan. One recent advertisement promised they could help folks be debt-free in "3 Easy Steps."

Yeah, right.

Getting out of debt is rarely easy. The truth is, it can be a painfully long journey back from the purgatory some debt can put you in. And many people are overwhelmed with debt these days, much of it because of credit cards. The average credit card debt for U.S. households in 2002 was $8,940.

As more people struggle to make even their minimum payments, they are turning to credit-counseling agencies for help. These agencies serve as debt middlemen. They negotiate with creditors on a debtor's behalf to, among other things, reduce the interest rate on a credit card and sometimes waive or reduce late fees and penalties. In return, debtors make one monthly payment to the credit-counseling agency, which then forwards the money to creditors.

In the past, credit-counseling agencies rarely charged for their services because they were financially supported by creditors, who saw the debt management plans, or DMPs, as a chance to recoup what they were owed.

But so many cash-strapped consumers have signed up for debt plans that creditors have cut back on their funding. In many cases, the debt plans are no better than what people who can negotiate on their own get. The cutback in funds by creditors has resulted in agencies routinely charging people a setup fee and a monthly fee. Some agencies charge as much as a full month's consolidated payment—usually hundreds of dollars—simply to establish an account.

Most problematic, say consumer advocates, is that there is more emphasis on debt consolidation and less on credit counseling. There has been a proliferation of agencies that critics call "debt mills," which try to sign up as many people as possible and put them in cookie-cutter debt programs. If you aren't careful, you could end up in worse financial shape than you were in before you signed up for one of these programs, contends a 2002 report, "Credit Counseling in Crisis," by the National Consumer Law Center and the Consumer Federation of America.

"There are a lot of good credit-counseling agencies out there, but there are also a lot of bad ones," said Deanne Loonin, a staff lawyer for the law center.

The credit-counseling report found that agencies often harm debtors with improper advice, deceptive practices, and excessive fees. Here are some of the typical complaints outlined in the report:

- Debt payments being sent late or not at all.

- Claims that fees for the debt-repayment plan are voluntary when they aren't.

- Excessive fees.

- Failure to adequately disclose fees.

Travis B. Plunkett, the legislative director of Consumer Federation, said no matter how desperate you are, take the time to evaluate all your options before signing up with a credit-counseling agency. "Unfortunately, when people take too long to deal with their debt problem, they often act in panic," he said. "But that can be a big mistake. Take a deep breath. Call around, and don't just respond to an e-mail or television ad."

According to the report, these are some reasons to reject an agency:

- *High fees.* In general, if the setup fee for a debt-management plan is more than $50 and the monthly fee more than $25, look for a better deal. "However, if the agency is offering extra services such as budget counseling or an educational program, it's reasonable for them to charge extra," Plunkett said. "But you don't have to spend hundreds of dollars to find a good credit-counseling agency."

- *Unreasonable promises.* Creditors, not agencies, determine which concessions will be made, said Lydia Sermons-Ward, a spokeswoman for the National Foundation for Credit Counseling, a nonprofit credit-counseling network. "Any agency that says they can guarantee a reduction in your payments or interest rate is giving you false information." In fact, many creditors are becoming increasingly unwilling to reduce interest rates for consumers who enter debt-management programs. More and more credit card issuers have increased the interest rate they offer to consumers entering debt plans, according to the credit-counseling report.

- *Suggesting that services are free.* Some agencies will tell you that their fees are voluntary but then will pressure you to pay the fees in full. If that happens, go somewhere else. Don't be pressured to pay. If the agency is vague or reluctant to talk about specific fees, take a walk. There are enough good agencies with low fees that you shouldn't pay an amount you can't afford.

- *Too short a relationship.* Any agency that offers you a debt-management plan in less than twenty minutes hasn't spent enough time looking at your finances. Keep in mind that even if the agency is a nonprofit, it is not necessarily a do-gooder organization. An effective counseling session—whether on the phone or in person—takes a significant amount of time.

If you need more information, try the National Foundation for Credit Counseling at (800) 388-2227. The member agencies also provide information online at www.debtadvice.org.

Besides the member agencies of the foundation, there are a few organizations whose mission is to provide a much more comprehensive approach to people's debt troubles. For example, there is Myvesta (800 MYVESTA or www.myvesta.org), a nonprofit consumer-education organization, which provides a range of debt, counseling, and educational services. As Steve Rhode, president and cofounder of Myvesta, said to me, many debtors need a complete plan to prevent them from returning to the same habits that got them into debt in the first place. "The primary focus needs to be on total solution options, which incorporates assisting the consumer through life and financial times and working with creditors."

So, can I give you a little advice? If you're in financial trouble because you're a poor money manager, signing up just for a debt plan is a temporary solution to a long-term problem you know you need to fix. If you want to use a credit-counseling company, find one that offers comprehensive counseling. Go into the office. Sit down with somebody. If you need some additional support try Debtors Anonymous (www.debtorsanonymous.org). The primary focus of the group is to help people stop incurring any unsecured debt one day at a time and to help compulsive debtors achieve solvency. To find a local Debtors Anonymous chapter in your area, go to the organization's website.

To be sure, debt plans have worked for some people. If, for example, you got behind in your bills because you lost your job or encountered a one-time financial crisis, a debt plan can get you back on track. However, if you have some real money issues, you may need some real counseling. If you don't address the behavior that got you deep in debt, a quick-fix debt-management plan won't help over the long term.

FIXING YOUR CREDIT REPORT CAN BE LIKE CLIMBING MOUNT EVEREST—BUT CLIMB ANYWAY

I'm constantly advising people to check their credit report. But what should you do if you find an error?

First, you should know that under the Fair Credit Reporting Act, the credit bureaus and any business that supplies them with data are supposed to correct inaccurate information in your report.

I use the word *supposed* because in practice, getting erroneous information removed from your credit file can be like climbing Mount Everest—a cold, hard, and exasperating expedition.

Just ask Judy Thomas. It took the Oregon real estate agent six years and a lawsuit to get TransUnion to remove the name and bad credit history of another woman from her credit file. Thomas's lawsuit resulted in one of the largest awards ever made in such a case. A jury agreed that Thomas should receive $300,000 for the harm to her reputation and health and a $5 million punitive award. The judge overseeing the case reduced the punitive award to $1 million while allow-ing the $300,000 in damages to stand, according to Michael C. Baxter, Thomas's Portland-based attorney.

Baxter, who specializes in representing consumers in disputes with credit-reporting agencies, said the Thomas lawsuit highlighted a major flaw in how credit bureaus investigate consumer complaints. "The bu-reaus go back to the source, and the creditor often just confirms the er-roneous information," he said. "It's crazy. I have a case in which the person would have been only five years old when an account was opened. It's hilarious."

It can also be maddening. "There were days when I went home in tears," Thomas said. "Creditors would say to me, 'Lady, just pay the bill.' But it wasn't my debt. The bad information would be taken off my credit report and then put back again."

Despite her ordeal, Thomas still believes it is best to try to get in-accurate information removed from your credit file. According to the Federal Trade Commission, here's what you should do:

- Tell each credit-reporting agency in writing what information you believe is inaccurate and request a deletion or correction. Provide your complete name and address. Your letter should clearly identify each item in your report that you dispute.

- Enclose a copy of your report with the items in question circled.

- Include copies (not originals) of documents that support your position.

- Send your letter by certified mail, return receipt requested, so you can prove that the credit bureau received the information.

- Keep records of everything and everyone you talk to. "If you have to start a whole new file cabinet, do it," Thomas said.

- You may need to send your letter to all three major bureaus (see page 80) if the information is incorrect in all of your credit files. You can also dispute information online with all three compa-nies. You will need a current copy of your credit report.

Here's what is supposed to happen after you've made your case:

- The law requires credit agencies to investigate disputed information and correct inaccuracies within thirty days of hearing from a consumer.

- The credit bureaus must forward all relevant data you provide about the dispute to the information provider. But I wouldn't wait for that to happen. Call and then send your own letter with copies of all documents supporting your position to whatever business or creditor is supplying the wrong data to the credit bureau.

- When both the information provider and credit-bureau investigations are complete, you must be given written results and a free copy of your report if the dispute results in a change.

- A reinvestigation may not resolve your dispute. If that happens, ask the credit agency to include your statement of the dispute in your file and in future reports.

If you don't get satisfactory action from the credit bureau, you have at least two recourses. You can complain to the Federal Trade Commission. To file a complaint go to www.ftc.gov, call toll-free (877) 382-4357, or write to the Consumer Response Center, CRC-240, Federal Trade Commission, Washington, DC 20580.

Unfortunately, the FTC does not resolve individual consumer problems. Nonetheless, your complaint might lead to some law-enforcement action.

Your second option is to file a lawsuit.

"The more people who file lawsuits, the more the consumer reporting agencies will have to change their methods," Thomas said. Baxter warned, however, that this type of case is hard to win and costly for the consumer. But if you have a particularly egregious case, go for it. You may find a lawyer to take the case on contingency, meaning the lawyer would get paid only if you win an award. The American Bar Association has a web page (www.abanet.org/legalservices/lris/directory.html) with links to state lawyer-referral programs.

When it comes to your credit report, your best defense is to catch errors early. Get a copy of your credit report at least once a year. Check it thoroughly, and immediately dispute any inaccuracies.

SAMPLE DISPUTE LETTER

Date
Your Name
Your Address
Your City, State, Zip Code

Complaint Department
Name of Credit Reporting Agency
Address
City, State, Zip Code

Dear Sir or Madam:

I am writing to dispute the following information in my file. The items I dispute are also circled on the attached copy of my credit report. [In the letter, identify item(s) disputed by name of source, such as creditors or tax court, and type of item, such as credit account, judgment, etc.]

This item is (inaccurate or incomplete) because [describe what is inaccurate or incomplete and why]. I am requesting that the item be deleted to correct the information.

Enclosed are copies of [use this sentence if applicable and describe any enclosed documentation, such as payment records, canceled checks, court documents] supporting my position. Please reinvestigate this (these) matter(s) and (delete or correct) the disputed item(s) as soon as possible.

Sincerely,
Your Name

Source: Federal Trade Commission

FOR A PRICE, KNOW THE SCORE ON CREDIT

You think your SAT score was important? Your credit score is the granddaddy of all grades.

Fair Isaac and Company of San Rafael, California, created the widely used computer-scoring model that assigns people a score based on information in their credit files. It is a three-digit number (generally ranging from 300 to 850) that is used by lenders to judge who might be a good credit risk. The higher the score, the lower the risk—and the lower the interest rate you might pay on a home or auto loan.

It wasn't too long ago that consumers, for the most part, were barred from seeing their credit scores. Now the three major credit bureaus—Equifax, Experian, and TransUnion—allow consumers to obtain their credit score for a fee.

There are two types of credit scores. The first is a FICO score, used by all three major credit bureaus. Then there are credit scores you can get free that use factors similar to but not the same as those used by Fair Isaac. Free scores are available from many online companies, such as E-Loan. In exchange for a free score, however, you may be bombarded with e-mails offering you various loan or consumer credit products.

You can get your FICO score for $12.95 from three websites: www.myfico.com, www.equifax.com, and www.transunioncs.com. Although Experian uses Fair Isaac's scoring formula, the credit score it sells to consumers for $14.95 is based on its own model. TransUnion also provides consumers with a credit score based on its own scoring system at no additional cost when you buy a basic credit report.

Should you spend the money to order your credit score? Yes. This is especially so if you are in the habit of paying bills late, carrying a stack of credit cards, or make minimum credit card payments. A look at your credit score might be just the kick in the pants you need to motivate you to better manage your debts and say no to taking on more.

"If your interest in credit scores is casual, then you should seek out a free score, since accuracy isn't very important," suggested Craig Watts, a spokesman for Fair Isaac. "But if you're thinking of applying for a loan and want to know what kind of reception to expect from lenders, then only the FICO score will do."

According to Fair Isaac, here's the national distribution of credit scores in the United States:

13 percent of people score below 600

11 percent score between 600 and 649

16 percent score between 650 and 699

20 percent score between 700 and 749

40 percent score above 750

Fair Isaac has introduced a feature on its website, www.myfico.com, that it says is an attempt to show people the link between their credit scores and the interest rates offered on residential mortgage, home-equity, and auto loans. The website shows national and statewide average annual percentage rates, updated daily. These rates are then matched to FICO score ranges.

For example, say you live in Florida. People with a credit score in the 720–850 range, on average, got a fixed rate of 5.737 percent for a thirty-year mortgage in early 2003. But people with a credit score between 500 and 559 got an average rate of 8.6 percent. On a $100,000 loan, that would mean the person with the lower credit score would have a monthly mortgage payment of $776, compared with a $583 payment for the borrower with the much higher credit score. Total savings over the life of the loan: $69,575. Of course, as interest rates go up, the difference in monthly payment rises also.

A calculator on the Fair Isaac website helps estimate what savings a borrower could realize if he had a higher credit score. For others, the rate information could be used to help negotiate a better rate on a mortgage, home-equity, or auto loan. "We hope this will help people control their credit and get better deals," said Sue Simon, a vice president at Fair Isaac. "We tried to aim this for people who have the most to gain by improving their credit score."

For instance, let's assume you live in California and you want to buy a new car. Right now you have a credit score in the 625–659 range. Based on data collected from lenders in California in early 2003, people in that range on average received an interest rate of 11.989 percent for a sixty-month new-car loan. But if you had paid down all of your credit cards a bit before applying for the car loan and pushed your score up into the 660–689 range, you might have qualified for a rate of 5.928 percent.

In early 2003, on a $20,000, sixty-month new-car loan, that would reduce your monthly payments by $59, according to estimates by Fair Isaac. Over the life of the auto loan you would save $3,527.

Of course, you can't run into a bank with any of this information

and demand a certain rate. The actual interest rate for which you qualify may depend on several other important factors in addition to a
credit score, such as your income, down payment, and debt-to-income
ratios. But what Fair Isaac is offering certainly provides a useful tool
that might help you get a better deal.

Everything You've Ever Wanted to Know About Your Credit Score but Had No Inkling to Ask

For some, especially those who aren't sure about their creditworthiness,
a credit score can help provide leverage if it turns out to be better than
they thought, though lenders often consider factors other than just
your score.

So, what factors can help boost your score or send it down? Take a
look: A thirty-day-late payment made just a month ago will count
against you more than a ninety-day-late payment five years ago. In
some cases, having a very small balance without missing a payment
may be slightly better than having no credit balance at all.

What about your track record for paying your bills? The first thing
any lender would want to know is whether you have paid credit accounts on time. But late payments are not an automatic score killer. An
overall good credit picture can outweigh one or two instances of late
credit card payments. By the same token, having no late payments in
your credit report doesn't mean you will get a perfect score. If you pay
your bills on time, keep credit card balances low, and apply for new
credit sparingly, you should be in good shape.

Having credit accounts and owing money on them does not mean
you are a high-risk borrower with a low score. But owing a great deal of
money on many accounts can indicate that you are overextended and
more likely to make some payments late or not at all. Part of the science of scoring is determining how much is too much for a given credit
profile. Generally you want to use no more than 50 percent of the limits on your credit cards. In general, a longer credit history will increase
your score. But even people with short credit histories can get high
scores. People tend to have more credit today and to shop for credit—
via the Internet and other channels—more frequently than ever. Fair
Isaac scores reflect this fact. But research shows that opening several
credit accounts in a short period does represent greater risk—especially

for people who do not have a long-established credit history. This also extends to requests for credit, as indicated by "inquiries" to the credit-reporting agencies (an inquiry is a request by a lender for a copy of your credit report).

Your credit score will reflect your mix of credit cards, retail accounts, installment loans, finance-company accounts, and mortgage loans. It is not necessary to have one of each, and it is not a good idea to open credit accounts you don't intend to use. So stop opening credit accounts with retail chains just to get that 10 percent discount. Having too many of such accounts, even if you never intend to use them, can hurt your score and ultimately cost you more by way of higher interest rates. If that happens, that 10 percent discount could end up costing you plenty.

As you can see, FICO scores consider a wide range of information on your credit report. However, according to Fair Isaac, they do not consider the following:

- *Your race, color, religion, national origin, sex, and marital status.* Federal law prohibits credit scoring from considering these facts, as well as any receipt of public assistance, or the exercise of any consumer right under the Consumer Credit Protection Act.

- *Your age.* Other types of scores may consider your age, but FICO scores don't.

- *Your salary, occupation, title, employer, date employed, or employment history.* Lenders may consider this information, however, as may other types of scores.

- *Where you live.*

- *Any interest rate being charged on a particular credit card or other account.*

- *Any items reported as child/family-support obligations or rental agreements.*

- *Certain types of inquiries* (requests for your credit report).

The score does not count "consumer-initiated" inquiries—requests you have made for your own credit report, in order to check it out. It also does not count "promotional inquiries"—requests made by lenders in order to make you a "pre-approved" credit offer—or "administrative inquiries"—requests made by lenders to review your account with them. Requests that are marked as coming from employers are not counted either.

Here are some of the more frequently asked questions and answers provided by Fair Isaac:

Q: How can I improve my FICO score?
A: Your FICO-score analysis will suggest things you can do to improve your score over time. Generally, people with high FICO scores consistently

- Pay bills on time.

- Keep balances low on credit cards and other revolving credit products.

- Apply for and open new credit accounts only as needed.

Q: What's the most important factor in a score?
A: FICO scores consider five main kinds of credit information. Listed from most important to least important, these are

- Payment history.

- Amount owed.

- Length of credit history.

- New credit.

- Types of credit in use.

Q: How often does my score change?
A: Your credit file is continually updated with new information from your creditors. The FICO score is calculated based on the latest snapshot of information contained in your file at the time the score is requested. So your FICO score from a month ago is probably not the same score a lender would get from the credit-reporting agency

today. Fluctuations of a few points from month to month are quite common.

Q: What are the highest and lowest FICO scores?

A: FICO scores range from 300 to 850. The higher the score, the lower the predicted credit risk for lenders.

Q: Does requesting that your credit limit be lowered help your credit score?

A: No, it won't help your FICO score if you have your credit limit lowered. FICO scores don't penalize you for having a lot of available credit. They are more concerned with how you manage the credit you already have. The best way to raise your FICO score is to pay down your current account balances and always pay your bills on time.

COSIGNING YOUR FINANCIAL LIFE AWAY

Despite all her tribulations, Big Mama had "good" credit by anybody's standard. In her entire life, she never paid a late fee. My grandmother managed to make ends meet by following several simple rules, one of which was to never cosign for anybody for anything.

I learned about this money rule the hard way. After graduating from college, I asked my grandmother if she would cosign a loan so I could buy a car. It wasn't an expensive car, just a basic Ford Escort. It didn't even have air-conditioning.

"Child, have you lost your everlasting mind?" she said, in what turned into an hour-long lecture about the dangers of cosigning. "You ain't going to mess up my credit. You better go out there and catch you a bus until the bank says you can get credit on your own." She went on to say: "If the bank, which has more money than me, doesn't think you are able to handle the loan, then what makes you think I can handle it if you don't pay it like you supposed to?"

I caught the bus until I could stand on my own creditworthy feet.

Big Mama was absolutely right. Think about it. When you cosign, you're being asked to take a risk that the lender wouldn't take. If the borrower was a good risk, he wouldn't need a cosigner. Under federal law, creditors are required to give you a notice that explains your obligations. The cosigner's notice, according to the FTC, states:

- You are being asked to guarantee this debt. If the borrower does not pay the debt, you will have to. Be sure you can afford to pay if you have to, and that you want to accept this responsibility.

- You may have to pay up to the full amount of the debt if the borrower does not pay. You may also have to pay late fees or collection costs, which increase this amount.

- The creditor can collect this debt from you without first trying to collect from the borrower. However, your state law might forbid a creditor from collecting from a cosigner without first trying to collect from the primary debtor.

- The creditor can use the same collection methods against you that can be used against the borrower, such as suing you, garnishing your wages, et cetera. If this debt is ever in default, that fact may become a part of your credit record.

I understand there may be times that you will break Big Mama's rule against cosigning. You may have a relative or friend whom you really want to help. If you do choose to cosign, consider the following recommendations from the FTC:

- Be sure you can afford to pay the loan in full.

- Try to negotiate the specific terms of your obligation. For example, you may want to limit your liability to the principal on the loan, and not include late charges, court costs, or attorneys' fees. In this case, ask the lender to include a statement in the contract similar to "The cosigner will be responsible only for the principal balance on this loan at the time of default."

- Ask the lender to agree, in writing, to notify you if the borrower misses a payment. That will give you time to deal with the problem or make back payments without having to repay the entire amount immediately.

- Make sure you get copies of all paperwork, such as the loan contract, the Truth-in-Lending Disclosure Statement, and war-
  ranties. You may need these documents if there's a dispute
  between the borrower and the seller.

- Check your state law for additional cosigner rights.

Cosigning may seem like no big deal, but it can ruin your credit,
even if the primary borrower is good for the money. Remember, life
happens. People lose their jobs, get divorced, get sick and die. You may
not be as dogmatic about this rule as my grandmother was, but if you
cosign, be sure you can make the loan payments if it comes to that.

HOUSE-POOR

I've talked about the evil lure of credit card debt and how your credit
score can determine how much you pay for your home loan; now let
me focus on the two assets that most people have to use credit to buy—
a home and a car.

First, let's discuss buying a home.

I know you have heard—probably from a real estate agent—that
you should buy as much house as you can afford. In the early 1980s,
when home prices were soaring, such advice might have made sense.
Back then it was a safe bet that almost any house would increase
tremendously in value, giving the buyer a big windfall in a later sale.

But that advice isn't always good. In many areas, certain segments
of the housing market, such as town houses and condos, have seen little or no appreciation. Home values don't always go up. This is especially true in black neighborhoods, where home values traditionally do
not increase as fast as home values in similarly situated white communities do.

Most important, many new-home buyers aren't putting down
much money. A 2 to 5 percent down payment is now common, down
from the old standard of 10 to 20 percent.

Although low or no down payments allow many buyers to get in
the door, they also may help kick them out the door later—when
they're forced to sell a house they couldn't really afford in the first place.

I cringe whenever I hear someone say their house is their best investment. A house is where you live. You hope that it will appreciate, and for many Americans it has, but you should plan for your house to just be the place where you lay your head. It is true that you should buy as much home as you can afford, but when I say it I mean something entirely different from what your real estate broker or banker means.

On paper your home deal might work. Your debt-to-income ratio or how much income you have to support your debt load including your mortgage might pass muster with a lender, but do the math honestly. The numbers that lenders crunch to get you into your home don't include the unexpected expense—a job loss, a divorce, or a hefty car-repair bill.

Lenders primarily look at two lending limits. The first is how much mortgage debt (including insurance and taxes) you can handle compared with your gross monthly income. Generally your mortgage shouldn't be more than 28 percent of your monthly income. For example, a person earning $45,000 a year should only carry a mortgage of $1,050 a month. The second limit adds on other debt (car payment, credit card debt). That limit shouldn't exceed 36 percent of your gross monthly income.

However, people do whatever they can to squeeze into a home. They borrow money to pay down their credit card bills to qualify for the home loan. But as soon as the ink on the settlement paper is dry, they have plans to charge those cards right back up. You want a home so bad that you ignore the fact that you are really stretching to get in the door.

Take this deal described to me by a real estate agent in the Washington, D.C., area. A couple living in a $70,000 home in the District wanted to buy a $200,000 place in the suburbs. They didn't have much money saved and were still paying off creditors after filing for personal bankruptcy. Yet a lender was willing to give them a loan to buy a $200,000 house—at a steep interest rate, of course.

"How do you advise people in that situation?" the agent said. "They are jumping out there just after having gotten through a bankruptcy. But they want the big, pretty house. If I tell them no, they will just go get another agent."

Here's another example. A home buyer has $37,000 in income; his only major debt is a $300 monthly car payment. He isn't putting any money down on a $129,000 house because he is using a V.A. loan-guarantee program that doesn't require a down payment. His monthly mortgage payments would total $1,200.

The numbers say he can handle the mortgage. But do the math. This guy doesn't have much room for error. If he has a major interruption in his income or a financial setback, he's in trouble. Remember the ratios are based on gross pay, not what you take home. Even with the mortgage-interest deduction, you have to carefully consider how much house you can afford.

Once you show up at the office of a Realtor or a mortgage lender, don't expect to be talked out of buying a house or talked into buying a smaller one. The ratios financial institutions use to make loans only tell people what they are capable of doing if everything goes right. So, what if something goes wrong? Many people are not adequately prepared or educated about the home-purchase process. They have no cushion.

With cleaned-up credit records, many new home buyers are living large. They buy a new car or a big-screen television or expensive furniture to go with the new house, and that is a formula for disaster.

Even many consumer advocates—who have been pushing for years to get lenders to make more home loans to low- and middle-income families—say they are concerned about home buyers who are able to purchase homes with little or no money down, tiny savings, and sizable credit card debt. "Lenders and real estate agents are not always making decisions that are in the best interest of every borrower," said John E. Taylor, president of the National Community Reinvestment Coalition. "There is a thin line between letting people participate in the dream of home ownership and placing them in a devastating position," said one official from the Mortgage Bankers Association.

As one housing expert put it, purchasing a house isn't like jumping into a pool and swimming around until you get used to the water. If you jump into the housing market and can't handle your mortgage, you may drown financially.

Don't base your mortgage planning only on the ratios used by a lender. Consider all potential expenses that aren't factored in to a loan application. For example, at one point I supported a disabled brother. Keeping that in mind, my husband and I bought a house far below what the lenders said we could afford. That cushion has also allowed us to send our children to private school and save for their college education.

If one day my husband loses his mind and runs off with some

home-wrecking hussy, I can afford the house payment on just my income. If one day I decide I just can't take the pressures of daily deadlines, I can afford to quit because we can afford the house on just my husband's paycheck. And we don't live in a shack. We have a two-story, four-bedroom colonial. But we moved to a lower-cost area because we wanted a nice home for an affordable price. The real estate agent thought we were being too conservative. "You know you can afford more house," he said to us.

"Yes, we know, but we bought what we can handle today, tomorrow, or the next thirty years," I said.

My husband and I don't think of our home as an investment. It's where we live.

When hunting for a home consider the following:

- Have a cash cushion. Even if you don't have to make a down payment, make sure you have enough money saved to tide you over if your income drops. Sure, you can squeeze into the house with little money. But look at your total financial picture. Maybe you should scale back and get a smaller house with a smaller mortgage note so you can keep some of your savings. This is particularly true for couples starting out. Remember, one of you might want to stay home after you have children. Get a big house note, and that option goes away.

- Buy a home you can live in for several years. I'm not suggesting you buy a "starter home." But buy a home you can live in for the duration. Use what I call the ten-year rule. Ask yourself if you could live in the house you are buying for ten years, even if you have kids or a relative has to move in. If your income rises or you want to move later, you are still in a great position because you've been able to save for the next down payment even if your present home doesn't appreciate.

- When calculating your mortgage payments, make sure you include room for savings. So many people are so focused on qualifying for a home that once the loan payments start there isn't much leftover to pay themselves first. When figuring out your ratios, add your savings or investment goal into the equation just like it was a debt payment.

- Take a home-buyer's education course. Most banks, mortgage lenders, and community housing groups offer workshops for new home buyers. Check with your state housing office for local programs. You can also get a lot of information from Fannie Mae and Freddie Mac (both of the groups are in the business to buy home loans to make more money available so lenders can make more home loans). Visit Fannie Mae's website at http://www.homepath.com. It offers a lot of information about buying a home, especially for the first time. Freddie Mac's web address is: http://www.freddiemac.com.

Today home ownership is an attainable goal for most people, but you have to let your gut be your guide. If deep down you feel you are overreaching your budget by buying a certain house, then you probably are.

PAYING OFF YOUR MORTGAGE

My grandmother couldn't wait to pay off her mortgage. Big Mama's goal was to retire with no house payment, and she reached her goal. She retired at sixty-five and died at eighty-two, giving her seventeen years without worrying about a mortgage.

However, many financial planners these days tell aging home owners not to worry about paying off their mortgage. Experts point to the tremendous tax break that home owners get. They argue that the money could be better invested.

Personally, I've been vacillating on this issue. I want the peace of mind of knowing that the roof over my retired head is paid for. Yet I'm not sure it's wise to make extra principal payments or pay off my mortgage early, because if I need my cash in the future, it will be tied up in my house.

Before paying off your mortgage, consider the following:

- Do you have an emergency stash of cash? You should have at the very least three to six months of living expenses saved. You may need to save more if you work in an industry hit hard by layoffs. Keep in mind that once you lose your job and your income drops, you may not be able to tap into your home equity by getting a loan.

- Do you have any higher-interest debt? If so, pay that off first.

- Have you fully funded any tax-deferred retirement accounts available to you?

- Do you need the money for other financial goals first, such as paying for your children's college education?

Finally, many of my readers tell me that they believe paying off a mortgage before retirement is worth the peace of mind even if a financial calculation proves otherwise. "[My dad] only held two jobs his whole life, neither of which offered a pension or other perks for retirement," one man wrote. "At the end of his working life, all he had for living expenses was the monthly Social Security check. By the time he retired at age seventy, he made sure the house—the largest living expense in any household—was paid off. And that, I think, is a key factor missing from your calculation whether to pay off the house: How near are you to retirement? Returns on investments are uncertain; the cost of a mortgage is not. You can be sure that by the time I hit retirement age, the mortgage will be paid off. And I'll thank Dad for the lesson!" The lesson for all of us: There are many variables to consider if you want to pay off your mortgage early. No one rule of thumb or calculation is best for everyone.

Think about your current and future financial needs. For example, my husband and I have decided to invest any extra money we have rather than make additional mortgage payments. We have three small children to put through college, so we don't want to tie our money up in our home.

However, if you are like Big Mama and you would feel more secure paying off your home, then do so if you have the means.

DON'T DRIVE YOURSELF TO DEBT

I've heard otherwise rational people say they *need* to buy a new car because their current car needs some repairs. During a seminar I was conducting, a woman raised her hand and said she and her husband needed help with a decision to buy a new car. Their old car needed about $1,500 in repairs, but they had been eyeing a car that cost $25,000. "How do you decide when it's time to buy a new car?" she asked.

I turned around and wrote down a simple formula on the blackboard. On one side of the equation I put down $1,500. On the other side I wrote down $25,000.

"I'm not a math genius, so you'll have to tell me," I said to the woman. "Which number is smaller?" That's your answer.

I know you're tired of cursing the clunker you've been driving because it's parked at the repair shop more than in your driveway. Or maybe you don't really need a new car, but your present vehicle is looking a little dinged-up. Perhaps you just miss that new-car smell. So, you've begun the hunt for a new car.

But there is another option. You could hang on to your old car as long as possible, especially if it's paid for. As the refrain of one of my favorite blues songs says, "It's cheaper to keep her."

Look at a theoretical case involving two popular 1996 models, a Honda Accord and a Ford Taurus. Say that each car has been driven 75,000 miles, mostly urban driving. On average, a consumer could expect over the next two years to pay repair costs of $1,000 for the Accord and $1,040 on the Taurus, according to calculations by Edmunds.com. That $1,000 (or $1,040) is definitely cheaper than financing a $20,000 new car, even at no interest.

Personally, I drive my car until it's breaking down so often that my mechanic is on speed-dial. I have only one rule when it comes to trading in my car. If it's breaking down unexpectedly and leaving me stranded, then it's time to buy another *used* car. I don't want to be sputtering on the Interstate. But if the problems are things that I planned to have repaired—brakes going bad, new muffler, air-conditioning—it's much more economical to just have the car repaired.

Perhaps at no other time has the used-car market been so good, thanks in part to all those folks who lease. But let's look at the question of whether it's time to buy a new car.

Setting aside such subjective considerations as image, comfort, safety, and reliability, Runzheimer International, a Rochester, Wisconsin–based management-consulting firm, took a look at the costs of keeping an older car versus buying a new one.

"New-car payments are the decisive factor," according to David Friedlen, director of product development and research at Runzheimer and car-cost expert. "Even though the new-model vehicle has a much greater trade-in value after four years and you save on repairs and maintenance, the monthly car payments more than counterbalance these other factors."

HAVE I GOT A DEAL FOR YOU!

Want a good car for a good price? This is the time to go the used-car route, especially if you are looking for a late-model vehicle. Perhaps at no other time in automotive history have there been so many high-quality used cars on the market.

What's going on?

Many two-, three-, and four-year leases are expiring. Car-rental companies are selling vehicles from their fleets because of a slowdown in travel. And because consumers often trade in cars when they buy new ones, the incentives that dealers have offered on new cars—cash rebates and low interest rates, including no interest at all—have resulted in a lot more trade-ins than the industry expected. All those factors have brought prices on used cars down, according to a spokesman for Cars.com, an online resource that helps consumers search for new and used vehicles.

A number of other excellent websites (Edmunds.com, Auto-Trader.com, Carfax.com, IntelliChoice.com) also help buyers in their search for reliable, safe used cars at fair prices.

"The Internet has made a big difference in the used-car market," said Bill Swislow, vice president and executive producer for Cars.com. "The Internet has allowed consumers to become more comfortable and knowledgeable about the car they are buying."

Buying a used car still comes with some risk. You could buy a lemon. The first used car I purchased from a private seller gave me so much trouble that I carried a box of tissues for all the tears I shed while waiting for roadside assistance. It was a good thing my grandfather was a tow-truck driver.

I made quite a few mistakes when I bought that piece of junk. First, I was in a rush. I wanted a car so badly that I didn't take the time to look around. I didn't check to see if that model had a good track record. I didn't have a mechanic inspect the car.

Fortunately, there are now many resources, Internet and otherwise, to help you research a vehicle's price, reliability, safety, and history.

You may want to start with the *Consumer Reports Used Car Buying*

Guide. For a very reasonable sum you get a comprehensive report on the most reliable used cars, SUVs, pickup trucks, wagons, and minivans.

To check for a history of safety recalls on a vehicle, *Consumer Reports* recommends calling (800) 424-9393 or going to www.nhtsa.dot.gov. Other safety sites to check include www.autosafety.org and www.lemonaidcars.com. Edmunds.com provides used-car reviews, prices, and advice.

For a fee, Carfax (www.carfax.com) will check a vehicle's history for hidden problems. You can order a Carfax report using the prospective auto's vehicle-identification number, or VIN, to detect such problems as a rolled-back odometer, previous use as a fleet or police car, or a major accident in its history. If you're still worried about buying someone else's trouble, you may want to try a "certified" used car. Many dealers are offering late-model, relatively low-mileage used cars and trucks with no history of major damage. These vehicles are usually more expensive but are often covered by a warranty that extends beyond the original factory warranty. IntelliChoice.com rates many of the certified or preowned used-car programs.

If you do your homework, you can save thousands of dollars by buying a used car. For example, I did a little research to find a good used car for under $10,000.

I looked over the *Consumer Reports* list of used cars that have shown above-average reliability. I picked the 1996 Toyota Camry LE. Then I checked with Cars.com, which found a 1996 Camry for $8,995 with 66,756 miles. The invoice price for a new Camry LE with similar features was $19,810, according to Cars.com. That's a difference of $10,815.

With deals like this available, I don't think I'll ever buy a new car again. And I know I won't have to, thanks to people who trade in perfectly good cars—often before they have even paid off their current loan.

I won't have to buy a new car thanks to people who think paying thousands of dollars over a three-year period to rent (oh, I mean lease) a car is good money management.

I just love people who lease. They provide us penny-pinchers with a wonderful opportunity to buy well-maintained used cars with relatively low mileage. After all, most lease contracts require the renter (um, lessee) to return the car in good condition with few dings and dents. Otherwise they have to pay a hefty wear-and-tear charge.

I know there are many reasons why people prefer a new car to a used car. Manufacturers are constantly upgrading their models and adding better safety features.

But if you wait just a bit, you can capitalize on those new features and get a great deal in the process. Remember, this isn't your father's used-car market anymore.

THE PATH OF LEASE RESISTANCE

Let me say up front that I will never lease a car. Nowhere in this book will you find details on how to lease a car. Giving you advice on how to lease would be like a minister telling his congregation not to fornicate and then saying, "But if you do, here's how to protect yourself."

I believe in buying the best car I can afford—and letting it rust off the road before replacing it. As long as the car is safe and reliable, I'll drive it for years, dings and all.

My first car was a pumpkin-colored Datsun that received more than its share of laughs from family and friends. I didn't care. It may not have been the best-looking car around, but I drove it proudly—knowing that I had paid cash for my used jack-o'-lantern. It's hard for me to understand why people find it so enticing to lease a nice car they wouldn't be able to buy—only to have to give it back three or four or five years later.

Don't listen to the auto dealers who promise no money down and low monthly payments. It's not true. You do have to make a down payment to get that low monthly payment. In addition, you may end up paying thousands of dollars at the end of your lease agreement because of wear and tear or the extra mileage you put on the car. When it's all added up you will have paid more than if you had scaled down your car choice and bought a used or new car within your budget.

Basically, leasing is just another way to rent what your paychecks can't purchase. With so many families overwhelmed with credit card debt and living so close to financial disaster, is it really fiscally wise to be leasing new cars every few years? Why not buy what you can afford and try to maintain the car so that you have many years without a car payment? Then take that money you would otherwise spend on a car note and save it or invest it.

I sympathize with people who worry about the decline of the stock market. But in everyday life, away from Wall Street, there are people who lose more money making foolish spending decisions than they'll ever lose—or make—in the market.

Car leasing comes to mind as one of those decisions. It came up during an appearance I made on *Oprah* to discuss how to find money in your budget to save and invest. As the show neared its close, I ended up in a verbal tussle with an audience member over the merits of car leasing versus buying. Sue, who had admitted that she had little or no savings, thought I was dead wrong when I said leasing makes no economic sense for most people. The show ended with Oprah asking viewers to go to her website to see Sue and me continue to go at it.

"Did you and the lady rumble after the show?" one viewer asked me later in an e-mail. Well, here's a transcript of the "rumble."

Oprah to Sue: You're leasing a car right now?

Sue: I'm just . . . (Sue pauses.) I'm in the business. (A fact that Sue failed to reveal during the network taping.)

Oprah and the audience: Oh . . . Ah . . .

Sue: No. Wait. Wait. I happen to know more facts about this subject than she does. For a certain person, [leasing] is the better choice.

Me: For a very small percentage of people, leasing works. But for the 99.9 percent of the rest of you all, it does not make sense. At the end of the lease you have no car. You have to pay more money to [buy] the car.

Sue: You have to look at your driving needs. You have to look at the interest rate. What are your driving habits? How much mileage do you drive? All vehicles depreciate in value.

Thankfully, there was another voice of reason on the show. There to back me up was Ric Edelman, a Washington-based financial adviser and bestselling author.

Ric to Oprah: Want me to break the tie?

And so he did.

Ric: If you look at leasing from a purely economic perspective and ignore the lifestyle issue, the best way to handle an automobile is to buy a used car and keep it for ten years. That is how you create wealth. However, let's recognize in the real world a lot of people won't do that. A lot of us are going to buy a new car because we just like the smell.

Me: But for two dollars, in a bottle, you can get that new-car smell.

Audience: (Much laughter.)

Ric: If you insist on owning a new car every three or four years—and Michelle is right, you should *not* do this, but if you insist on being dumb, Sue is right. You should lease. Leasing has lower ownership costs during the three-year period. But remember, between the two . . . Sue will drive a more fun car. Michelle will get rich.

Maybe I won't exactly get rich, but I'll save a lot more money than people who lease cars.

At the height of the leasing craze in the late 1990s, about 30 percent of new-car drivers leased vehicles instead of buying them. With the average price of a new car at about $20,000, drivers have to extend loans over four to six years to keep payments reasonable. Leasing payments can typically be less than loan payments on a new car. That makes leasing seem attractive.

In 2002, if you had leased a $22,490 Honda Accord EX V-6 for three years with a down payment of $1,350, it would have cost you about $350 a month (plus taxes and fees), according to data from Edmunds.com. The leasing people compare that payment with financing the purchase of that same car, same down payment, for thirty-six months at a 9 percent annual percentage rate. With those terms, you would have paid about $685 a month (plus tax and fees). So, $350 versus $685—no contest, right?

The reality is that most consumers don't finance for thirty-six months. For most consumers, sixty-month financing is now the standard, and seventy-two-month financing is becoming increasingly popular. Using the same APR and down payment, the Accord would have cost about $445 a month (plus taxes and fees) for five years. And, most important, it will still be worth a good chunk of change at the end of the loan if cared for properly.

Leasing for three years cost about $13,500 (assuming you get the entire security deposit back). But you don't get to keep the car at the end of the lease unless you pay more money. Financing for three years costs about $26,000, but at the end of the loan period you own a car worth about $14,000.

Leasing makes sense for only a few people. Current tax law considers many of the expenses of a leased car used for business tax-deductible. Leasing advocates will say that leasing offers consumers a way to drive a car they want. Leasing, proponents argue, allows consumers to drive a more expensive vehicle than they can afford to buy.

Think about that logic: You, too, can drive a car you can't afford.

—

10

FINANCIAL BOOT CAMP

We all need a little reminder about the basics when it comes to our finances. So in this chapter I explore everything from the problem of ATM addiction, to balancing your checkbook, to cosigning to this fella called FICA.

THE CHECK IS IN THE MAIL

When was the last time you paid a bounced-check fee?

Perhaps no other consumer banking issue, with the possible exception of the fees banks charge for automated teller machines, generates so much consumer ire.

The average bounced-check fee is now $30. Nonsufficient funds or NSF fees have risen steadily over the last several years. Bankers say the fee is so high because they want to discourage people from bouncing checks.

I have only one rule when it comes to writing checks. Never, ever, ever write a check if you don't have the money in your account. This applies even if you have your paycheck direct-deposited. Why? Because anything can happen to delay a payment and you can end up being stung with a humdinger of a bounced-check fee.

Be sure to check your bank's policy on how they clear checks. In some cases they may have a big-to-small processing policy, meaning they will cash the biggest check first. For example, suppose you write four checks. In all, the checks total $2,000, including a $1,500 payment for your mortgage. But some computer glitch in your direct deposit results in a delay in your paycheck so you don't have sufficient funds in your checking account to cover all four checks. As a result, you have $500 in your checking account, which would have covered the three smaller checks. But because your bank cashed the mortgage check first, the others bounce. So instead of getting one bounced-check fee of $30, you have three for $90.

Ever wonder why a check takes so long to clear? Even with advances in technology, bankers say the process of clearing checks remains largely a manual job. Here's how it works:

1. A consumer deposits a check.

2. That evening, the check is sent to a central location where it is encoded with the dollar amount. The check is then sorted and bundled with other checks going in the same direction. Bankers say that the sheer volume of checks means that most banks only spot-check signatures.

3. The check is then rushed overnight to either a branch of the Federal Reserve Bank or some other central clearinghouse.

4. Upon receipt the clearinghouse or Federal Reserve grants the bank in which the check was deposited provisional credit for the check. As soon as provisional credit is received, the depository bank can invest those funds.

5. From the clearinghouse, the check is sent to the bank upon which the check is drawn and the bank deducts the amount from a consumer's account. If the check is bad, it goes back through the system, although not through all the same steps. The law allows banks to hold local checks up to two business days, and out-of-state checks and ATM deposits up to five days.

Do yourself a favor; don't try to beat the banks at a game they know all too well. You can say the check's in the mail, but make sure the funds are in your account to back that check whether you've mailed it or not.

CUT YOUR ATM ADDICTION

I know that ATM stands for "automatic teller machine," but for many people it has come to mean "always taking money." I want to spend some time talking about the use of ATMs because this is a convenience that has seriously compromised many people's ability to manage their cash.

When was the last time you used your ATM card?

If you're a typical bank customer, you won't have trouble remembering. It was at least twice this week already. And each time you withdrew about $20.

In fact, consumers value their ATM cards more than they do their computer, newspaper, or cable television, according to a study commissioned by the Pulse EFT Association, one of the nation's largest electronic funds-transfer systems. Using ATM cards to make purchases debited from a checking account ranked second only to the home telephone as the most valued consumer convenience, according to the Pulse survey. The research firm surveyed 2,200 adults with checking, savings, or share-draft accounts in sixteen states from the Great Lakes to the Gulf of Mexico.

There's no question that if you are in a bind and need a bit of cash, having access to an automated teller machine is a good thing. But the ability to withdraw money on a whim at all hours of the day or night can also encourage undisciplined spending.

The Pulse survey and other reports about ATM use offer clear proof that we have become a nation with an unhealthy addiction to having quick access to our cash. In fact, the latest automotive navigation systems can give drivers directions to the nearest ATM.

How many times have you been out on a Saturday and suddenly discovered that you are running low on money halfway through your various errands? No problem. Just whip out that ATM card and withdraw $20—for a movie, a quick purchase at the mall, or a burger and milk shake on the way home.

Star Systems, an electronic payment network, found that one out of every five ATM or debit card transactions it processed in 2001 took place on a Saturday.

Retail locations with ATMs on the premise see their sales dramatically increase, according to the ATM Connection, which sells automated teller machines. Nightclubs, for instance, can expect to see 70 to 80 percent of the dispensed cash stay at the club. ATM Connection contends that cash retention among large retailers is more than 30 percent.

"The big profit is from the additional sales from the thousands of extra dollars available in your facility," the company said in its online sales literature.

Just think about the fees that so many people are willing to pay to withdraw money from ubiquitous ATMs.

More than 65 percent of the bank customers surveyed by Pulse said they had used an ATM at a financial institution other than their own to withdraw cash.

The average fees charged by big banks for their own customers to use other banks' ATMs increased from $1.27 per transaction in 1999 to $1.49 in 2002, according to a bank-fee survey by the U.S. Public Interest Research Group, the national lobbying arm of the State Public Interest Research Groups.

Since 1996, ATM fees have nearly tripled. Whereas customers were usually assessed a $1 fee for using an ATM, they now pay an average of $2.86—with one fee going to their bank and another to the owner of the ATM. In larger cities, those fees sometimes jump to as high as $4.50 a transaction—even if you withdraw as little as $20.

"People are living from twenty dollars to twenty dollars," said Ed Mierzwinski, consumer advocate for U.S. PIRG. "This is a big problem because it means people are paying high fees to use ATMs and they are not keeping track of those fees or what they are spending the money on."

Like many other bank customers, I had become dependent on having easy access to my money. I had convinced myself that I wasn't in any financial danger. I wasn't charging on my credit card. I was just getting a little cash now and then. But those quick cash withdrawals add up.

Take a look in your wallet. Is it stuffed with ATM receipts? If so, you can stop wondering where all your money is going. It's going into an abyss that you can't even remember a week later.

The question is, how grateful should we be for the 24-7 access to our money?

In some situations, ATMs are a godsend. Running for an airplane and out of cash? Not to worry; an ATM is likely not far from the gate. But while automated teller machines have liberated us from long bank lines, they have also wreaked havoc on our budgets.

It wasn't until my husband and I began using Quicken's personal-finance software and our bank's online banking service that we knew how hazardous to our financial well-being our ATM cards had become. In one year, we had used the cards to withdraw an embarrassing amount of money from our checking account. Oh, we knew some of the money went for lunches at work, movies, video rentals, clothes, medicine, and any number of other small-ticket items, but we couldn't say with certainty where all the money had gone.

For many bank customers, constant trips to the ATM have become a bad habit that needs to be kicked.

So, how do you get the ATM devil off your shoulder?

It'll take discipline.

My husband and I limit our ATM visits. We each get an allowance to be taken out in one ATM trip a week. Additional ATM stops must be approved in advance, unless it's an emergency. (Money for an unplanned night at the movies because you need a break from your rugrats doesn't count.)

Once, during a trip to the mall, my husband and I decided to get a bite to eat with our small children. When we checked our wallets, we could come up with only about $7, and that was after digging for all the loose change in my purse. Not far away was an ATM. It would have cost us $3 to withdraw money from the machine.

That just wasn't going to happen. I hate paying somebody just to get access to my cash.

The temptation was great, but we resisted. We fed the whole family with those few bills and change. The only person not happy was the pizza guy—who had to count $3 in change.

ATMs are convenient. But the downside of this technology is you don't have to plan for your cash needs. You can walk out the door with just an ATM card.

Do you want some control over your cash-flow problem? Schedule your trips to the ATM. Withdraw whatever money you actually need for the week or month, and make it last. Then tuck that card away.

Try this for a month, and I bet you will stop wondering why you're always broke. You will have more money because you will have beaten your addiction to fast cash.

With a little willpower and planning you can shake the need to get quick cash, and you will be surprised at how much money you can save as a result.

WILL THAT BE CASH, CHECK, CREDIT, OR DEBIT?

The familiar and now almost deadpan question from store clerks, "Will that be cash, check, or credit card?" is now increasingly being updated to include "or debit?"

Financial institutions continue to aggressively pitch debit cards or check cards to consumers in hopes that such cards will become one of the more frequently used forms of payment by checking-account holders—saving the banks on check-processing charges and bringing in fees from both merchants and customers.

The banks also have identified a new potential income stream: Many banks collect fees from their customers when they make a debit purchase, and they also receive what is called an interchange fee from merchants based on the amount of the transaction.

These two motivators, coupled with the convenience of debit cards for customers, have led to marketing campaigns for debit-card products. Visa calls its debit product the Visa check card, while Master-Card's is called MasterMoney. The two can be used just about anywhere a credit card is accepted.

Though debit cards are convenient, there are drawbacks. First, because the cards are directly linked to checking accounts, unauthorized use results in a loss to the customer's account at least until the customer clears up the matter with the bank.

Basically, if a thief drains your checking account, you have to fight with the bank to get your own money back. Meanwhile, your other checks could bounce and you could face bounced-check fees, cash-flow problems, and other hassles. If a thief misuses your credit card, you don't usually have to fight to get the disputed charges removed from your account.

The big selling point of debit cards is the ease of use. True enough. It's easy for you and easy for a crook.

Many of the new debit cards are now almost indistinguishable from credit cards, except that the costs of purchases are directly subtracted from a customer's checking account either immediately or one to three days later. Sometimes customers are required to key in a secret personal-identification number (PIN).

While debit cards have been around for years, their popularity is picking up with consumers as more retailers install the "point-of-sale"

(POS) terminals that allow bank and credit-union customers to transfer funds directly from their checking accounts to the bank accounts of retail businesses.

Many people use them now to avoid piling debt onto their credit card. With the debit card, you are using your own money. It's a good strategy to curtail your spending, but you should also understand the risks involved.

If somebody steals your debit card, the money is coming out of your checking account. This puts you in a very different position than with fraudulent charge card purchases. The burden is on you to prove the transaction was fraudulent. You have to get the bank to give you back your money. With a credit card, if you report the loss right away, there is no immediate loss of your personal money. Under federal law, if someone steals your credit card, you're only responsible for paying the first $50 of unauthorized charges. Often, credit card companies won't even hold you liable for the $50.

If your debit card is lost or stolen, someone could have a passport to your checking account. If you don't use your debit card often, it may be days before you notice any money missing.

The protection for your debit card isn't as good as that for a credit card. For example, your liability under federal law is limited to $50, but only if you notify the issuer within two business days of discovering the card's loss or theft. Your liability could jump to $500 if you put it off. If you wait more than sixty calendar days from the time your bank statement is mailed to report the loss, you may have no protection at all. Ultimately, if a consumer complies with the regulations, she can get her money back, but it could be a hassle to clear it up in the interim.

There are some key distinctions with a debit card. The first is an "online" or direct-debit card. Most bank customers already have debit or point-of-sale (POS) capability and may not realize it. When bank customers access an ATM with their plastic card, they are using it online. Those transactions are immediately subtracted from an account and require a PIN.

Most ATM bank cards double as a debit/POS card. POS transactions can be made with these cards at gas stations, grocery stores, or other retail outlets that have access to regional or national ATM networks, such as MOST. Just look on the front or back of your ATM card and match the logo with the signs posted at a retail outlet. However, be aware that your bank might charge a fee for the transaction.

The other kind of debit card looks like a credit card but acts more like a check. This "off-line" or "deferred-debit" card does not require a PIN. When this card is used, the customer signs a receipt and the money is usually subtracted from his or her account within three days, not unlike a check. In many cases a retailer doesn't even know a customer is paying with a debit card.

You may not even realize you have a debit card. Many banks just replace your standard ATM cards with upgraded ATM cards that have a debit feature. You may also receive in the mail what looks like a credit card when in fact it is a debit card. In fact, my bank automatically sent me a debit card with the off-line feature. I promptly called them and asked that they send me a debit card that always requires a PIN.

Remember, no matter what the commercials say, a debit card is not a credit card. With off-line debit cards there is the potential to overdraw your account if you don't keep track of your purchases.

FICA AND ALL THAT: A PAYCHECK PRIMER

I remember how excited my nephew was the day he got his first paycheck. He had all kinds of plans for his newfound wealth. As he began to examine his pay stub, however, he let out a yell so loud that my neighbor's dog started barking. "Aunt Michelle, what the heck is FICA, and where is all my money?" he shouted. "I've been robbed."

"No, Tom," I said. "You've been taxed."

I think it's appropriate that we refer to the document attached to our paycheck as a stub. *Stub* is defined as something cut short or stunted.

When you start a new job, you are asked to fill out a W-4 Employee's Withholding Allowance Certificate. On the W-4 form you report your marital status and the number of allowances you want withheld. This information allows your employer to calculate the amount of federal income tax to withhold from your pay. You can file a new Form W-4 at any time, and you can choose to have more or less tax withheld from your paycheck. On the W-4 you will find listed:

- *Allowances.* You are entitled to take federal withholding allowances for yourself, your spouse, and your dependents. A single worker with no children might elect to take one allowance; if so, the number on this line would be 1. Allowances reduce the amount of income that is subject to withholding. You can adjust the number of allowances depending on your situation. For example, many people with large itemized deductions such as mortgage interest take extra allowances so they will have more take-home pay. At the end of the tax year, they then claim the interest deduction on their tax return. And, just so you know, if an employee claims more than ten exemptions, his employer has to report this to the IRS.

- *Addl. amt. (additional amount).* On this line your employer would list any additional withholding you have authorized. Many people who have nonwage income may have extra tax withheld so they won't be hit with a big tax bill.

  Your pay stub includes federal and state income taxes deducted from your pay. You'll also find reference to the Federal Insurance Contributions Act, or FICA, which consists of payments to the Social Security retirement-supplement system and the Medicare hospital-insurance program. Under FICA, the employee and the employer each pay half of the taxes (for a total of 12.4 percent for Social Security and 2.9 percent for Medicare). The self-employed pay the entire tax themselves.

  If you have a second job, that employer has to withhold for the Social Security tax, even if ultimately the withholdings are refunded because your total exceeds the annual limit. Employers are required to separately display the two components of FICA.

  Here's a breakdown of the taxes on your stub:

- *Federal withholding.* The amount of income tax withheld is based on marital status and the number of allowances indicated on your W-4.

- *Fed MED/EE (Federal Medicare Employee Employment Tax).* The Medicare tax you pay is 1.45 percent of your taxable income, with no yearly maximum.

- *Fed OASDI/EE (Federal Old-Age, Survivors and Disability Insurance Employee Employment Tax), otherwise known as the Social Security tax.* You pay 6.2 percent of the first $87,000 of your wages for 2003.

- *State withholding.* Any state and/or local taxes withheld from your pay.

- *Before-tax deductions.* Any money that is exempt from income taxes, including medical insurance, flexible-spending accounts, and voluntary tax-deferred retirement contributions, such as to a 401(k) plan. Voluntary retirement contributions are not exempt from Social Security and Medicare taxes.

- *After-tax deductions.* Deductions that are not exempt from income taxes and FICA. These include life insurance, long-term disability insurance, union dues, and United Way or other charitable contributions.

- *Total gross.* The running tally of what you have earned for the current pay period or YTD (year to date) before any withholdings or deductions.

- *Fed taxable gross.* This is gross earnings that are subject to federal income tax.

- *Employer-provided benefits.* Benefits paid for by your employer, such as matching contributions to a retirement savings plan. The items in this section do not represent deductions from your pay.

- *Net pay.* The amount of earnings you ultimately get to take home after all taxes and deductions.

DON'T LEND UNCLE SAM YOUR MONEY

I used to pray for a tax refund. After being taxed all year, the last thing I wanted to do on April 15 was give the Internal Revenue Service any more of my money. This was a case, I figured, where it was definitely better to receive than to give.

But instead of rejoicing about a refund, I should have been trying to figure out how to have that money show up regularly in my paycheck. That's what I do now, but I know many people still count on getting a refund. In 2002, the national average tax refund was $1,966 according to the IRS. That's about $164 a month that could be used to pay down a credit card with a high interest rate.

"So many people are dependent on this windfall that they fail to realize it's really their money they're getting back," said Donna LeValley, a tax lawyer and contributing editor of J. K. Lasser's *Your Income Tax 2002*.

Ideally, you want to break even when it comes to your taxes. You want to neither give nor receive.

The best way to strike that balance is by increasing or decreasing your "personal allowances" on your W-4 form—the one you filled out when you started your current job. The more allowances you claim, the less money is withheld from your paycheck.

Many people just ignore the W-4. But as your tax situation changes—you have more children, more deductions, get a second job—you should fill out a new form so your employer doesn't withhold too much or too little. For 2003, the value for each allowance is $3,050. The W-4 form has a worksheet to help you figure out how many personal allowances to take based on projected deductions and tax credits.

I do have to caution you: If you don't have enough money withheld, not only will you have to write a big check to the IRS, but you could be subject to a 9 percent penalty for underpaying.

If you have access to a computer, you can use the withholding calculator on the IRS website, www.irs.gov. (In the search box, type "withholding calculator.") But you can do it yourself using the W-4 worksheet. I asked LeValley to walk me through the form using the example of a single male taxpayer with no children and a gross income of $45,000 a year.

Based on the 2002 W-4, a single person who is not claimed as a dependent on someone else's return would enter the number 1 on Line A.

If you are single and have only one job, you get another allowance. Therefore, you enter the number 1 on Line B. If the man is married and has children, he would be able to add one allowance for his spouse and one for each dependent child. There are additional allowances for the child tax credit, head of household, and child- or dependent-care expenses.

Since our single guy is not claiming any dependents, however, he ends up with two allowances.

But wait. The guy bought a house at the beginning of the year and expects to have $10,000 in deductible mortgage interest. He also plans to contribute $3,000 to an individual retirement account. He likes getting a big refund. As a result, he doesn't change his W-4. With his $45,000 gross income, LeValley calculated that his employer will withhold federal income taxes of $6,278.76 a year, or $523.23 a month, not including taxes taken out for Social Security and Medicare.

Now look at what would happen to this guy's take-home pay if he changed the number of allowances to reflect the mortgage-interest deduction and IRA contribution.

Because he can itemize, the W-4 instructs him to use the "Deductions and Adjustments Worksheet." He has $13,000 worth of qualifying tax deductions. After some simple computations, the deductions are converted into two additional personal allowances. He now takes four allowances.

His gross income is still $45,000, but the amount withheld is $4,658.76, or $388.23 monthly, according to LeValley. That's a difference of $1,620, or almost $135 a month, not including other federal or state taxes. And he would still get a refund in 2003 of $608.76, according to Sam Serio, a spokesman for the IRS.

"Overwithholding is like the Christmas passbook accounts banks set up years ago," Serio said. "Come Christmas you had money for presents, but you earned no interest throughout the year."

If you are concerned that you will waste your own money during the year, set up an automatic payroll-deduction payment to a savings account.

Bottom line: Don't treat your tax refund as a windfall, because it's not unexpected or unearned.

If the following fits your financial situation, you might need to update your W-4:

- *Life change.* You go through a marriage, divorce, birth or adoption of a child, purchase of a new home.

- *Change in earnings.* You or your spouse start or stop working, or one of you quits or takes a second job. You had income that will either be decreased or increased because of interest income, dividends, or capital gains. You are entitled to itemized deductions or tax credits for medical expenses, job-related expenses, charitable contributions, education credit, interest on a student loan, IRA deduction, alimony expense.

Now, I know a lot of people like getting a big fat refund check at the end of the tax year, but that's a big fat mistake. Just think about that logic. Would you give your Uncle Bunky $1,000 or $2,000 to hold for a year without it earning interest, just because you couldn't trust yourself to save it or invest it?

Of course you wouldn't. So why give it to Uncle Sam?

CHOICES FOR CONSERVATIVE SAVERS

In a later chapter I'll give you more basic investing advice, but here I want to go over the basic choices for folks who want to stay clear of the stock market.

When it came to investing, my grandmother had one strategy: Protect your principal. Big Mama put all of her money into a simple passbook savings account. She didn't invest in stocks. The only bond she ever bought was the adhesive material that held her dentures in place. I never succeeded in getting my grandmother to put her money anywhere else.

Big Mama believed you could build wealth without Wall Street.

When she died, she wasn't a wealthy woman. But she had managed to amass enough money to take care of her financial needs during her retirement.

You might not want to play the stock market either. But there are other virtually risk-free choices that will give you a bit more return on your money than a savings account. Here are some alternatives to start with:

- *Certificates of deposit.* With a CD you invest a set amount of money (generally a minimum of $500 or $1,000) for a stated period of time, typically at a fixed interest rate. If you need your money before the CD matures, you'll probably pay a penalty. For a CD with a term of one year or less, you may pay three months' worth of interest for early withdrawal. "If you factor in inflation and taxes, CDs usually are at best break-even," said Morris Armstrong, a fee-only certified financial planner based in New Milford, Connecticut.

Armstrong noted that if a CD pays 4 percent and you are in the 31 percent tax bracket, then your return is 2.76 percent. "If inflation is higher, then you are actually losing purchasing power," he said.

That's why long-term commitments to fixed-interest accounts such as CDs should be done carefully, advises David W. Bennett, a Los Angeles–based certified financial planner. You don't want to lock up all your money in a long-term CD at one interest rate in case rates increase dramatically.

Cheryl Costa, a financial adviser based in Natick, Massachusetts, says to consider "laddering" your CDs. Laddering helps protect you against swings in interest rates. Let's say you have $10,000. You might put $2,000 each into one-, two-, three-, four-, and five-year CDs. Each time one of the CDs matures, you could reinvest the proceeds in a new five-year CD. "When you ladder in this way, you still have money becoming available every year, but eventually you are earning the five-year CD rate on all of your investment," Costa said.

You can use shorter terms (six months, one year, two years, et cetera), but generally the longer the term, the higher the interest rate. In fact, if rates are low, you might consider starting with a shorter-term ladder of three months to one year.

- *Money-market deposit account.* A money-market account is simply a savings account that is federally insured, with check-writing privileges. The advantage of a money-market account is that you can get to your money whenever you want—without a penalty. The disadvantage is that some banks may impose a monthly fee and you could be limited to a fixed number of transactions per month. Check around at credit unions, small banks, and savings and loans for the best rates. One of the best places to check for rates nationally and in your local area is www.bankrate.com.

Money-market accounts should be used for money you may need in the short term. This is where you may want to keep money for a home down payment or for that years' worth of living expenses that you should be saving.

- *Money-market mutual fund.* This is a mutual fund that invests in short-term debt instruments such as U.S. Treasury bills and top-rated corporate debt. These funds earn a variable interest rate. Shop around for rates. Look in your local newspaper or try www.bankrate.com, which lists both local and national rates. These fund accounts are not insured the way money-market accounts at insured financial institutions are. Technically, when you invest in these funds your principal is not guaranteed. But the risk of losing your principal is extremely low.

  A money-market fund can also be used for an emergency fund or as a place to park cash temporarily. Be sure to pay attention to fund expenses, which can vary greatly. "Expenses eat up a good portion of a money-market fund's yield," said Daniel Roe, a certified financial planner based in Columbus, Ohio. "That's why you see some funds yielding well below 1 percent now. Generally, money-market funds issued by the larger no-load fund companies offer the best rates."

- *Treasury bonds.* Series I inflation-indexed savings bonds, or "I-bonds," are issued by the U.S. Treasury. I-bonds are sold at face value, so you pay $100 for a $100 bond. The earnings rate is a combination of a fixed interest rate plus the rate of inflation, adjusted semiannually. You can invest as little as $50 or as much as $30,000 a year. You can buy I-bonds from most banks, credit unions, and savings institutions, or over the Internet at www.savingsbond.gov.

  You can defer federal taxes on earnings for up to thirty years. The bonds are also exempt from state and local income taxes.

Keep in mind that the enemy of every saver is inflation and taxes. Inflation decreases your dollar's value. If you are planning for your financial needs in the future, you'll need to protect the purchasing power of your money.

Ultimately, if you choose to stay off the road that leads to Wall Street, just be forewarned that you'll need to save a lot of money for a long time so that the effect of compounding can make up for your conservative investing.

11
—
BROTHER, CAN YOU SPARE A DIME?

Family and finances often don't mix. But what are you going to do? In the section that follows I'll go through some of the situations you may find yourself in when it comes to your money and your loved ones. I believe family should help one another out, but you have to set limits. You may have to say no sometimes. Above all, you have to protect your finances first.

How many times have you heard this request from a relative or friend: "Hey, can you spot me a couple hundred to pay my rent this month? I'm good for it."

Despite all the warnings we get about lending money, it's inevitable that at some point you will want to help a friend or relative by lending him some money. More likely you will be guilt-tripped into giving a loan. This happens often in families. As soon as someone begins to make a little bit of money, he finds himself doling out dough to a lot of relatives. If someone needs a down payment on a home, he gets called. The relative with the "good" job ends up being the family banker. Neither a borrower nor a lender be is a good rule to follow until or unless someone has an emergency.

Professional lenders have all kinds of sophisticated tools to advise them on how likely they are to get their money back and from whom. But just how should regular folk go about being a good lender or borrower?

There are some basic rules that can help the family banker or the perennial borrower.

First, as a borrower, be straightforward about what you can pay back and when. Don't duck and dodge. If you don't foresee paying back your mama or coworker when you agreed to, say so. If you won't ever have the money, come clean. They deserve the truth. Remember, a deadbeat is not necessarily someone who's broke but someone who chooses to hide from or ignore his obligations.

When you do get back on your feet and get some money, don't put your family or friends last in line to get paid. I understand how it happens. You figure family can wait for their money. After all, it's not likely your relative will throw you out on the street like the company that holds your mortgage. Nor is it likely that family will report your bad debt to the three credit bureaus.

But they deserve something. Put Mama ahead of MasterCard.

Above all, borrowers should drop "the attitude." What gives you the right to become annoyed when asked to come up with the cash you owe?

If you lend money, however, you have to learn to deal with this kind of behavior. The solution: Don't lend money when you know you'll get ulcers trying to collect it.

If you lend somebody your rent money and don't get it back in time to pay your landlord, you should kick yourself.

It's not selfish or uncaring to cover your own expenses first. Besides, if you say no when you can't afford to be an ATM, it may actually force someone in your life to get a grip and find an alternative to their chronic cash-flow problems. Perhaps that someone needs to get a second job instead of treating you like his personal banker.

Now, there will be the occasion when you lend money you really, really want back. This is the time to put your expectations for repayment in writing. (See sample of a personal loan agreement, pages 127–28.) Record how much was borrowed and set a payment schedule. Maybe the borrower will live up to the agreement. Maybe not. At least when you drag her behind into small-claims court you have proof of a bona fide personal loan agreement.

Don't be timid about enforcing the loan terms. If the borrower wasn't too proud to ask for the money, don't be shy about asking for it back. Be persistent but not a pain.

Disclaimer: This loan agreement is not a substitute for the legal advice of an attorney. No guarantees are made regarding the legal suitability of this form.

SAMPLE PERSONAL LOAN AGREEMENT

The lender(s) _____

The borrower(s) _____

Length of loan (weeks/months/years): _____

Total loan amount: $_____

Annual percentage interest rate charged: _____%

Repayment conditions: The borrower(s) agree(s) to repay the agreed-upon loan installment of _____ on the _____ day of each month/week.

Late charge: Any payment not paid within five (5) days of the due date shall be subject to a late fee of $_____.

Total payment due at the end of this loan agreement: $_____

Prepayment: The borrower(s) has/have the right to prepay the entire loan amount at any time. Interest will only be due for the time the loan is outstanding.

Co-borrowers: All borrowers listed on this agreement shall be equally responsible for paying the entire balance due on the loan. In other words, if one borrower decides not to pay, the co-borrower will still be responsible for paying the entire loan balance, including any interest and late charges due.

Default: If for any reason the borrower(s) fail(s) to make _____ number of payments on time, the loan shall be in default. The lender(s) can then demand immediate payment of the entire remaining unpaid loan balance, including any interest and late fees.

Legal fees: If this loan results in legal action for nonpayment, the borrower(s) agree(s) to pay any attorney or court fees associated with the collection of the unpaid loan balance.

As a legal adult 18 years or older I am fully responsible for paying back the full amount of this loan.

Notarized Signature of

Borrower: _____

Co-borrower: _____

Lender(s): _____

_____

Date of loan agreement: _____

Notary signature: _____

Notary Seal

Date: _____

Mostly, you should be realistic about a borrower's ability to make good on a promise to pay you back. You've heard the lines (or lies) before: "I swear I'll pay you back." "Next paycheck, I'll give you your money." "As soon as my tax refund comes in, I'll send you the money I owe."

Been there.

If someone you care about needs money, and you know or even suspect (from experience) that you will never be repaid, you ought to kiss the cash good-bye and give it out of the kindness of your heart.

I suggest you even create an account for just this purpose. If you have a needy family or always-broke buddies, set aside a pot of money (if you save regularly, this shouldn't be a problem) that you can afford to lend/give. It will make your life so much easier and stress-free.

But when that money runs out, shut down the family bank. It may seem cruel, but ultimately you have to be sure your financial needs are taken care of first before you open your personal bank vault. Otherwise, you both may be standing on the corner asking a brother if he can spare a dime.

WHEN YOUR HOME IS THE FAMILY HOTEL

Charles Schwab & Company and the black-owned mutual-fund company Ariel Capital Management have spent the last several years looking at the saving and investment habits of black and white households. One of their most interesting findings is that blacks tend to be more responsible for their extended-family members.

In one survey, 813 black households and 816 white households with incomes of $50,000 and higher were questioned about their family obligations. The survey results found that African-American household incomes were stretched further to support more people. What particularly caught my attention was that 27 percent of African-American households financially support friends or family beyond those living in their own home. That's compared with 12 percent of the white households surveyed.

Although blacks are more than twice as likely to be helping extended-family members, this isn't just a black phenomenon. For many people there might be a time when you have to open your home to a relative or friend in need. I can personally attest to this kind of income sharing. In fact, I joked to a colleague that one of the reasons I didn't quit my job and stay home after I had my second child was that my family couldn't afford it—and I wasn't talking about my husband and kids.

In the spirit of helping family, my husband and I agreed to let my nephew move in with us for a while. During the time he lived with us I learned a great deal about the right and wrong way to help someone become a working, valuable contributor to society. First off, I was very unprepared for how unprepared my nephew was for the real world. Like many teens and an equally large number of adults, he wanted a great-paying job, a fancy apartment, and a luxury car—while expending the least amount of effort. For example, his idea of looking for a job was to get up around 11 A.M., glance through the want ads, and call it a day by two after having made a few telephone calls. He complained that he couldn't look for a job because he didn't have a car. Of course, he couldn't be bothered with catching a bus or the subway.

When I was growing up with Big Mama, she had a pretty strict rule about grown children living in her house. "If I'm getting my tired bones out of the bed to go to work, then every able body in the house has to be working or at least go looking for a job like it is their job," she said.

In my nephew's opinion, he had to wait for just the right position. It didn't seem to matter that he didn't have any money or savings to help with expenses. Fast-food jobs or any position that required some muscle were beneath him.

He also didn't think he should pay rent. After all, he argued, we were family. I just rolled my eyes and established a $100-a-month rent payment, with the understanding that it would be adjusted when he got more than a part-time job.

That day came—he got a good full-time position—and I upped his rent to $300 a month to help cover more of his portion of the utility bills and groceries.

"Doesn't rent include food?" my nephew blurted after I announced his rent increase.

"Well, William," I said, "when you get your own place, be sure to ask the apartment manager what day of the week you should expect him to drop off your bag of groceries."

One month he came up a dollar short on his rent. Naturally I asked for my dollar.

"What?" he asked incredulously. "You actually want the one dollar?"

"Well, if you were living in an apartment you couldn't go to the rental office and pay two ninety-nine if your rent was three hundred dollars. They would charge you a twenty-five-dollar late payment just as if you hadn't paid your rent at all. They would want their dollar, and so do I."

My nephew left the room and returned with my dollar.

On another occasion he asked if he could pay his rent late. He wanted to use the money to buy summer clothes.

"Let me get this straight," I said. "You want to pay June's rent in July? If you want to buy clothes, I suggest you get another job to supplement your income."

His answer: "What, you want me to work myself to death?"

This comment came nine months after my nephew moved in, so I was a much wiser and saner person. I simply chuckled and politely asked for my rent money. No argument. No need to get my blood pressure up.

Believe me, I was no pro at handling a live-in relative. I was quick, unfairly so, to get angry when my nephew wouldn't look for a job the way I thought he should. I had no patience in dealing with the constant battles over the money he owed us or asked to borrow.

Ultimately, with the help of my husband, who has the patience of Job, I learned to respect my nephew as an adult and listen to his goals and concerns. I also realized I had to remain calm but firm in communicating what I expected him to contribute to the household.

Your goal should be to help the person living with you develop a plan to live on his own, otherwise he isn't going to be any good to anyone.

Eventually, after much hair pulling, my husband and I sat down with William and developed a live-in agreement. With my nephew's input, we came up with a written document to govern the conditions under which he could continue living with us. (See the rental agreement on pages 132–33.)

The first thing you should agree on is rent. I firmly believe that unless an adult relative is not working because she is going to college, she should pay a fair share of the expenses. Look at it this way. Children or other relatives will never learn to be on their own and manage their own money and bills if you don't teach them to be responsible. And you do that by setting certain expectations. It's a lesson I learned well from my grandmother. At the age of fourteen, when I got my first summer job, she said I had to use some of my paycheck to buy my own school clothes. From then on, whenever I had a job, she made me use some of the money to help with my expenses.

In the case of my nephew, we decided to charge him rent even during his unemployment periods. The agreement was that after he got a job, he had to pay the rent he couldn't cover when he was out of work. That motivated him to start looking for any job because the amount he owed was growing rather quickly. I wasn't playing. I meant business.

Disclaimer: No guarantees are made regarding the legal suitability of this form.

SAMPLE RENTAL FORM

This Rental Agreement is made with the following tenant(s):

_____

_____

_____

The tenant(s) will occupy the residence located at:

_____

The tenant(s) agree(s) to the following terms:

Rent: The total monthly rent is $_____. If there are multiple tenants each will be responsible for the following monthly rent amount: _____. Each tenant is responsible for the full amount of his/her portion of the rent even if another tenant fails to pay his/her share.

Rent due date: Rent shall be paid on the _____ day of each month directly to _____.

Late Fee: Failure to pay rent by due date will result in a $_____ (I suggest $25) late fee assessed for each monthly rent payment not paid on time. A partial payment of rent is considered to be late and therefore a late fee will still be assessed.

Loss of employment: Each tenant is still responsible for paying rent even if he/she is not employed. Until the tenant is reemployed, the amount of rent will continue to accrue. Arrangements can be made to pay past-due rent; however, the home owner must approve any such plan. Once the tenant is again employed, the full rent is due as stipulated in this agreement.

Living arrangements: The bedroom(s) will be allocated as follows:

_____

_____

_____

Shared space: The following are conditions of the shared space:

_____

_____

_____

_____

_____

Utility charges: Each tenant agrees to pay _____% of the utility charges, _____% for gas and/or electricity, and _____% of the water bill.

Telephone charges: Each tenant will pay _____% of the monthly telephone service charges and will be responsible for all of their personal long-distance calls.

Food: Each tenant is responsible for providing for their own meals or they will be assessed _____% of the weekly/monthly grocery bill.

Household chores: The tenant(s) will be responsible for the following household chores:

_____

_____

_____

Overnight guests: Each tenant must obtain permission from the owner of the home prior to the stay of any overnight guest(s). No overnight guest(s) may stay longer than _____ consecutive nights.

Smoking: Smoking _____ is _____ is not allowed in the residence.

Vacating the residence: The tenant(s) must give the home owner at least _____ notice that he/she plans to move out of the residence.

The parties agree to the above-stated terms. Any changes to this rental agreement must be made in writing and signed by the owner of the residence.

Tenant(s) signature/date:

_____

Landlord(s) signature/date:

_____

Second, we set my nephew's rent based on a simple calculation. We estimated that most people spend about 30 percent of their income on housing. When William got a part-time job, we asked that he pay that percentage in rent based on his net salary. This way we could begin to show him how much of his income had to be used for housing. And we agreed that when he got a full-time job his rent would go up based on his new take-home pay.

Next we worked on helping him develop a budget (see pages 135–38) that included a required savings goal. We didn't take the rent money he paid us and save it for him. It was his responsibility, as an adult, to save for himself.

When he didn't have a job and wasn't looking for one, he had to do household chores. After many days of washing dishes, mowing the lawn, and cleaning the basement, he was motivated enough to get out of the house and put in job applications wherever he could.

One year and three months after moving in, my nephew announced that he was ready to move out. He had found a great desk job. When he made the decision to move out, he came to us with a written budget detailing how he could afford his rent and other expenses. I cried. He had decided to skip getting cable because he realized he couldn't afford it. (Hallelujah!)

This is like anything in life; you have to set the expectations high. Most people will rise to the occasion. Love means showing people how to be financially independent.

WHEN YOUR ADULT CHILD COMES HOME TO ROOST

Imagine you've seen your son or daughter off to college. You close the door and whirl around in excitement. You yell, "Peace at last, peace at last, thank God almighty, peace at last!"

But the celebration is short-lived. A few years later your graduate is coming home, not just for cake and ice cream for her graduation party but to stay, for a few months or maybe a few years.

Increasingly, adult children are returning home to live with—or, in some cases, live off—their parents. One online job service surveyed college students in 2003 and found that 61 percent of them said they planned to live with their parents after graduation. In an earlier survey

(*cont. on page 138*)

SAMPLE BUDGET

Major items that should be on your budget sheet:

Income: Enter any and all disposable income you receive from pay-checks, interest, investments, alimony, child support, parents, etc. This is your take-home pay.

Housing: The household category is designed to make your budget easy to manage by lumping many items into one category. List all expenses you have between paydays. Try to keep this item to no more than 30 percent.

Transportation: If you have a car, the name of this game is to get the cheapest car possible. Buy used. Don't lease.

Savings: This is possibly the most important of all the categories. It is absolutely necessary that you make plans for your financial future and put money away to pay for it. Your short-term savings (crisis fund) are used to cover unexpected and irregular expenses. Your long-term savings will allow you to fulfill your ultimate long-range goals (paying off your student loans, paying cash for a car, buying a home). You should always save at least 10 percent of your income. How you divide it between long and short term savings is up to you, however a 50–50 split seems to work best. If you believe in tithing, you will have to save 20 percent of your income.

The Budget Worksheet

Match Your Expenses to Your Income

Income + Expenses	Estimated	Actual
Monthly Gross Income (what you wish you could keep!)	$_____	$_____
Monthly Net Income (the pitiful amount you actually take home)	$_____	$_____
Savings (PAY YOURSELF FIRST— include tithing if that's something you believe in)	$_____	$_____

Income + Expenses	Estimated	Actual
Rent/Mortgage	$_____	$_____
Utilities:		
Gas/oil	$_____	$_____
Electric	$_____	$_____
Water	$_____	$_____
Telephone (including the cell phone you don't need)	$_____	$_____
Groceries:		
Food	$_____	$_____
Household supplies	$_____	$_____
Transportation:		
Subway/bus	$_____	$_____
Gasoline	$_____	$_____
Car payment (you better not be leasing)	$_____	$_____
Car maintenance (get a roadside assistance plan)	$_____	$_____
Work-related expenses (lunch, shopping during lunch—just kidding)	$_____	$_____
Internet access	$_____	$_____
Cable (which is not a need)	$_____	$_____
Insurance:		
Health	$_____	$_____
Life	$_____	$_____
Disability	$_____	$_____
Auto	$_____	$_____
Other _____	$_____	$_____
Entertainment/recreation:		
Meals away from home	$_____	$_____
Movies/concerts/theater	$_____	$_____
Health club, etc.	$_____	$_____
Other _____	$_____	$_____

Income + Expenses	Estimated	Actual
Personal:		
Clothes	$_____	$_____
Grooming (e.g., haircut,		
dye job)	$_____	$_____
Other _____	$_____	$_____
Miscellaneous (specify):		
Birthday gifts	$_____	$_____
Money for friends		
or family	$_____	$_____
_____	$_____	$_____
_____	$_____	$_____
Total Income	$_____	$_____
Total Expenses	$_____	$_____
Do you have a surplus or deficit?	$_____	$_____

BUDGET TIPS

Pay Yourself First

You must begin a practice of putting aside a set amount every time you get your hands on some money. If you wait until after you pay your bills, you won't save. Set up an automatic way for money to go directly into your savings account. Follow this rule, and you will begin to have more money.

Know Exactly What You Are Spending

Rather than saying, "I think I spend about $200 a month on groceries," be accurate about your monthly expenditures for various items. Once you have a running total for several months, you can develop an average and adjust your budget up or down accordingly.

Credit Cards

You will notice that on the sample budget there is no line item for "credit cards." You used those cards to buy something, so specify in your budget what you charged. Remember you are using other people's money. You are buying stuff with money you don't have and are not sure you're going to have next month, otherwise you would have paid cash for it.

Incorporate Your Goals

A budget is only as good as the goals attached to it. For example, you may decide that you want to get rid of your credit card debt. But it's not enough to just say that. Figure out how much you need to put toward that debt each month. Start slowly, with a fairly easily attainable goal, and then "test" yourself with a more difficult (and rewarding) goal as you get more proficient at your budgeting process. For example, let's say you have charged a total of $1,500 on your credit card. If your minimum payment each month was $30 on a card with 19.9 percent interest, it would take you more than 25 years to pay off your debt! Even worse, you would end up paying a total of $6,000, even though you only borrowed $1,500! If you doubled what you paid each month to $60, then it would take only two and a half years to pay off your debt and you'd pay a total of only $1,900.

24 percent said they planned to live at home for more than a year. Some experts say the slowdown in the economy is leading to an increase in the number of these "boomerang" adult children. And mounds of debt is a major reason more young adults are moving back home.

Nellie Mae, a subsidiary of the better-known Sallie Mae and an originator of postsecondary-education loans, reported in 2003 that undergraduate student-loan debt has increased significantly since 1997. The average undergraduate debt is $18,900, up 66 percent from $11,400. The median undergraduate debt rose 74 percent to $16,500 from $9,500. Those who attended private four-year colleges borrowed most (average $21,200/median $18,400), followed by those who attended public four-year colleges (average $17,100/median $16,200). Those who borrowed the least attended public two-year institutions, and their average student debt was $8,700 (median was $7,700).

Nellie Mae also reported that the percentage of college students with four or more credit cards had climbed from 27 percent in 1998 to 32 percent in 2000. The average credit card debt rose 46 percent, from $1,879 to $2,748. Nearly 10 percent of students owe more than $7,000.

So what should you do if Junior or Princess wants to move back home? Charge rent? Share utility bills? Scream?

The advice on this particular topic varies greatly, as it should. But you know your child. So act accordingly.

If your adult child is living beyond his means, you shouldn't feel guilty about asking for a financial contribution in return for accommodations. Why should you struggle or put off your retirement while this grown person happily lives life as a spendthrift?

On the other hand, if your child has always been responsible, you could use the request to move home as an opportunity to help ease him into what will be a lifetime of financial obligations.

I moved back home to live with my grandmother after I graduated from college. Big Mama didn't charge me rent. "Baby, just save your money," she said.

Even so, I would slip cash into her handbag. I paid some of the utilities and bought groceries.

Big Mama didn't ask for rent, but she had a long list of rules. For instance, she demanded that I save a set amount of money from my paycheck every week. I couldn't park in her space in front of the house. I couldn't leave shoes under my bed. If I was going to be late, I had to call. Actually, she would put the chain on the door if I didn't come home at what she considered was a decent hour.

Her house. Her rules.

Whether you are elated or deflated about an adult child moving back home, be sure to have a conversation with your new boarder about the situation. To get you started, here are some pointers:

- *Determine how long the child really plans to stay.* Don't leave it open-ended, otherwise Junior will be thirty-seven years old and still handing you his laundry.

- *Don't put your own finances in jeopardy to help support the spendthrift ways of an adult child.* Think about the words of the flight attendant instructing passengers on emergency procedures before takeoff. Parents are told to put on their own oxygen mask before tending to their children. No matter how often I hear this advice, I still squirm. How can I take care of myself first? That's not what a parent is supposed to do. And yet it is exactly what you must do. Similarly, if you fail to secure your retirement because you are enabling your adult child to wear you down financially, you both could end up gasping for air.

- *Unless your adult child is paying off some heavy debts or has a specific savings goal, such as buying a home, ask for some help paying household expenses.* I think every able-bodied adult bringing home a paycheck should contribute monetarily.

- *Establish consequences if your child doesn't honor your agreement.* A friend's son moved back home and agreed to pay rent. But he always paid late. So his mother began charging him a $25 late fee. He started paying on time. Charging a late fee might seem excessive, but good bill-paying habits have to start somewhere.

- *Don't let your child get too comfortable.* You're a mama, not a maid. Your child should be required to help with household chores. Don't allow your home to be used as a hotel.

- *Be careful about cosigning.* Actually, I recommend you don't cosign for any loan. I can't tell you how many stories I hear of parents cosigning for their adult children only to be left having to pay off cars and outrageous credit card bills. Understand this: If you cosign for a loan or credit card, that means you are agreeing to pay the *entire* debt if the primary borrower doesn't make the payments. If your adult child cannot or will not pay his loan or credit card bill, that bad debt will be reported on your credit report too. Cosigning may also limit the amount you can borrow in the future.

- *Trust, but verify.* If your adult child says she is coming back to pay off bills or save, make sure she keeps to that plan. If you notice far too many weekend shopping sprees, it's time to renegotiate the living arrangement. Don't be suckered by your own kid. The ultimate goal should be to help your children become responsible, self-sufficient adults.

- *Put all agreements in writing.* (See rental agreement, pages 132–33.) I know this is your baby, but in many cases the living situation should be treated like a business arrangement. Writing it down shows just how serious you are. If you see something going on that you don't like (shopping sprees, shoes under or on the bed), don't be afraid to amend the rental contract.

If putting your agreement in writing seems too heartless or businesslike and not warm and cozy like a mommy and daddy should be, at least have a conversation about the living arrangement. Get all expectations—yours and your child's—out in the open.

It's fine by me if you never want your adult child to leave home and everybody is happy. But if you had plans for your senior years that didn't involve picking up behind some nasty, disrespectful, slothful adult child, take control of the situation, otherwise your boomerang baby may never leave the homestead.

I WAS MY BROTHER'S KEEPER

I was barely twenty-one years old and just out of college when my grandmother announced that she was "bone tired" of caring for my brother Mitchell, who also lived with Big Mama. Mitchell suffered from seizures because of his epilepsy.

I never imagined that as a young adult I would have to take care of my brother, who was two years younger than me. I don't think anyone can really prepare you for the emotional challenge of taking financial responsibility for a disabled sibling.

"In many ways helping a sibling is more difficult than dealing with a parent or a child," said J. E. McNeil, a Washington, D.C.–based attorney. "This is somebody you are an equal to, and it makes it hard to deal with a lot of the issues of independence." Many people with epilepsy live normal, productive lives. Mitchell, who suffered from epilepsy since infancy, wasn't so fortunate.

Taking care of my brother was often a full-time job. He was always in some medical or financial crisis. I had to deal with the frustrating and often nonsensical policies of the social service system. I paid his medical bills during periods when he wasn't covered by Medicaid. On several occasions, I had to threaten to call in our family attorney—even though we didn't have one—when Mitchell's employers tried to fire him because of his epilepsy.

Most important, I had to supplement whatever income my brother could earn.

At times I wanted to control every aspect of his life in an effort to minimize the things that could go wrong. But my brother hated that, and fought to maintain his own identity. "I'm not a baby," he would insist.

After dozens of arguments, he and I finally managed to develop a relationship that preserved his sense of independence but allowed me to stay close enough to oversee his finances.

Financial and legal experts say my experiences were fairly typical. Here are a few guidelines to help you deal with a sibling who has a disability or continually needs help with financial problems:

- *Set limits.* This was one of the hardest things for me to do with my brother. I felt bad that he suffered so much. So whenever he asked for money, I would feel guilty if I didn't give it to him. But the financial drain was too much. Ultimately, I had to learn to say no and mean it. We finally agreed on a number of expenses I would cover. For example, I would take him grocery shopping every month, pay to replace his glasses, or give him extra money for clothes.

- *Keep control of some of the money.* On two occasions Mitchell received lump sums of money. It wasn't easy, but I persuaded him to let me put the money in a trust account, and I invested it in government-backed securities. I was the trustee for the account and made it clear to him the money was for emergencies only.

- *Open a joint bank account.* A checking account seemed like a bad idea, because of the risk of overdraft problems, so I opened a joint savings account. The money was Mitchell's, but I had the bank send me a duplicate copy of the monthly statement so I could oversee it. One month I noticed my brother had spent almost $20 on ATM fees. He didn't understand that he was being charged $3 every time he used an ATM operated by a bank that wasn't his own. I put a stop to that immediately. With a fixed income, he couldn't afford such charges. We also banked at the same financial institution, which allowed me to transfer money to him easily.

- *Seek help from nonprofit organizations.* Don't try to be a martyr. There are wonderful organizations that can help you. In our case Abilities Network, a nonprofit that helps individuals with disabilities, assigned my brother a counselor—free of charge—who assisted him with such things as job training and placement. She helped him develop a budget, go shopping, find housing, and apply for state and federal benefits. One year, his counselor even helped my brother prepare Thanksgiving dinner for our family.

- *Elicit help from family members.* Don't try to do it all by yourself. Ask other relatives to help out, and keep them informed. If they resist helping with big items, then get them to do some small things, such as donating food or clothing.

- *Have fun.* I did things with my brother that weren't always associated with solving some financial or medical problem. He gave me away at my wedding. My husband and I took him on vacations. We took him to the theater and the movies. Mitchell's twin brother helped him get a job as an umpire with a Little League team.

- *Challenge the system.* When Mitchell was turned down for Social Security disability, the nonprofit advised me to hire an attorney to appeal. It was a lengthy process, but not only did my brother win the benefits, he also got back payments from the original date of his application.

None of this will be easy. It took more than a decade for Mitchell to achieve a relatively stable life. We had our share of fights, and I fussed at him a lot. But we always tried to work it out. Mostly, I stopped feeling sorry for my brother—and that really empowered him to take greater responsibility over his life. Without warning Mitchell died from a massive seizure in 1997. He was thirty-two.

Before his death, Mitchell had been doing quite well. He was a regular volunteer for the American Red Cross. He was living on his own. And when Mitchell couldn't find a roommate, my husband and I paid half the rent and utilities. Mitchell was finally living the independent life he had so desperately wanted.

If you find yourself caring for a disabled sibling, here's some additional advice:

- Budget money to help with your sibling's expenses such as medical bills and supplies. This way you won't be blindsided all the time.

- Offer your sibling a monthly stipend until he is out of financial trouble. This will help you avoid putting out a lot of cash at one time.

- Be careful before cosigning or guaranteeing payment for services or goods. If a medical provider insists, then guarantee to pay only up to your sibling's assets. If you cosign or guarantee a payment, creditors won't hesitate to go after you.

- Get a durable power of attorney, which allows you to make decisions if your sibling is unable to. You can find a boilerplate power-of-attorney document at most stationery stores. But it might be worth the money to hire an attorney to be sure the power of attorney is properly documented.

- Get life insurance. If you are caring for a sibling and have limited funds, consider taking out a small policy that will cover burial costs, maybe around $5,000.

- When preparing your will, make provisions for your sibling. Put it in a trust with instructions on how you want it used. Name someone you trust as the trustee.

- Don't be embarrassed to help your sibling apply for public-assistance programs. These systems are there to provide such help.

PLAN FOR YOUR DISABLED CHILD'S FUTURE

Nearly 1 in 5 persons—53 million people—said they had some level of disability in 1997, while 1 in 8—33 million—reported they had a severe disability, according to a 2001 report by the U.S. Census Bureau.

Among people twenty-five to sixty-four years of age who have a severe disability, only 48 percent had health coverage, compared with 80 percent for people with a nonsevere disability and 82 percent of those with no disability.

The Census Bureau also found the following:

- Among the population age fifteen and over, 25 million had difficulty walking a quarter of a mile or climbing a flight of ten stairs, or they used an ambulatory aid, such as a wheelchair, a cane, crutches, or a walker.

- About 18 million individuals age fifteen and over had difficulty lifting and carrying a ten-pound bag of groceries or grasping small objects.

- About 7.7 million people age fifteen and over had difficulty seeing the words and letters in ordinary newspaper print (even with glasses).

- About 14.3 million people age fifteen and over had a mental disability, including Alzheimer's disease, senility or dementia, or a learning disability.

- The poverty rate among the population twenty-five to sixty-four years old with a nonsevere disability was 10 percent compared with 8 percent for people with no disability. The poverty rate for people with a severe disability is much higher: 28 percent.

- In 1997, 9.7 million people age sixteen to sixty-four had a disability that prevented them from working and another 7.2 million were limited as to the kind or amount of work they could do.

What does all this mean? For some parents it means facing the fact that if you have a child with a disability he or she may need financial help well into—and perhaps all of—their adult lives.

James Cotto, a financial planner in New York, said he has seen many families where a parent is seventy-five, with no plans in place to care financially for her forty-five-year-old adult disabled child once she dies.

"Because of medical advancements, many of these individuals have longer life expectancies than in years past," wrote Minoti Rajput in an informative article in the August 2001 issue of the *Journal of Financial*

Planning. "Further, more are living with their families in their own communities, as opposed to being placed in institutions."

Rajput, a financial planner who specializes in working with families raising disabled children, says improper planning for the future needs of these individuals is understandable, but it is a mistake that often affects the quality of their lives and the people left to care for them.

A lot of parents do what my grandmother did. They count on other adult children to pick up the slack. But that might not be feasible, or the siblings may not want the responsibility.

As a guide, Cotto suggests that parents consider some of the following basic planning strategies:

- Ask nonprofit organizations to help you deal with your child's specific disability. Ask for recommendations for professionals who can help. I took this advice after my brother was turned down for Supplemental Security Income, which is administered by the Social Security Administration. A nonprofit organization working with us recommended an attorney who helped my brother successfully appeal that decision (see chart for SSI payment amounts, opposite page). Supplemental Security Income, or SSI, pays monthly benefits to people who are sixty-five or older, or blind, or have a disability and who don't own much or have a lot of income. SSI isn't just for adults. People who get SSI usually get food stamps and Medicaid. Medicaid helps pay doctor and hospital bills.

- Make sure that any financial plan you devise does not jeopardize government benefits. There are strict guidelines on the assets recipients can have. But you can establish a trust that doesn't endanger benefits. Cotto suggests parents set up a "special needs" or "supplemental needs trust" as an umbrella for assets. The money in the trust can be used to pay for things the government benefits don't cover, like entertainment. There are a lot of nuances to establishing this type of trust, however, so seek professional help.

- Think about your child's future housing needs. Many parents assume they will leave their home to their adult-aged child. But in the case of a special-needs child, this is often unrealistic.

SUPPLEMENTAL SECURITY INCOME PAYMENT AMOUNTS, 1990–2003

The following table shows the monthly maximum SSI payment amounts for an eligible individual and for an eligible individual with an eligible spouse:

YEAR	AUTOMATIC INCREASE	ELIGIBLE INDIVIDUAL	ELIGIBLE COUPLE
1990	4.7%	$386	$579
1991	5.4%	407	610
1992	3.7%	422	633
1993	3.0%	434	652
1994	2.6%	446	669
1995	2.8%	458	687
1996	2.6%	470	705
1997	2.9%	484	726
1998	2.1%	494	741
1999	1.3%	500	751
2000	2.5%	513	769
2001	3.5%	531	796
2002	2.6%	545	817
2003	1.4%	552	829

Source: Social Security Administration

- Look for a financial planner who has worked with families in your situation. But don't be scared into buying inappropriate financial products. If you can't afford an expensive insurance policy, don't buy it. Look for alternatives that meet your financial situation. For instance, if you have equity in your house, you could arrange to have it sold upon your death and the proceeds placed in a special-needs trust.

These are only suggestions, and any financial plan should be tailored to your own particular situation. The important thing is to *have* a plan—whether you do it yourself or hire a financial planner. Here are some Internet sites that may help:

- http://www.disability.gov. The U.S. Office of Disability Employment Policy created this site to provide one-stop online access to resources, services, and information available throughout the federal government.

- Health-mart.net provides comparative hospital pricing and quality data by disease. Be sure to click on the picture for "Patients" to avoid paying a fee.

- http://www.ssa.gov/notices/supplemental-security-income. This link will give you information about how to apply for disability benefits from the Social Security Administration. On the site, for example, you can find information about the amount of income you can have each month and still receive SSI. The amount depends partly on where you live. You can call (800) 772-1213 to find out the income limits in your state.

CAN WE TALK?

More precisely, can we talk about what adult children aren't talking about with their aging parents?

A report by AARP found that a third of adult children say they don't talk with Mom and Dad about their parents' finances. Likewise, a third of older parents consider the subject taboo when talking with their adult children. It's a sensitive topic. How do you open up a conversation about finances with the people who fed, clothed, and disciplined you? How do you step into the role of being their caretaker or, at the very least, watching over their financial well-being?

Neither is it easy for parents to reverse roles and discuss finances with their children.

My grandmother was fiercely independent and private. As a result, it was incredibly difficult to raise the subject with her. She refused to get a will. She wouldn't consider moving from her home even as her health deteriorated.

The AARP survey noted that three in ten adult children suspect their parents need help at some point but have not asked for it.

If you are one of the fortunate people whose parents have organized their financial affairs and shared their information with you, consider yourself blessed.

I wasn't so lucky. Big Mama's idea of discussing her finances was pointing to a big beige purse she kept locked in her bedroom closet. "Everything you need to know is right there in that purse," she would say. "You can look through it if I get sick or die."

But Big Mama was wrong. Everything we needed to know wasn't in her purse. Which led to confusion and some heartache afterward.

Ask yourself, do you know the details of your aging parents' assets and liabilities? Do you know where all their bank and brokerage accounts are? If you don't have a clue, or fear broaching the subject, your family could be headed for a lot of headache and heartache. Trust me, I've been there. Talk now. Don't wait for a crisis.

Start by creating a legal and financial profile of your parents. On the legal side, try hard to persuade them to get a will. Talk with them about medical directives so someone can make decisions for them or declare their preferences for treatment if they are unable to speak for themselves. The legal profile should also include durable powers of attorney, which allows someone to handle their financial affairs.

The financial profile should include such information as Social Security numbers, insurance coverage, Medicare numbers, health records, and financial status (debts, savings, investments). Encourage them to do what the mother of a good friend did: She put all her pertinent documents in a big metal box.

So, how do you open a conversation with your aging parents about their finances?

- *Be direct.* Just ask. Encourage them to discuss their situation and their wishes. Point out that having the conversation doesn't mean you have to take over their affairs. Conversely, aging parents should be careful about turning over their finances to an adult child who might not have their best interests at heart.

- *Or try the indirect route.* For example, you might start by bringing up the situation of an older friend who needs help or the experiences of an older person featured in the news. Watch for openings in which your parents might mention a need or small problem that could become a major impediment to independence.

- *Make a list.* Give your parents a list of questions or concerns, and schedule a time to sit down and talk.

- *Get outside help.* If your parents remain reluctant to talk about their finances, try to persuade them to hire a lawyer or financial planner.

Once the conversation gets going, here are some of the areas to discuss, according to AARP:

- *Housing.* Are your parents in a house or apartment that is still appropriate for their needs? Could simple modifications make it easier or more convenient for them, such as grab bars for the bathroom? Where would they prefer to live if they become incapacitated? Check out assisted-living facilities.

- *Finances.* What are your parents' current and future needs? Are they in a position to meet those needs? Do they need help getting government or pension benefits? Do they need financial assistance to make their resources last?

- *Insurance.* Do your parents have adequate health or long-term-care insurance? Do they need help determining their needs, filling out forms, or paying for insurance?

However tough this conversation might be, don't put it off any longer. In this case, talk isn't cheap. Getting these matters cleared up can save everyone a lot of time and money.

12

—

HEART CURRENCY

I'm a little embarrassed to admit that I watch *Judge Judy*. I'm drawn to the show mostly because of the cases involving financial disputes between former lovers. I have to agree with my grandmother when she said, "Some people ain't got no common sense."

With some of the reality television shows you aren't always sure the participants are real—even though the show's producers swear they are. Still, I wanted to know if there are people out there who could really be that crazy in love.

Turns out there are.

Take Beatrice, for example, a thirty-something paralegal I interviewed for my *Washington Post* column. She bought a $300,000 home with her boyfriend in the Washington, D.C., area. Two years after moving in together, they broke up and Beatrice moved out. But she continued to help pay the mortgage.

"I went into it with my feelings all the way," she said. "But you have to think, 'What if things don't work out?' I didn't have a plan. I thought he was it. I loved him."

Bless her heart, the woman fell in love and lost her everlasting mind.

Sadly, lawyers say they see this all the time. Couples lend each other money, allow their sweethearts to use their credit cards, rent apartments together, and cosign on car loans.

When the breakup comes— as it does more often than not— financial fights often complicate it. Some people, like Beatrice, have been forced to file for bankruptcy protection—all because when they opened their hearts, they opened their wallets too.

When you're dating and things are good, it's easy to think that making a major purchase together is no big deal. But it is. Legally, you don't have the same protections as married folk. It's tough enough separating your finances when you're married and have some legal protections.

Unmarried partners can get some protection if they draw up legal documents—for a fee—to help untangle their finances should the relationship fail. But people in love are always doing foolish things. For example, why would you sign up for a joint credit card? Do you really want to be paying for your man's pants when he's long gone and taking them off for another honey? The credit card issuer isn't going to care who made the charges. Both of you are on the line for the entire amount. If she skips out, the bank is coming after you. If he decides to blow off the debt, you are on the hook.

Okay, so maybe you didn't cosign for a credit card, but perhaps you are doing something equally asinine. You are allowing your special someone to charge things on your credit card.

"Let's face it," said John Garza, a bankruptcy lawyer. "Anybody and their grandmother can get a credit card these days, so if your boyfriend or girlfriend can't get one, you should think twice about letting them use yours. If the bank doesn't think they are going to pay and won't give them a card, then why should you?"

I know you love him. He's down on his luck. You're crazy about each other. Tough. Probably neither of you can afford the credit card bills anyway. Besides, what do you really need to buy on a credit card—clothes, restaurant meals, furniture?

I know your mama warned you about cosigning. It's a potentially dangerous financial situation to put yourself in, particularly if you are only dating. Studies of cosigned loans that go to default show that as many as three out of four cosigners are asked to repay the loan.

Cosigning means you are agreeing to pay that debt in full if the primary borrower cannot. Don't count on the lender buying some sob story. Don't count on being allowed to pay half either. You will be held completely responsible.

Cosigning can also affect your ability to get credit. For example, suppose your ex is making the mortgage payment on a house you bought together but you've now moved out of, and you want to buy your own place. You may have trouble getting a loan even if your ex is paying the mortgage as agreed. That's because creditors count every debt obligation. Your signature on a car loan or mortgage makes you liable for that debt, therefore it might make you less eligible for more credit.

I understand that you may feel guilty about not helping your significant other, but you have to have the heart to say no. It's okay to say to your honey: "I love you and everything, but if you need money, ask your mama." Note to Mama: Don't you cosign, either.

EXCHANGE CREDIT REPORTS BEFORE YOU
EXCHANGE WEDDING VOWS

The couples had gathered in the conference room of their church for a premarital session on finance, but they weren't ready for what they heard.

The session facilitator made a recommendation that had almost everyone gasping. She told them to share their credit reports with their intended. It should be one of the first things you do before getting married, said the financial adviser. "Lord have mercy!" one participant exclaimed. Increasingly premarital counselors are urging couples to share their credit reports. I think this is a marvelous idea. What better way to get to know your honey than to see how he's handled his money? Couples need to talk about their finances before they get married, and poring over each other's credit report provides a great way to open the conversation. In fact, get all three reports from the three major credit bureaus to be sure you have a full picture of your sweetheart's finances.

Unfortunately, many couples never get around to discussing their individual financial situation or how they plan to handle their money once they get married. In fact, many couples don't talk about their finances at all. They won't even tell each other how much they earn or discuss major purchases. In one premarital counseling session I attended, the planner said 80 percent of the couples who sign up for the sessions had never had a conversation about money—and probably wouldn't have if not for the course.

Of course, talking about money doesn't always bring folks together. After signing up for the premarital sessions at her church, financial adviser Annette Singletary (no relation) said about half of the couples decide to postpone their wedding or call it off altogether. Many of them cited financial differences or debt problems.

That's a statistic church organizers are actually pleased to see, because it indicates the couples weren't ready to get married in the first place.

What's often the cause of the breakup over money? Different priorities about spending and saving. It's interesting to me how couples will spend a year planning a wedding and less than a couple of hours planning their financial life. Again, we get back to putting your priorities first.

My husband and I talked about money before we were married. And it's lucky we did, because we were worlds apart.

I wanted a half dozen or so different bank accounts. The way I had planned it, there would be my accounts (a savings and checking to which he would have no access), his accounts (a savings and checking to which I would have no access), and two joint accounts (a savings and checking to which we would both have access). After I presented my thoughts on money and marriage, my husband laid out his plan. He suggested we look at setting up our financial household like a business partnership. We would pool our income into one joint checking-and-savings account to pay our bills and save for the future. In his mind there was no yours or mine, only ours. It didn't matter who earned more because it was our money. He figured that by combining our resources and being completely honest with each other about our finances, we could achieve more.

At first I balked. In principle, his idea sounded good. But his way, to my mind, meant giving up some of my financial independence, something I had worked hard to achieve.

Ultimately, after many, many talks, I decided he was right.

By joining forces and keeping their finances together rather than separate, couples can learn to lean on each other—using the financial strengths each brings to the marriage. For example, if one spouse is frugal, that person can help the other become less of a spendthrift. On the other hand, a frugal spouse can be helped to loosen up on the purse a little and have some fun.

Now, if your partner has some serious issues about how she handles her money, joint accounts might not work. But I really don't believe separating everything because your partner bounces checks or can't stop charging on his credit card is the answer. It's only a temporary solution to what will become a very permanent problem. Get counseling, not separate accounts.

Whether you are getting ready to walk down the aisle or you're already married, consider these tips for better money harmony:

- *Get your credit reports, and share the information.* As hard or embarrassing as this may be, it's important that each partner knows all about the other's financial situation before and during the marriage.

- *Develop a budget.* It doesn't have to be an elaborate plan, but it can be the beginning of some enlightening—albeit heated—discussions. For those getting married, let your wedding be your first test at budgeting together. If you (or your parents) decide to spend $10,000 for the wedding, try cutting it back to $8,000 and save or invest the difference.

- *Make a date to talk about your money.* Personally, I know how difficult this recommendation can be. In many families, duties are often divided up out of necessity. In our family, my husband is the treasurer. Ideally, try to meet at least once a week for an hour.

- *Set financial goals for the relationship.* By setting goals, you can establish priorities and define what kind of lifestyle you want to lead. For example, you need to know if your spouse wants to retire early, open a business, go back to school, or change careers. Each of those decisions will affect the relationship and your financial future.

- *Agree on spending limits.* I highly recommend this one. My husband and I have an agreement not to spend more than $200 without discussing it with each other first. We have to agree or come to a compromise before a purchase can be made. I mentioned this to a single girlfriend, and she was horrified. "I'm not asking any man for permission to spend my own money," she said. But it's a good check-and-balance system. It's less a matter of asking permission than of discussing how a large purchase will affect the family finances. Incurring a lot of debt might result in one of you working overtime, which means time away from the family. By talking about it together you might decide the purchase isn't worth the sacrifice.

- *Learn to negotiate.* Some of the biggest arguments over money result when one partner wants to spend money on something the other doesn't approve of. My husband and I found a solution to that problem. We have an agreement not to spend money on a particular purchase until a compromise has been reached. There is a downside to this practice. It took six years before we could find a dining room set we both liked.

- *Educate yourself as much as possible about how to manage your money.* Subscribe to financial magazines, then use the articles as a basis for discussion.

However you decide to handle your money, be open and honest. Wealth building in a marriage should be a team effort. It's also one of the best ways to pass on healthy financial habits to your children.

FINANCIAL OPPOSITES DO ATTRACT

I am always amazed and amused at the way couples handle their money. I once asked couples to share their experiences about marriage and money. The responses described situations that ranged from domestic dictatorship, with one partner trying to control all the money and doling out an allowance as if the spouse were a child, to household anarchy, with husbands and wives treating saving as an annoyance to be avoided at all costs. What surprised me the most was the lack of communication between people who are supposed to be sharing a life together.

For example, one woman wrote that her husband lost nearly $20,000 in the stock market. It's not just the lost cash that upset her, she said, but the fact that she didn't even know he had invested that kind of money, at a time when they had large bills to pay.

One man wrote about his wife's unique method of handling her personal checking account. Each month when the written statement from the bank arrived, she simply took the bank's word on her current balance and recorded that in her checkbook. And what did the wife say when her husband asked about this blind acceptance of the bank statement? "Balancing the books was what the bank got paid for doing, and they were good at it."

Some couples cooed that they had found the perfect financial formula for their marriage.

One couple was so intent on making sure everything was fairly split that they had devised an elaborate formula. "Since I weigh 200 pounds and she weighs 110 pounds, we didn't think a 50/50 split [of food costs] would be fair," the husband wrote. "Therefore, we developed a 70/30 formula loosely based on our weight as a percentage of our total resting bed weight." The couple swore the strategy worked for them. They wrote, "We have very few arguments over money. . . . We have been managing our money this way for fifteen years, and the food ratio has not changed, since we both watch our weight and our money."

Whatever.

Most couples admitted that they often found themselves living out the old adage that opposites attract. "My husband and I rarely see eye-to-eye on our finances," said one wife. "He always wants to spend, spend, spend, while I wish to spend wisely, but mostly save."

It's not just wasteful spending that can drive a spouse a little batty. "I am married to the Coupon King," one woman wrote. "I can't even read the newspaper because there are holes where he has cut out the coupons. Our children, relatives, and friends are trained to avoid using major appliances during peak time," when electricity costs are higher. The cost cutting doesn't stop there. "One morning when I was home from work, he became upset because I used the coffeemaker instead of the microwave for a cup of coffee," she said. "Confronting me before I had that cup of coffee, he chastised me about peak-time usage."

Over the years I've received many letters from couples who want to know how they should handle their finances. The choices are many.

I know couples who don't divulge to their spouses what they earn. They divvy up all the bills and keep secret the balance in their individual bank accounts. Other couples do a combination of things. They pool a portion of their money but keep separate accounts for the rest.

If what you are doing now works, you may not need to heed my advice in this area. But obviously what many couples are doing isn't working. As I said previously, I don't believe in separate bank accounts.

"How can you share a bed and create children together and not share your money?" my pastor once asked during a sermon.

While the rest of the church was shouting "Amen!" and "Hallelujah!" one woman sitting behind me was shaking her head in disagreement. "He would understand if he had a husband who bounced checks all the time and was messing up the money," she whispered to the woman sitting next to her.

Getting a separate account is not the only answer if your spouse has a problem handing money. Eventually your spouse's mismanagement of money will affect the family. To me it's akin to having a spouse with a drinking problem. Would you say, "Honey, go drink in a separate room and I'll handle everything over here?" No, you wouldn't. You should get help to manage this problem together.

In reality, couples have to do what keeps the peace. But I will say this: If you want harmony and happiness in your marriage, you and your spouse should have the same values about money.

For example, while dating my husband I insisted that I had to have a one-carat diamond engagement ring. My husband did some research and discovered that if he wanted to get me a high-quality diamond, he could afford only two thirds of a carat. So that's what he budgeted and saved for, and that's what he gave me.

In the end, I realized that was the kind of man I wanted for a husband. He wasn't going to spend more than he could afford. It's just what I would have done. It was a value I respected.

Let these stories be a lesson to you. Opposites might attract, but the quickest way to pull your marriage apart is failing to set goals together.

A GOOD-BYE KISS FOR MYTHS OF LOVE AND MONEY

Let me address a few of the many misguided notions you or your partner may have about money. Here are some of my favorite misconceptions:

- *How much he spends is an indication of how much he loves me.* In a survey by Money Management International, a credit-counseling agency, the men polled said they would spend $121 on average on Valentine's Day. The women said they planned to spend $83. "Far too many consumers will spend way too much on a Valentine's Day gift," said Rudy Cavazos, director of corporate and media relations for Houston-based Money Management. I say, stop the madness. Love means never keeping score on what your sweetie is spending.

- *A guy should spend two months' salary on a diamond engagement ring.* Who do you think came up with that ridiculous guideline? A diamond-sales and marketing firm, that's who. Ten percent of the reported 2.3 million couples who get engaged each year do so on Valentine's Day, according to the Diamond Trading Company. Aren't those couples lucky that Diamond Trading would pass along its little gem of advice on how much a ring should cost? Ignore such nonsense. On a salary of $50,000 a year, you'd be out $8,333 before taxes. Spend what you can afford. If your intended has some arbitrary ring price or diamond size in mind, speak up now or forever hold your peace. But trust me—if you start your marriage off with this kind of spending, you may not have any peace, financially or otherwise.

- *Everything has to be equal.* After more than a decade of marriage and talking to many experts, I hate to tell you this, but everything won't be equal all the time. So many couples derail their relationship by trying to precisely divide up the money and bills so that whoever is earning more (or less) pays a "fair share." They end up acting like two spoiled siblings fussing over who got the bigger slice of pie. I had one reader actually say she hid purchases from her husband because if she didn't, he'd feel compelled to match her spending even if he didn't need anything. This is just another example of why the divorce rate is so high. If you're married and working toward the same financial goals— a house, a secure retirement for the two of you, or a college fund for your children—everything doesn't have to be split down the middle or divided up to approximate each person's income. You aren't roommates. It is important, however, to set up a system in which you both agree on how the bills will be paid and how much to save from each paycheck. Each of you should have some spending money to do with as you choose.

- *You shouldn't marry for money.* Yes, you should. But it's not what you think. I'm not saying you should try to find a rich husband or wife. But what do married people have at retirement that divorced and never-married people don't? They have a lot more money, according to Janet Wilmoth, an assistant professor of sociology at Purdue University. Her research showed that for every dollar the continuously married person has accumulated, the never-married person has about 23 cents (and this is holding constant for income and children). The divorced person who never remarries has 25 cents. The potential financial benefits of marriage include increased home ownership, insurance coverage for spouses, larger savings, and survivor pension benefits. For example, you have to be married at least ten years to qualify for Social Security benefits based on your former spouse's employment record.

13

—

IT'S NOT PLAY MONEY

Parents often ask me at what point they should begin to discuss money with their children.

Here's my standard answer. You should begin to talk to them about money the moment they begin to ask for stuff. That means if at the age of two they want to go to McDonald's, you ask them if they have the money to pay for the Happy Meal. Okay, so they won't have a clue what you mean, but ask anyway.

My oldest daughter and I constantly talk about money—most of the time about why I won't spend it. Nonetheless, that doesn't stop her from asking. She asks. I say no. She pleads. I say no again with an explanation. She whines, throwing in a tear or two for good measure. I ignore her. She glowers at me. I laugh and put my arms around her and repeat for the hundredth time why I choose not to indulge her every whim for toys, candy, or fast food.

I tell her that I choose not to spend based on her demands because we are saving for her college education.

"That's not fair," Olivia said once as she scrunched up her mouth and eyes. "I don't even know what college is."

"Well," I said, "college is where you go to learn so you can get a good job so you can move out of my house so I can have some peace and quiet."

Remember, you are the adult. It's your responsibility to use every opportunity you can to teach your children what they need to know about money, including how to spend wisely, save, and invest. It's your best chance that they will become savers, not spendthrifts—and won't have to live with you into your retirement (see Chapter 11 on boomerang children).

I'm certainly no paragon when it comes to teaching my children about money. But I do know that the example my husband and I set will teach them more about managing money than anything else will.

That is true for most parents, according to the American Savings Education Council and the Employee Benefit Research Institute. For several years the two nonprofit groups have commissioned a Youth and Money Survey. Each year the results come back the same. Nearly all of the surveyed students age sixteen to twenty-two say they are likely to turn to their parents for financial information.

"Unfortunately, many parents are missing a bit of the mark when it comes to educating their children about money," said Dallas Salisbury, chairman and chief executive of ASEC. "Parents both overestimate what kind of condition they're in and underestimate the kind of influence that they can have."

While most parents apparently think they do an excellent or good job of managing their money, their financial habits suggest that they aren't practicing on a day-to-day basis what they may be preaching to their children. And believe me: Your children do notice. For example, don't tell them cash is king unless it does rule in your house. In the Youth and Money Survey only about four in ten parents report that they paid off their credit cards each billing cycle. This generation of children is growing up with credit as king.

When it came to budgeting, many parents were less likely to plan how much they will spend and stick to their plan. Fewer than half of those surveyed said they stuck to a spending plan most of the time.

When asked to describe what exactly they had done to teach their children about financial matters, 56 percent of the parents could think of only one thing. Thirty-one percent could come up with only two things, and 8 percent said they had done nothing or didn't know what they had done.

"The bottom line is that most parents, on a regular basis, likely have a major impact on the financial attitudes and behavior of their kids—both positive and negative," said Salisbury.

Janet Bodnar, an executive editor at *Kiplinger's Personal Finance* magazine, agrees. Bodnar says parents have to recognize and capitalize on teachable money moments.

"If your kids keep asking to go to McDonald's, don't just say no or tell them you don't have the money or just give in all the time," Bodnar said. "Explain to them where the money comes from. And maybe next time your kids may not be so quick to ask to go to McDonald's."

Children really do live what they learn. If you want them to know how to handle their money in a responsible way, you have to start doing just that in your household.

If a man empties his purse into his head, no one can take it away from him. An investment of knowledge always pays the best interest.
                                        —Benjamin Franklin

TO GIVE OR NOT TO GIVE AN ALLOWANCE, THAT IS THE QUESTION

I never got an allowance.

With a low-wage job and five grandchildren to raise, allowances were a luxury my grandmother couldn't afford. I certainly never dared ask to be paid for any chores around the house—unless, of course, I wanted to cut down a switch for my own spanking.

These days, however, millions of kids are on their parents' payroll. In a survey by researchers at Ohio State University, half the children surveyed got a regular allowance. The median amount among kids between the ages of twelve and eighteen who get allowances was $50 a week. The highest-paid teens got more than $200 a week.

But half of all teens aren't getting any money, and of the half that do, 25 percent get less than $7 a week. Not surprisingly, parents who earned less gave smaller allowances. As income rose, so did the allowance.

The allowance survey was based on lengthy personal interviews conducted with nearly nine thousand randomly chosen teenagers participating in the National Longitudinal Survey of Youth. It was sponsored in part by the Labor Department and profiled in an issue of *American Demographics* magazine. "Allowance" was defined as any money disbursed to children by parents, other relatives, or guardians.

The survey findings had talk-show hosts and financial experts complaining that parents are overindulging their kids by handing out such large amounts of money.

But most revealing was that the coauthor of the study, Jay Zagorsky, told me he found little research to support a widespread notion that an allowance, or lack of one, has some connection with a child's future financial responsibility.

Apparently a lot of parents think that it does. In fact, many experts recommend that if you want your kids to learn about money, you should give them an allowance—even if it's a modest amount.

There are numerous books advocating allowances: *Allowance Kit, Junior! A Money System for Little Kids, Monthly Money: Allowance & Responsibility System for Kids and Teenagers, 101 Ways Kids Can Spoil Their Parents . . . and Increase Their Allowance,* and *Rich on Any Allowance: The Easy Budgeting System for Kids, Teens, and Young Adults.* These books tackle such issues as the amount you should dole out and whether the money should be tied to chores or given free and clear.

There are experts who say children will be ruined if they don't get an allowance and others warning that they'll be spoiled if they do. I don't blame parents for being confused.

Zagorsky said he was a little surprised at all the media hype, which focused on the $50 amount, even though half of the kids got no allowance at all. That $50 is the median amount among those who do, meaning half of the reported allowances were higher and half were lower.

So, should children get an allowance?

If so, how much?

The Ohio State study found the median allowance for a teen in a household with a family income of $70,000 to $80,000 is $70. Is that too much? Is it unreasonable that children should profit as the family finances get better?

The answers to these questions really don't matter—at least not if your goal is to teach your children how to handle finances.

"Giving a child an allowance doesn't guarantee that they will be good money managers," said Don Blandin, president of the American Savings Education Council. "It's not about giving them a buck or seven bucks. It's just as important to talk to them about finances in the home as best you can."

Ultimately, children are most likely to learn how to handle money from watching how their parents handle their money. My grandmother never made enough to give me an allowance. But watching her scrimp and save helped me establish healthy values that I stick by to this day.

However, if you choose to dole out some dough to your kids, here's my own little do-and-don't list:

- Be consistent. Set up a regular payday for them. Decide how often you will be paying your child (weekly, biweekly, or monthly). According to *Zillions,* the kids' magazine published by Consumer Reports, the average allowance for kids eight to fourteen is $5.82 a week, based on a 1998 survey of over one thousand children.

- Decide what will and won't be covered by the allowance, and put it in writing. All interested parties should read and sign an allowance agreement. Yes, even five-year-olds should sign or print their name. (See sample allowance agreement, pages 166–67.)

- Don't pay for regular chores. Kids should do chores because they are members of the household, not employees who ought to be paid for their work. Most of us aren't running a family business, so if you begin to put a price on chores, you could find yourself putting your kids on a permanent payroll. If you want, you could pay for extras the children might do, such as washing your car.

- Require that a certain percentage of the allowance (at least 10 percent) be saved. To encourage your child to save, you may want to match every dollar they save with the understanding that the match can only be used for long-term saving goals.

- Take out taxes. If this is supposed to be a real-life money-management exercise, then show them how taxes affect their net pay. I suggest taking 15 percent. You can give some or all of the money to a charity. You might also require them to contribute to their college fund.

- Follow the money. I firmly believe that as parents we still should have some say in how the allowance is spent. You better believe my daughters won't be buying tight shorts and tank tops. My son won't be allowed to buy violent video games.

SAMPLE ALLOWANCE AGREEMENT

I hereby agree that I will pay my son(s)/daughter(s) the sum of $_____ every week/month. (Pick a regular day so you won't forget if the allowance was paid).

Your allowance will be given under the following conditions:

1. The allowance will not be tied to any specific chores or grades. You are a member of this household and as such you are responsible to help around the house and get good grades without being paid.

2. A minimum of _____% of the allowance must be put away for savings. [If you tithe as a family, then your child should also tithe their 10 percent from their allowance.]

3. _____% of the allowance will be withheld for taxes. [This will give you an opportunity to discuss how taxes affect the amount of money they will net when they get a real salary. This money can be divided between charities and or a college fund. You should let the child choose the charity.]

4. Each dollar saved will be matched with an additional $_____. The matching money must be used for an agreed upon savings goal [e.g., bicycle, computer]. The matching money cannot be withdrawn from the bank or spent without prior approval. [This may give your child more incentive to save].

5. The following expenses are to be paid out of your allowance: [e.g., school lunch, CDs, movie tickets, gifts for friends; choose a certain number of expenses but don't overdo it.]

6. Your allowance cannot be spent on the following items:

_____.

7. Every month you must prepare a budget indicating how the allowance will be spent.

8. No advance on the allowance will be given. No exceptions! [This is your chance to teach your child that they have to live within their means or budgeted allowance.]

9. Once a year, on your birthday, there will be an allowance review meeting. At that time we will negotiate a possible raise in your allowance.

Parent and child agree to the above conditions.
Parent's Signature

_____

Child's Signature

_____

Date of Agreement

_____

- Make them create a budget. Again, if you say you are giving them an allowance, show them how to manage their money, then show them how to create a budget. Even small children can do this.

- Keep the issue of allowance and punishment separate, especially if the misbehavior has nothing to do with money.

- Have regular allowance reviews. This will allow you to adjust up or down the allowance you have set.

PAY YOU, PLEASE

One Saturday afternoon I asked my then thirteen-year-old niece to keep an eye on my two little ones for about twenty minutes so I could do some paperwork in the den. "Are you going to pay me?" she asked, palm extended.

"Let's see, are you going to pay me for all of the food you eat around here or the lights you turn on to do your homework or the water you use to wash your hair?" I asked her.

"Pay you? Please."

I was reminded of this little negotiation with my niece as I listened to child-care consultant Celia Martin Boykin read her essay "Our

Charge to the Children" during a service at a church in Washington. It's a sermon that a lot of parents need to hear as they confront the raw greed of our children. Here's part of what Boykin said: "I expect you to take out the trash, to say 'please,' 'thank you,' and 'excuse me.' I expect you to go to school, study, and get good grades. But I will not pay you to do what you are supposed to do. I will not pay you to take out the trash, because you are a member of this family, you live here. I will not pay you to say 'please,' 'thank you,' and 'excuse me,' because it is the thing to do, it is socially appropriate behavior."

At this point so many of the Sunday churchgoers were on their feet shouting and applauding Boykin that she had to pause while the congregation calmed down. Then she continued: "I will not pay you to go to school, study, and get good grades, because school is your work, your job—the only obligation you have until you get out of high school, and it is a benefit to you. And I will not pay you to be honest and kind. . . . I may reward you with a hug, we may celebrate by shopping together . . . but I will not pay you and promote a misplaced and undeserved sense of entitlement."

When Boykin finished her presentation, I sprang to my feet with a loud "amen," praising her for articulating how many of us besieged parents, aunts, uncles, and grandparents feel about raising children who are increasingly putting their palms out to get paid—for everything.

I have to say I'm not always sure when I should pay up. Unfortunately, there really doesn't seem to be consensus from experts on when it's appropriate to pay your children and for what.

Should you pay your child for good grades?

Before I had any children, I didn't see anything wrong with this idea. I thought, "What better way to encourage your children to do their best in school than to give them a cash incentive?" After all, it works in the real world. Workers get paid for good performance.

I asked Boykin, who has run various child-care centers in the area and now helps clients establish their own. "It's just a sophisticated bribe," said Boykin, whose three children are grown now. "Once you start paying them for good behavior or grades, there is a potential that they will put a money value on everything. If you do pay, I think you can set yourself up, and you may find that you have to keep paying. Then the stakes and monetary amounts keep getting higher."

If you decide to give your children an allowance, make it mean something. The primary reason to give an allowance is to teach your child how to handle money.

PUT THE WRAP ON CHILDREN'S BIRTHDAY BILLS

My three children are quite the socialites. But nothing seems to generate more stress for me than the birthday parties. Those parties have created a small but not insignificant dent in our household budget.

One year my husband added up our "birthday bills" and was amazed to find we'd spent several hundred dollars. So when I opened the invitation from a coworker for her son's birthday party, I got a surprise that warmed my cheap little heart. There was a note with the invitation asking guests to bring a book to exchange instead of a gift. I was so happy, I wanted to party.

"I looked around at all this stuff that Robbie has in toy boxes, bins, and baskets and I decided he needs no more toys," my friend explained. "I really wanted him to know what fun is without expecting toys."

This is a lesson that shouldn't be lost. Many of us are overindulging the kids in our lives, and we aren't stopping to think what kind of consumers we're creating.

"I figured the parents of the kids whom I was inviting didn't need the expense and the headache of trying to buy a toy for a three-year-old who has everything," said my friend. "So I decided then and there that this party would be about creativity."

I'm certainly not calling for a moratorium on giving or receiving gifts at birthday parties. But shouldn't we consider toning down our largesse? Kids are getting so much stuff it's hard for them to appreciate it all. I can't count the number of times I've been at a birthday party and watched the birthday boy or girl tear open gifts as though they were bags of chips. They sit in the honored position as gift after gift is handed to them with barely a moment in between to really cherish each one. It's "gimme," rip, "gimme," rip, "Can I have the next present, Mom?" Rip. "Is there more?" Rip. "Can I go play now?" Then all the presents get piled on a table to be toted away and dumped in the kid's room.

Now, you might be inclined to say, "It's just a birthday party." But year after year of overindulgence will make it harder to teach your children about moderation later. Already we have an epidemic of overspending among adults. Perhaps this is how it starts.

So, try some of these tips to help get a handle on these out-of-hand birthday-buying blues:

- Once, I invited a small group of my daughter's friends to a free neighborhood Easter-egg hunt in lieu of a big party. Then we just had cake and ice cream afterward. It was a cheap party, and the little tykes didn't trash my house. Look for free events in the community or at nearby museums. Have the party guests arrive at the event and then go back to your home for the food festivities.

- Consider forgoing gift giving, at least occasionally. Do as my friend did. It's okay to break the routine by coming up with alternatives to presents. For example, you could ask each guest to bring a nice, used toy that their kid no longer plays with to give to the birthday boy or girl or exchange with other partygoers.

- In the spirit of recycling and charitable giving, require that your child give away one toy for each new toy he receives.

- If you must have gifts, then set a price limit.

14

—

WHEN LIFE AND DEATH HAPPEN

AN INSURANCE PRIMER

The awful truth is that the people who need insurance the most will probably not have enough of it. I know this has been on your to-do list forever. But you know when you'll find out that you need it? When you can't get it because the worst has already happened. So let's run down the kind of insurance you need to get before you make another trip to the mall, place another order for some useless infomercial product, or plan your next vacation.

- *Health insurance.* Count your blessings if you're fortunate enough to have health insurance through your employer. You might gripe about the increasing costs in your copayments, but at least you have coverage. Millions of Americans either have no health insurance or the coverage they have isn't enough for all their medical expenses. This is particularly true for minorities. The Census Bureau reports that between 1998 and 2000, 19.5 percent of blacks had no health insurance, compared with 10.1 percent of whites. About 33 percent of Hispanics were uninsured. The statistics come down to this: Minorities are more likely to be uninsured or underinsured. That means that when they develop health problems, they have to pay for medical costs out of pocket or go without treatment.

    For several years I covered bankruptcy for the *Baltimore Evening Sun* and later for *The Washington Post.* I reviewed hundreds of bankruptcy petitions. A common misconception (thanks to the credit card companies' lobby machine) is that most people filing for bankruptcy are spendthrifts who now want to stiff their creditors. In fact, many people end up filing for bankruptcy because they can no longer handle the crush of medical bills. For many people a catastrophic illness can quickly deplete their life savings.

Most Americans (65 percent) get their health insurance through an employer. Lose your job and you're likely to lose your health insurance. There was a time when group health coverage was available only to full-time workers and their families. That changed in 1985 with the passage of the health-benefit provisions in the Consolidated Omnibus Budget Reconciliation Act (COBRA). Now, if you are terminated or you lose your health coverage because of reduced work hours, you can buy group coverage for yourself and your family. But the problem is that most workers can't afford to pick up the coverage. Only 7 percent of unemployed workers or their families used COBRA in 1999, according to the Kaiser Commission on Medicaid and the Uninsured. It's no wonder.

Are you ready for sticker shock? In 2001 the average family had to pay $600 a month to continue their health insurance under COBRA. For an individual the cost was about $225. That's because under COBRA you have to pay the full health premium, including the part that your employer used to pay, plus a 2 percent administrative fee. That would take a big chunk out of the average monthly unemployment benefit of $925 per month.

If you are entitled to COBRA benefits, your health plan must give you a notice stating you have a right to choose to continue benefits provided by the plan. You have sixty days to accept the coverage. Depending on your circumstances your COBRA coverage can last eighteen to thirty-six months.

I know this will be a hard choice. But if somehow you can manage to carry this coverage until you get another job, try to do it. This is why I've been nagging you about building up your savings so it can see you through tough times like this. (More later on what to consider in choosing your health insurance plan.)

- *Home owner's insurance.* You had to get this if you got a loan to buy your home. But did you get enough? Remember to period-ically review your policy and make sure you have 100 percent replacement-value insurance, which means enough to rebuild your home. You don't need to include the cost of the land. Make sure you have an automatic yearly adjustment for inflation. And please don't neglect to get replacement-cost coverage for your personal belongings. It won't be enough to get what's called "ac-tual cash value," which is replacement cost for belongings minus depreciation for use or age. Replacement-cost coverage is going to cost about 10 to 15 percent more, but unless you plan on sav-ing up the difference between the two types of policies, pay for the extra coverage. Don't forget to take an inventory of your household items. My home was broken into once and many items were stolen. However, I was able to get everything re-placed with no trouble because I had kept my receipts and taken pictures of the big-ticket stuff.

  What I'm about to suggest will just be ignored by many peo-ple, but I'll say it anyway. Raise your deductible if you want to save money over the time you have to own home owner's insur-ance. Normally, the standard home owner's policy comes with a deductible of $250. This is the up-front amount you pay before the insurance company pays you anything. But if you increase your deductible to $500, you could save up to 12 percent; to $1,000, up to 24 percent; to $2,500, up to 30 percent, depend-ing on your insurance company, according to the nonprofit USAA Education Foundation.

- *Renter's insurance.* Unfortunately, only about three out of every ten renters purchase this insurance, according to the Insurance Information Institute. But is your stuff less valuable than what home owners have? Sure it isn't. Then why have you neglected to protect it? The rates for rental insurance vary, but generally it's pretty affordable. Policies generally cost $130 to $200 a year with a $250 deductible.

- *Long-term-disability insurance.* This is your paycheck-protection policy. Long-term-disability insurance is coverage that is in-tended to replace some or all of your income, typically 50 to 60 percent, up to a specific maximum, if you are disabled and unable to work. This insurance is perhaps more important than life insurance. According to the U.S. Census Bureau, in 2001 nearly one in five people classified themselves as disabled. The sad fact is that your family finances will more likely be impacted by a disability than by death. A worker at age thirty-five has about a 24 percent chance of being disabled for more than ninety days during the remainder of his or her working life. If your employer offers this insurance, get it. Just so you know, you will be required to pay taxes on your long-term-disability benefits if your employer paid for your policy.

However, if you buy your own policy with after-tax dollars, it's not taxed. You need to account for the tax status of your disability benefits. If you're going to be taxed on the amount you receive from a plan paid by your employer, you might need to get a supplement policy to replace what is lost to taxes on the first policy. You will want to be clear on how the company defines a disability. Some policies pay benefits if you are unable to complete the duties of any occupation. Others pay benefits if you are unable to perform the major duties of your current occupation. Just be sure that you understand how and when your benefits will be paid.

- *Auto insurance.* For starters, when was the last time you shopped for car insurance? Twenty-nine percent of consumers reported that they have not shopped for insurance in at least five years, according to Progressive Auto Insurance. Of those respondents who said they have not shopped for auto insurance in 2001, 19 percent have spent more than ten years with their current auto-insurance company and report having never shopped for auto insurance. Additionally, of those consumers who have been with the same auto-insurance carrier for seven to ten years, 42 percent said they are extremely *unlikely* to shop for auto insurance. The study found that the cost of a six-month auto-insurance policy for the same driver with the same coverage could average $524. The national average for an auto insurance premium is $683.

- *Long-term-care insurance.* Long-term-care insurance provides coverage for care or assistance in a nursing facility or in a home or community environment. Although fees vary widely, an extended nursing-home stay can cost as much as $4,000 a month. Such insurance is expensive, and the older you are when you buy it, the higher the cost of the monthly premiums. Policies purchased at age sixty-five average $1,800 a year for four years of comprehensive coverage; at seventy-nine, they average $5,600 a year. A major reason for purchasing long-term-care insurance is to avoid depleting your life savings with a prolonged nursing-home stay and to preserve savings and other assets for children and grandchildren.

Benefits from a long-term-care policy can range from $75 daily to more than $175. Benefits generally start after a waiting period of thirty or ninety days from the time you are deemed unable to care for yourself. Premiums vary depending on age at the time of enrollment and the level of benefits chosen. Some experts recommend people hold off on buying a long-term-care policy (even though premiums are lower the younger you are when you enroll) until they reach their fifties.

Don't be pushed into buying this insurance before you absolutely have to. Even buying it at age fifty or older means you could spend thirty to forty years paying premiums before you need to use the insurance. When I turned forty, I checked with my financial planner to see how much my yearly premium would be if I waited until I reached fifty. The difference was $10 per month.

This type of insurance is being aggressively sold because the cost of long-term care is so catastrophically high. Insurance salespeople will argue that you can't predict the future and you could walk out of your home tomorrow, fall down with a debilitating illness, and wish you had purchased long-term-care insurance. Of course you could also be struck by lightning.

DO A CHECKUP ON YOUR HEALTH PLAN

In 2002 my husband and I learned that our seven-year-old daughter, Olivia, had developed a rare condition brought on by juvenile rheumatoid arthritis. Doctors told us she could die if they couldn't stop cells known as macrophages from attacking and destroying her red and white blood cells. Essentially, Olivia's immune system was attacking her own body. It wasn't until that moment in a staff room at Children's National Medical Center in Washington when I found out the gravity of Olivia's condition, that I fully appreciated how fortunate I was to have a good job. Without it, I wouldn't have access to the kind of health insurance needed to get my daughter's illness treated.

Olivia spent six weeks in the hospital. Months later we had a stack of billing notices as thick as two telephone books.

When I sat by Olivia's bed and watched her breathe through an oxygen mask and moan in her sleep from all the drugs she had to take, I couldn't help wondering how much more scared and stressed I would have been if I hadn't had adequate medical coverage.

I had chosen my plan, Kaiser Permanente, the way I picked my bank. The HMO was convenient. It had a large medical center near my home. Sure, I had looked at the type of coverage the plan offered and how much the copayment was compared with other plans available through my company. But there was so much I didn't check out. I should have found out which hospitals were affiliated with our plan. I didn't know that Children's, one of the nation's top pediatric hospitals, was where we would, luckily, be referred for specialty care for our children.

"Which health plan you choose can have important consequences for the quality of health care you get, the convenience of getting that care, the ease and pleasantness of dealing with the plan, and your total health care costs," say the editors of Consumers' Checkbook, an independent, nonprofit information service.

About the same time Olivia was admitted to the hospital, I received Consumers' Checkbook's *Guide to Health Plans*. This publication is full of important and potentially lifesaving advice. It can be ordered with a major credit card at (800) 213-7283 or on the web at www.checkbook.org.

The medical crisis my daughter went through taught me that if you want to receive good care in any plan, it often comes down to really knowing the rules and enlisting the help of the care providers who are part of the plan. Here are some key things to do or ask, according to Consumers' Checkbook and other experts:

- *Find a good primary-care physician.* This "is essential to getting good care in any type of plan but especially critical in an HMO, where this doctor will be the gatekeeper controlling access to all other services," according to the health-plan guide.

- *Understand how to get a referral for specialty services.* This is why you want to select not just a good doctor but also one who is good at navigating your plan's referral system. I don't think my daughter would be alive today had it not been for our pediatrician. She put in a request for a referral to a specialist the moment it appeared that Olivia's condition was unusual. When a referral didn't come through fast enough, she ran interference. It was a specialist at Children's who diagnosed Olivia's rare syndrome.

- *Find out who authorizes what treatment you will need during a hospitalization.* I think by far the best thing Kaiser has done is station one of its own physicians at Children's. That doctor has been a godsend. He coordinated daily with the wonderful team of physicians who were assigned to Olivia. He worked for Kaiser, but he became our doctor, our advocate—and now he is our friend. Not once did we have to fight with some bureaucrat about paying for a procedure or drug, no matter how experimental or expensive.

- *Find out which services are covered and what limitations and exclusions there are.* You may be surprised to find out that your policy has what is called a lifetime limit, which is sort of like a credit card limit. It establishes a monetary ceiling for how much will be covered for the life of your policy. Data from the Kaiser Family Foundation show that the lifetime limit often depends on the size of the company you work for. The larger the company, generally the higher the lifetime limit. Overall, says the foundation, 63 percent of employer-based health-insurance plans carry a lifetime limit of $1 million or more, 21 percent carry no maximum value, and 6 percent carry a limit of $1 million or less.

- *If your policy has a low lifetime limit and you're married, consider carrying insurance through both of your jobs.* It may be possible to use one health-care plan until it is maxed out and then switch to the second. Having a lifetime benefit of $1 million may seem sufficient, but keep in mind that the limit takes into account all previous treatments for various illnesses per individual covered under the plan. With the cost of medical care, you could hit that lifetime limit sooner than you think. But with two policies, once you max out on the primary plan, you can submit the additional charges to the secondary policy, says Joe Luchok, communications manager for the Health Insurance Association of America. Here again, check the second plan to find out what it will cover.

If you follow the basic tips I've outlined, maybe you won't have trouble with your medical coverage. Maybe you still will. At the very least become an informed consumer before a medical crisis hits. Go dig out your health-benefits book and read it cover to cover. Ask lots of questions even before you think you need the answers.

I'm grateful that when tragedy struck, I didn't have to worry about the cost and quality of the medical care my precious and precocious little girl received. But I'm also aware of and still troubled by the way insurance worries could have made things work out differently.

GET A LIFE—INSURANCE, THAT IS

Life insurance is one of the most important financial safety nets you should have, but it is also one of the most confusing to buy. The fact is that many people fail to get life insurance, pay too much for what they do have, or get too little coverage.

So, let me cut to the chase. You hate having to buy life insurance. I feel the same way. Theoretically, it's not much different from buying car insurance. In the case of term life insurance, you purchase a set amount of coverage for a specified period of time, after which the premium can be adjusted depending on your health and age. In both cases, if you miss a payment, the policy can be canceled.

Term life insurance, like car insurance, has no cash value until something bad happens. What irritates you is that if nothing happens—you don't get into a car accident or you don't die—you've spent all this money for nothing. But you do get something in return. You are getting protection against a catastrophe you don't have the cash to cover. Frankly, I know you would rather do anything than read this section of this book. But life is tough, so read on.

First, let me discuss who does and doesn't need life insurance.

- *A child.* I know you love your children and their death would be devastating to you. However, the death of a child isn't usually financially devastating to a family. If you're worried about paying for the funeral if the unthinkable does happen, then start a small savings account. If you're disciplined enough to pay $20 a month for a small life-insurance policy, why not just put that money in the bank? Even $20 a month earning just 2 percent in a simple savings account would grow to more than $6,200 in twenty-one years. This is a case where buying a life-insurance policy for a child is a waste of money.

- *Single person with no children or other dependents.* Enjoy life and thank your lucky stars that you don't need to worry about buying life insurance. Life insurance is bought to replace income that won't be coming in because you're dead. If you're only supporting yourself, once you're gone there's nobody to support, thus no need for life insurance. There are a few caveats. If a relative or friend has cosigned for any of your purchases, you should consider life insurance, otherwise you will leave your relative with the bills to pay. If you are concerned about burdening your family with funeral costs, then buy a small policy to help pay for that expense. But again, a better use of your money is to set aside your burial money in a savings account. Get someone you trust (your mom, dad, or a favorite older aunt) to cosign on the account, and tell that person that the money is to be used to pay for your funeral expenses. If you get a joint savings account, the money in the account won't be part of your estate since it will go to the joint-account holder upon your death. The best part is that if you don't die, you have a nice little bit of money saved.

- *Single person with dependent children.* Sorry, the party is over. You absolutely need life insurance. If your children rely on just your income, it's critical that you get life insurance.

- *Married person with no children.* If you fit this profile, think about what your spouse will need after you're gone. Do you have a mortgage and other household expenses that take two incomes to pay every month? If so, you might want to get some life insurance. But if your spouse can live comfortably without your income, you may not need it.

- *Married person with dependent children.* Same as the single person with children. You should buy insurance to cover the income that won't be coming in once you're gone.

- *Stay-at-home parent.* The temptation here is to buy life insurance just for the partner with a paycheck, especially if money is tight. Wrong move. Think about how much your spouse will have to pay someone to take care of your children. Then add to that maid service, a cook, a driver, a social secretary. See what I mean? It will take a lot of money to replace the services the stay-at-home parent is now rendering for free.

- *Married person with adult children and not far from retirement.* Once the children are out of college or have left to go live on their own you should evaluate how much insurance you really need at this point. You should still consider the expenses your spouse will have in case you die, but if you've been saving and you have a nice little nest egg (pension, Social Security, retirement savings in taxable or tax-deferred accounts), you might not need life insurance anymore.

If you determine that you need life insurance, the question is how much and what kind. There aren't any real rules on how much is the right amount of insurance. You should have enough to make up the difference between the lost wages and the benefits your family will get from various other sources such as Social Security, your pension, any savings, and retirement investment accounts. Ultimately, you want enough insurance so that your survivors can invest the life-insurance proceeds and live off the interest payments. Just as a reference point, the average amount of life-insurance coverage per insured household is $196,200, according to the American Council of Life Insurers.

Think Term

A reader made an interesting comment in response to a column I wrote on life insurance. "Term life insurance has always seemed to be a waste of money to me," a reader said. "I get nothing at the end of the term. But the premiums for whole life would be prohibitive at this time."

That made me think: Is term life insurance a waste of money?

Term life provides protection for a specific period of time, typically one to thirty years. It pays a death benefit only if you die during the term of the policy. Some policies can be automatically renewed at the end of the coverage period, and some can be converted to permanent insurance without the need for a medical exam.

Many people prefer permanent life insurance, also known as a "whole life" or "cash value" policy, because it builds up that cash value. While the permanent policy is in force, you can borrow against it or use the accumulated value to pay premiums.

So, as to the reader's concern: Is term a bad deal?

The short and simple answer is no.

"Term allows you to buy the most amount of insurance for the least amount of money," said Paul Graham, chief actuary for the American Council of Life Insurers. "With term you are getting the protection you need at the time you need it. That's why people should buy insurance. You buy it because you know you have a family, and if you die they won't have your salary anymore. Insurance gives them the opportunity to stay on their feet."

To me this issue is much like the debate over buying versus renting. I often hear people say that when you rent rather than buy a home, you aren't getting anything back for your money.

But you are getting something in return: a roof over your head, even if it is rented. It's not as if you're going to live on the street until you can afford to buy a house. Renting isn't always a bad deal if that's what you want or all you can afford.

"For many people, term insurance is just fine," said Emily M. Chiang, a certified financial planner based in Virginia. "Don't short-change your family in the life insurance department because you want a cash-value policy you can't afford. It's better to have term than nothing at all."

If you do buy term, here are the basic types of policies available, according to Graham and the Insurance Information Institute:

- *Renewable term.* This policy has a provision allowing you to renew coverage at the end of the term without having to show evidence of insurability. The company has to renew your policy even if your health has deteriorated. But the premium rate can rise with each renewal.

- *Level term.* This provides a fixed premium for a certain number of years, usually ten or twenty, while the death benefit remains unchanged. The advantage is that you lock in a certain rate for a certain period of time. The disadvantage is that the premiums will tend to cost more than the premiums charged in the earlier years of a renewable policy.

- *Decreasing term.* The death benefit in this type of policy decreases over its term. For example, you might start with $100,000 of coverage, with the amount decreasing by $10,000 each year for ten years. The premium usually remains the same over the term of the policy. Decreasing the death benefit allows you to keep the premium the same as you grow older; the alternative might be to keep the same amount of coverage but see the premium rise over the years. Graham said this type of policy isn't very common, but he called it useful for people who, for example, just want enough life insurance to pay off their mortgage.

- *Increasing term.* With this kind of policy, the death benefit gradually increases over the life of the policy. You may start with a $100,000 policy and increase the death benefit $10,000 each year for ten years. The premium will also increase each year. This kind of policy may be appropriate if you see your insurance needs growing in coming years because, say, you expect to have more children.

One feature to consider when buying term is a convertible option. Premiums for convertible policies are usually higher than for nonconvertible policies. Once the policy is converted, the premiums for the permanent coverage will be higher than those of the term policy if you keep the same death benefit.

Of course, there are some people who argue that you don't always need life insurance. True. There are many people who don't need this type of insurance. But if you decide you've got to have it, get as much as you can afford, which may mean buying term.

As Chiang said to me: "Always view life insurance as a gift of love for your survivors."

The Devil Is Always in the Details When It Comes to Permanent Insurance

Without a doubt, life insurance can be a pain to purchase and understand. A survey by the National Association of Insurance Commissioners found that only 28 percent of people with insurance—life, auto, home, health, or disability—really understood the details of their coverage.

And some types of insurance are more complicated to buy than others. For example, the Consumer Federation of America released a report warning consumers about the difficulty in purchasing a type of permanent insurance called variable universal life (VUL).

"Variable universal life insurance policies are so complex that they are difficult for most consumers to purchase intelligently," said James H. Hunt, the Consumer Federation's life insurance expert and a former Vermont insurance commissioner.

I'll get back to that later, but let me give you a brief overview of permanent life insurance:

The biggest selling point of permanent life is the cash value it can accumulate. Permanent policies are known by a variety of names: whole, ordinary, universal, adjustable, and variable. If you're thinking about purchasing permanent insurance, such as VUL, here are your basic choices, according to the American Council of Life Insurers:

- *Whole life or ordinary life.* Whole life policies stretch the cost of insurance out over a longer period to level out the otherwise increasing cost of the premiums. Part of your premium is used to pay for the death benefit, and the insurance company invests the rest, which is where the cash value comes from. Eventually you can use some of the cash buildup to pay the insurance premium. You can also borrow against the policy.

- *Universal life or adjustable life.* This kind of policy allows you, after your initial payment, to pay premiums at any time, subject to certain minimums and maximums. This type of policy usually guarantees a modest interest rate. A portion of each premium payment is used to pay for the insurance, some is used to pay fees, and the rest goes into a cash account. This type of policy is interest-rate sensitive. The cash value grows more in a higher-interest-rate environment.

- *Variable life.* This type of policy combines a death benefit with a cash value. The premium you pay (again, less certain fees such as commissions and investment-management and administrative charges) is invested. You can allocate your money among a variety of investments (typically mutual funds that invest in stocks, bonds, money-market instruments, or some combination of the three). Anyone selling this type of insurance must be registered to sell securities with the Securities and Exchange Commission. The cash value is not guaranteed and grows according to how well your investment choices do.

And then there's the VUL, a hybrid of universal and variable types. Its main attraction is as a tax shelter, the Consumer Federation's Hunt said. Under current tax law, investment earnings of VULs and other cash-value policies are not taxable if the policy is held until death.

But an array of VUL charges can more than offset the advantage of this insurance product, Hunt warned. "I think a VUL is the most useful and suitable for professional people, the self-employed, or people making significant incomes who are not eligible for either a 401(k) retirement plan or other tax-deferred plans that reduce their taxable income," he said.

The American Council of Life Insurers took issue with some of Hunt's conclusions, particularly his assertion that buying a VUL policy isn't easy.

"Actually, VULs are quite easy to understand if the individual's goal is to obtain permanent insurance, with premium payment flexibility and choice of accumulation investment vehicle," said William Schreiner, an actuary for the council.

Schreiner said that when buying a VUL, it comes down to asking yourself three questions: Do you want permanent insurance? Do you want flexible premiums? And do you want an investment vehicle attached to that policy? If you answered yes to all three, then a VUL could be right for you.

Whichever type of insurance you choose, here's the most important tip: Don't use the insurance salesperson as your only source of information. Would you ask only your grocer which foods and how much to buy for your family? I hardly think so. Certainly get advice from your insurance agent, but also do your own research. There are so many good independent resources on the Internet. If you don't have a computer, go to the nearest public library. Many allow you free Internet access. One of the best sites I've found is www.insure.com. Another site with good basic information belongs to the Insurance Information Institute (www.iii.org). The American Council of Life Insurers has a brochure called "How to Buy Life Insurance"; you can get it on the web at www.acli.com/ACLI/Consumer/Default.htm.

Buying life insurance is one of life's big annoyances. It *is* rocket science. But if purchased correctly, it can be a great benefit to your survivors.

When deciding to buy life insurance, here's what to consider:

- *How much insurance do you really need?* Consumer advocates argue that the purpose of life insurance is to provide income for your dependents if you die. So, unless you are going to do a lot of research, don't view it as an investment. There are often better ways to invest, such as mutual funds. If you have children, ask yourself how you want to provide for them. The insurance should cover funeral expenses, taxes, and debts. Then consider other future child-raising expenses, such as child care, dance classes, summer camp, or college costs.

- *How much insurance can you really afford?* Don't be intimidated by a salesperson into purchasing life insurance you can't keep up. What good is an insurance policy with an investment component if you let the policy lapse because you can't make the payments? The best bargain is usually term life insurance, especially for low- to moderate-income folks. For $5 you can buy Consumer Federation of America's thirty-page *Buyer's Guide to Insurance*. Here you will find advice on purchasing the four primary types of insurance: life, health, auto, and home owner's or renter's insurance. It also covers disability-income insurance, long-term-care insurance, and what to do if you don't get a fair insurance-claim settlement. To obtain *A Buyer's Guide to Insurance,* write the Consumer Federation of America at 1424 16th Street NW, Suite 604, Washington, DC 20036. Include a mailing address and a check or money order for $5 made out to CFA.

For people with limited incomes, cash-value insurance can seem like an easy way to set aside money and invest at the same time. But get someone to look over the policy before you buy it. The Consumer Federation of America will do it for a fairly reasonable fee. For $55, they'll evaluate any cash-value life-insurance policy. That's not small change, but it could save you a bundle of money over the long term. If you're thinking about buying a cash-value policy, get an independent look at what's being sold to you. Consumer Federation's actuary will also evaluate existing policies. Additional policies can be evaluated for $40 apiece if submitted at the same time. To read more about CFA's Rate of Return (ROR) service, go to www.consumerfed.org.

There are also firms that offer low-load insurance or insurance quote services for a fee. These firms give rate comparisons of the best-priced term life insurance with quality companies, including no-load (no-commission) and low-load (low-commission) policies:

Insurance Information Inc., (800) 472-5800 (charges a $50 flat fee; does not sell insurance)

SelectQuote Insurance Services, (800) 343-1985

USAA, (800) 531-1433

Quotesmith, (800) 556-9393 (www.quotesmith.com)

FINDING PEACE OF MIND FOR THE LONG TERM

If you decide the time has come to buy long-term-care insurance, you'll probably find the issues you have to contemplate bewildering.

Long-term-care insurance is not easy to buy. There are more policy options, conditions, and restrictions to think about than there are ice-cream flavors at Baskin-Robbins.

Before buying this insurance, sort through all the issues carefully. For starters, consider who will sell you a policy. Rick Epple, a Minnesota-based fee-only financial planner who advises clients on what to consider when buying a long-term-care policy, lists these options:

- *An insurance broker.* Look for an independent insurance agent who works with a number of companies so you can find a policy that best matches your needs.

- *Your employer.* The National Association of Insurance Commissioners notes that a growing number of employers now offer LTC insurance as part of employee-benefits packages. In many instances, although not always, group coverage is less expensive when purchased through your employer. One advantage of an employer group plan is that you may not have to meet any medical requirements to get a policy, according to the association. And many employers also let retirees, spouses, parents, and parents-in-law apply for coverage.

- *Professional or service organizations.* These groups may provide discounted rates for you and your spouse. For example, AARP makes long-term-care insurance available to its members.

- *A financial planner.* You may want to hire a financial adviser who can coach you through the process of determining whether LTC insurance is right for you and help with selecting a good and affordable policy.

When you are ready to search for a policy, here are some of the main points to consider, according to Epple and John Ryan, a Denver-based insurance broker, certified financial planner, and adviser to fee-only financial planners:

- *Complete coverage.* A good, comprehensive policy should provide coverage for stays in nursing homes and assisted-living facilities, as well as for in-home care.

- *Inflation protection.* There are basically three kinds of inflation protection, according to Ryan. Simple inflation protection means the benefit increases by the same dollar amount each year. For example, a $100 daily benefit that increases by $5 a year will be $200 a day in twenty years. Compound inflation protection means your daily or monthly benefit is adjusted each year over the previous year's amount. Since the increase, which is usually 5 percent, is compounded, the annual increase will be higher each year. Under compounding, the $100 daily benefit will be $265 a day in twenty years. The third protection against inflation is a CPI rider, which gives you the right to buy more protection at intervals based on the consumer price index. Just so you know, the more inflation protection you get, the more you'll pay. Most experts recommend the compound option, which can increase your policy premium by as much as 50 percent or more. A general rule is to get the compound option if you are sixty-five or under. Get the simple inflation option if you are over sixty-five.

- *Daily/monthly benefit limit.* Get the average cost per day for nursing-home care in your area. To find out what that is for your state, go to www.quotesmith.com. If you are looking for ways to save money on an LTC policy, you could get a lower daily-benefit limit and supplement it with your own savings should you need long-term care.

- *Benefit period.* Get coverage for at least five years. The average stay in a nursing home is between two and three years. If you are worried about needing care for a longer period, or if you want to make sure you won't wipe out your estate, consider a lifetime benefit policy. Keep in mind that the longer the benefit period, the more expensive the policy. Ryan recommends buying a policy with five to six years of coverage for the husband and a lifetime benefit for the wife. As he points out, statistically wives live longer than their husbands.

- *Elimination period.* This is how long it will take for your policy to kick in after you become disabled. Get a ninety-day-or-longer elimination period. "I much prefer my clients go for the longer elimination period and increase their benefit period," Epple said. If you opt for a longer elimination period, you will need some savings. For example, if you have a ninety-day elimination period and it costs $150 per day for care at a nursing home, you will ring up a bill of $13,500 before your insurance kicks in.

- *Understand how your claim will be paid.* Many policies will reimburse you. That means you get paid back for the expenses you incur. On the other hand, an indemnity rider pays a flat daily rate no matter what the costs are if you qualify for benefits. An indemnity rider could add about 10 percent to the cost of your policy.

- *Portability.* If you buy your coverage through your employer, verify that you can take it with you if you leave your job or retire.

Here are some of the conditions under which you may not need long-term-care insurance:

- If you have the resources (typically over $2 million) to pay for long-term care. Of course, this also depends on your annual expenses. Even $2 million could be eaten up if you needed years of long-term care.

- If you would qualify for Medicaid because you have limited assets. Keep in mind that neither employer health insurance nor Medicare usually pays for long-term-care expenses in a significant way. Medicare will pay for short-term, skilled care. Medicaid is the federal and state health-insurance program that pays for medical treatment, including nursing-home care, for people with limited income. To qualify for Medicaid you first have to spend down most of your savings.

- If you cannot afford the premiums. This may seem obvious, but remember, you could be paying for the insurance for years before you need it. So make sure you can comfortably pay for the premiums while you are working and once you retire.

According to Epple, you should consider getting long-term-care insurance if:

- You are satisfied you've done enough independent research, all of which points to taking out a policy. He recommends reading *A Shopper's Guide to Long-Term Care Insurance,* produced by the National Association of Insurance Commissioners (www.naic.org).

You can get one free copy of the guide by calling the NAIC at (816) 842-3600. AARP is also an excellent source of information on the topic. For a list of tips and resources, go to www.aarp.org and search for "long-term care."

- You want to protect your assets. Long-term care is expensive. You could wipe out your life savings before you qualify for any public assistance.

- If you want to stay independent and have choices about who cares for you. "A person going on Medicaid may have limited choices as to which facility they can get into," Epple said.

Still not sure what to do? Here's what Epple recommends for clients in the following situations:

- A single male (or female) in his fifties, with no children, who plans to retire soon with a good pension, $2 million in assets, and no desire to leave an estate to anyone. He doesn't mind if he has to spend all his assets until he qualifies for Medicaid. In this case, long-term-care insurance isn't recommended.

- A couple in their sixties, both in good health, with an estate of $1 million. They want to leave an inheritance. They can easily afford premium payments now and in retirement. They want the best if the need for long-term care should arise. They don't want to be a financial burden to their adult children. In this case, Epple suggests long-term-care insurance.

- A sixty-five-year-old couple with assets of $150,000. They live on Social Security and a small pension. All income goes to pay for needed living expenses. It would take only a few years to go through their savings before they qualify for Medicaid if long-term care were needed. Long-term-care insurance in this case does not make economic sense.

One Couple's Long-Term Journey

Gary and Jen Comfort decided in their late fifties that it was time for them to get long-term-care insurance. "We started to recognize that if one of us needed long-term care, we could wipe out all our assets pretty easily," said Gary.

Comfort, a retired Air Force officer and research analyst for a non-profit defense think tank, did what every expert says is essential before buying long-term-care insurance: his homework. He said it took three months of research before he felt ready to buy a policy. I think what this couple found could help you if you're in the market for this type of insurance.

For example, the Comforts felt it was vital to get inflation protection, even though it can double the cost of your premiums. "Unless you have inflation protection, you might still find yourself having to spend down your assets," Comfort said.

The cost of long-term care is eye-bulging. The average daily rate for nursing-home care in 2002 was $168 for a private room and $143 for a semiprivate room, according to a survey by MetLife, a provider of insurance and other financial services. The average hourly rate for home care was $37 for a licensed practical nurse and $18 for a home health aide.

But when it comes time to select the amount of coverage you want, base your decision on your family situation, not statistics, Comfort advises. "The pamphlets will inform you that the average stay in a nursing home is relatively short—two to three years. So lots of folks save costs by purchasing coverage for only a fixed period, perhaps five years," he said. "But those assumptions are based upon the 'average' stay."

For the Comforts, it was especially important to make sure they have enough coverage because they have an adult daughter with a disability. "We must leave her some assets, and we could not afford to take the risk of going broke with a limited-term LTC policy," Comfort said. "I think that one purchases insurance to guard against calamitous losses. So, since we can't be certain that we won't need many years of coverage, we bought policies that provide against that calamity."

The Comforts ended up buying a policy with a lifetime benefit.

One issue that was extremely important to the couple was picking a financially healthy insurance company.

As part of his research into long-term-care insurance, Comfort said he checked the ratings of all the companies he was considering.

A number of rating services analyze the financial strength of insurance companies. Be sure to find out how the agency labels its highest ratings and the meaning of the ratings, the National Association of Insurance Commissioners recommends.

Here are just a few of the rating services the association suggests using:

- Moody's Investors Service, (212) 553-0377; www.moodys.com.

- Standard & Poor's Insurance Rating Services, (212) 438-2400; www.standardpoor.com.

- Weiss Ratings, (800) 289-9222; www.weissratings.com.

Finally, the Comforts ran into a problem that made them very uncomfortable. "I was amazed at the reluctance of companies and their agents to let me see the actual policy contract," Gary Comfort said. "Each company would provide me some form of outline of coverage and tell me that after I bought the policy, I would receive the actual contract. I find that approach ridiculous for what is likely—second only to one's home—the largest financial expenditure of one's life."

Depending on the policy, consumers do have a right to cancel their contract after signing. In most states you have thirty days to do this, but in some you have less time. Check with your state insurance department to find out how long the "free look" period is. Regardless of the free-look period, Comfort said he wanted all information up front, before he signed on the dotted line.

"For example, many companies require that the plan of care be approved by a long-term-care coordinator who is either named by the insurer or must be approved by the insurer," Comfort said. "In my view, such a coordinator could wind up becoming a restrictive gatekeeper. It is this type of detail that is often not in the sales brochures but is clearly spelled out in the contract."

In the end, this is what the Comforts bought: Jen Comfort's policy has a $150-a-day limit with 5 percent compounded inflation protection, a sixty-day waiting period, and an unlimited benefit period. Gary Comfort's policy is the same except that his daily benefit is $100 (he expects to use his military pension to make up any difference). Their combined premium is $3,555 per year.

If you want to be comfortable with your long-term-care insurance, do what the Comforts did: research, research, research.

WHEN YOUR SLIP IS PINK

What can you do to prepare for a layoff? It used to be that many workers could count on continuous employment. IBM workers used to boast about their job security. But today for hundreds of thousands of employees the possibility of being laid off at some point during their working lives is very real. So, I asked several personal-finance specialists what they would recommend workers do if they expect to be laid off. Here's what they suggest:

- *Discontinue 401(k) contributions, and lower the withholding on your paychecks.* Typically, during extended unemployment, cash flow is needed and tax deductions are not. When faced with monthly bills and no future paychecks, you need to preserve as much cash as possible. If you were to contribute that extra cash to your 401(k) and later you needed to withdraw it during unemployment, you could be looking at a penalty of 10 percent in addition to the income taxes due. Also, if you are facing a prolonged period of unemployment, your taxable gross income is likely to be lower for the year. Therefore, you may want to decrease the amount of withholding on your final paychecks. Do this only when you are reasonably sure you face a layoff. As an alternative you could just reduce the amount you contribute to your 401(k) and put in just enough to get the company's match. That way you can start storing up some cash but you won't miss out on the free matching money.

- *Make minimum payments on credit cards for ninety days.* Generally, you should absolutely pay more than the minimum credit card balance due each month. But if you are laid off or are in fear of being laid off, having a cash reserve will become very important. Once you are back at work or the threat of being laid off has passed, you can resume larger payments on your credit cards.

- *Maintain cash reserves in a money-market fund.* Don't tie up your cash (such as severance payments) in long-term or illiquid investments. This is not the time to risk your cash in the topsy-turvy world of the stock market. Don't risk holding money for short-term needs in long-term investments.

- *Collect all unemployment and severance benefits you're entitled to.* Many people are reluctant to claim unemployment benefits when they are out of work. But unemployment is an insurance fund that has been contributed to on your behalf by your employer. Just as you claim insurance reimbursements for medical expenses, you should not hesitate to put in for unemployment benefits.

- *Maintain health insurance.* Your employer may have paid all or part of your health-insurance premium. As part of your severance, you may be able to negotiate with the company to continue your current coverage for a period. If not, most employers are required by law to offer the option of continuing your health insurance up to eighteen months through the health benefit provisions of COBRA (the Consolidated Omnibus Budget Reconciliation Act), but you will have to pay for the coverage plus an administrative charge. Although this could add a significant expense (as much as $600 for a family), the alternative could be worse. Having a serious medical problem without health insurance could trigger further financial difficulties. If your company plan is particularly expensive, you could reduce your premium by getting a policy with higher out-of-pocket expenses that still has good catastrophic coverage.

- *If you own a home, arrange for a home-equity line of credit to get you through tough times.* This is a loan that is approved for a certain amount. When you want to borrow some of that amount, you simply notify the bank how much you want and the amount is transferred into your checking account. Many banks provide checks so that borrowers can tap the funds that way. If you have a line of credit and are then laid off, it can provide a cushion until you are back on solid ground. This should be used as a last resort, but it can be a real lifesaver. Having the line of credit and not using it will usually involve a fee—possibly as much as $100 a year—just to keep it open. If you never draw on the money, obviously you will never pay interest. Look at the fee as the price of insurance for a rainy day.

- *Cut expenses.* Most people have significant room to cut expenses by reducing entertainment expenditures. This does not mean excluding entertainment altogether. Go to bargain movie matinees, or eat out during early-bird specials to save money. Having fun and a positive attitude will also help you land a job more quickly.

WHEN YOU'RE PLANNING THEIR "HOMECOMING"

When I got the call telling me my younger brother Mitchell had died of a massive seizure, I doubled over as if I had been sucker-punched in the stomach. Mitchell had epilepsy. He was thirty-two. My grief and guilt felt like someone was pushing a fifty-pound weight down on my heart. I could hardly breathe.

When it came time to make the funeral arrangements for Mitchell's "homecoming," as they call it in my faith, I tried not to let my heartache get in the way of planning a simple, low-budget funeral. My brother had a small insurance policy, but anything it didn't cover I had to pay for. I was following my grandmother's example. Big Mama was determined not to go broke burying my grandfather after he died of lung cancer.

I'll never forget the exchange she had with the funeral director. When he pulled out the casket catalogue, he immediately flipped to the pages showing expensive caskets of polished hardwood lined with fine fabric. Big Mama didn't pay him any mind. She flipped the pages back to the basic boxes. She chose a plain, gray metal casket that cost about $700.

"Of course that model will do," the director said. "But don't you think your husband deserves the best?"

"Lee Kelly got the best I could give him when he was alive," Big Mama said. "Besides, he's dead. He won't know if I'm burying him in a pine box or a bedsheet."

The director tried another tactic. He switched from "deserving" to "preserving." He recommended a higher-priced casket that could help preserve my grandfather's body.

"Why?" Big Mama asked. "Will he know when it rains?"

"Surely, you will want flowers," the director said as he began to flip to that section in his book.

"Why?" Big Mama asked. "He surely won't be able to smell them."

Big Mama also nixed getting limousines for the family, saving herself a couple hundred dollars. "I have a car and I know where the funeral home is, and the children and grandchildren have cars, and those that don't can ride with those that do," she said.

In the end, my grandfather and brother had dignified but inexpensive funerals. Even in my most mournful moment, I knew the amount of money I spent on my brother's funeral was no reflection of my feelings for him.

Perhaps at no other time are people more vulnerable than when a loved one passes away. Who wants to comparison-shop for funeral homes, caskets, or burial plots while grieving? And that's exactly what some providers in the funeral industry count on—consumers too consumed with sorrow to be concerned about saving money.

There are many decent funeral directors out there. But there are also unethical death-care providers just waiting to prey on the bereaved. They withhold price lists, overcharge for caskets, and lie about what services or products are required by law.

For instance, a casket is not required for cremation, despite what some will imply. And some funeral homes will still try to charge a casket-handling fee if you provide your own casket from an outside source, although such fees are illegal under federal law.

Even relatively scrupulous providers often persuade grief-stricken relatives to spend far more than necessary.

Funerals are now among the largest purchases most consumers will make. The cost of a funeral in 2003 ranged from $5,000 to $10,000. Caskets alone can cost thousands of dollars, with the average priced at about $2,000. But what often drives prices up, however, is our own guilt.

There is nothing disrespectful in living—or dying—within your means.

My grandmother lived several years after my grandfather died, and the money she saved on his funeral helped support her during her retirement years. As Big Mama said, "It doesn't make good sense to bury good money in the ground."

Bury These Misconceptions

Most death-care providers are honest, but others are more than willing to take advantage of grieving family members. Here are some common misrepresentations that you might hear from a funeral director:

"Embalming is required by state law." No, it isn't, except in rare circumstances.

"You can buy your casket somewhere else, but we'll have to charge you a handling fee." Under federal law, they can't.

"You need to buy a casket for cremation." Not true.

"This burial liner [or vault] will preserve the body indefinitely." No, it won't. Besides, why does this matter? Are you planning to reopen the casket? Don't go for this extra frill.

"We can't discuss prices over the phone." This is an attempt to get you to come into their office where it's easy to make the sell. The Federal Trade Commission's Funeral Rule requires funeral homes to provide prices over the phone if the consumer requests it.

Here's what you might hear from the salesperson at the cemetery:

"This burial liner [or vault] is required by state law." Actually, the cemetery usually requires it.

"You must buy your monument or marker from us." Not true. They're available from third-party sellers, including some on the Internet.

"Buy one plot, get one free." This is an offer often made to married couples but one that may come with many strings attached. For instance, the plots might not be next to each other. Adjacent plots could cost extra.

Prepaying for a Funeral

Long before my grandmother died, she made me promise to handle her funeral and burial. "You better put me down like I want, or I'm coming back from the grave and haunt you for not doing right by me after I pass on to meet my maker," Big Mama said.

Big Mama was obsessed with planning every detail of her funeral. It was also important to her that there be enough money to cover her funeral expenses. But instead of prepaying for her funeral, as an increasing number of seniors are now doing, Big Mama decided to keep control of the money designated for her burial.

Prepaid burial and funeral plans aren't new. But competition in the death industry has resulted in a stepped-up effort to aggressively market "preneed" contracts. The AARP says annual spending on preneed agreements exceeds $25 billion, up from $18 billion in 1995. In a 1999 survey, AARP noted that of the people questioned aged fifty and

older, two in five said they had been contacted about the advance purchase of funerals or other burial goods and services.

There is a certain logic behind prepaid funeral and burial plans—
lock in today's prices for tomorrow's death. Many people also want to
ensure that their families are not saddled with the costs of a funeral.
And rightly so. The average cost today is about $5,000, according to
the National Funeral Directors Association. Burial can add another
$2,500.

Thirty-two percent of Americans aged fifty and over, or roughly 21
million, have prepaid some or all of their funeral and/or burial expenses, AARP reports. Those who prepay tend to be at least sixty-five
and have annual household incomes of $5,000 to $40,000.

The problem with prepaying is that many consumers may be paying too much. Others might think they are taking care of all the costs,
but after they die, relatives discover that the contracts don't cover all
the expenses.

Worse, some families' contracts have not been honored—the funeral home went out of business, or the money was mishandled.

Consumer Reports does a great job highlighting the many pitfalls of
prepaying for funerals. An investigation by the magazine showed that
many people pay top dollar for prepaid funeral contracts. National funeral chains, which may keep the name of a local company they've
bought out, are the biggest promoters of prepaid funerals and charge
the highest prices, according to *Consumer Reports* and AARP.

"Prepaid plans benefit struggling funeral chains more than they
protect your pocketbook," according to *Consumer Reports.* "Paying
today for the promise of services and merchandise delivered years from
now is always an iffy proposition for the buyer."

There isn't anything necessarily unethical about the funeral industry selling prepaid funerals. Many preneed contracts are honored. But
for me, there are just too many risks.

Before my beloved Big Mama died, she arranged to use money
from her life-insurance policy to pay for her funeral. She also made me
promise to use money in a joint bank account we shared to supplement
whatever costs the policy didn't cover.

It is thoughtful to plan your funeral, and many people do it to spare
their loved ones grief. But think carefully before prepaying for it. A
number of states govern the prepayment of funeral goods and services,

and some state laws do a good job of protecting consumers' money. Others offer little legal protection. So, before buying a preneed funeral contract, do some research. AARP has a wonderful section on its website on preneed funeral and burial agreements. Go to www.aarp.org. If you don't have access to a computer, call AARP at (800) 424-3410. The Federal Trade Commission also provides advice on planning and paying for a funeral. You can find the information at www.ftc.gov/bcp/rule-making/funeral/, or call (877) FTC-HELP (877-382-4357). The National Funeral Directors Association (www.nfda.org or 800-228-6332) offers tips on prepaying as well as a funeral price list).

As an alternative to prepaying, AARP urges consumers to put their burial preferences in writing and keep control of their money. Instead of a prepaid plan, AARP suggests earmarking a certificate of deposit or life-insurance policy, or opening a designated savings account jointly with a family member who has right of survivorship so funds are not taxed.

WHERE THERE'S A WILL

"A will is for rich folk," my grandmother liked to say. "Besides, I don't want to hear no fussing while I'm still on this earth."

Big Mama was right about a lot of things when it came to her finances, but she was wrong about not having a will. Despite all my pleas, she didn't have one when she died.

The burden of having to make so many hard decisions—hopefully without hurting anyone's feelings—pushes will-writing way down on our to-do list. In that my grandmother was typical of most people. Seventy percent of Americans under forty who have children don't have wills.

For me it was painful enough dealing with the death of the woman who had raised me since I was four years old. But nothing prepared me for the squabbling over her furniture, jewelry, televisions, house, car, and all the rest of the things she accumulated in her eighty-two years on this earth. In fact, some of the bickering began even before Big Mama was put in the ground. The arguments about my grandmother's modest estate left some lasting scars in my family.

Please, don't underestimate the need for a will. Wills aren't just for rich folk. If you think about it, we all have something to pass on that could make things a little better for a relative or friend. A paid-off car could be given to a relative who's now catching a bus to work. Savings, even a small amount, could help a sister or brother buy books for college, or aid a parent on a fixed income.

If you don't get a will, decisions about your money and belongings will be left to the state—and your assets could be given to a relative you haven't spoken to in years, or don't even know. Don't assume that your children, sisters, or brothers will do the right thing with your money and possessions. Trust me, somebody will fight over something. Having a will doesn't guarantee that your family won't go to battle, but it might prevent an all-out war.

If money is an issue, just get a simple will. There are do-it-yourself versions, on paper and on computer software. Don't forget to have the will witnessed and notarized. Don't have any of your heirs serve as a witness. If you can afford it, it's best to have the will done by a lawyer. A lawyer can help deal with tricky issues that may not be covered by the boilerplate do-it-yourself versions. Depending on where you live, the cost could range from $300 to $500, though a complicated will will probably cost much more.

Finding a good lawyer is never easy. Lord knows I've had enough bad experiences with attorneys who took my money to solve family problems and did practically nothing. But don't let prior experiences keep you from getting a will. The best way to find a lawyer is through recommendations from friends or family members. You can also check with the local bar association. Interview at least two lawyers before you decide which to hire.

One of the reasons it's so hard to write a will is the very reason it's so important—choosing a guardian for your children if you pass away. That's where my husband and I got stuck. We ticked off who smokes, who's too old, too sick, or too tired from trying to raise their own kids.

But do pick somebody. Nobody will raise your children the way you would, so just accept that fact and choose the best guardian you can. Here are key things to consider when writing your will:

- *Revocable or living trust.* If you have a blended family or have specific instructions on how you want to dispose of your assets, you should consider a revocable or living trust. It allows you to bypass the probate process. It also allows you to manage your assets as if you were still alive. For example, you may want your money to be invested for a child's education. You also can arrange for your children to take loans against the trust to put a down payment on a home.

- *A living will.* These are your instructions on what to do if you become mentally or physically incompetent—if you don't want to be kept alive on a respirator, for example, or prefer to be cremated instead of buried.

- *Pour-over will.* This would allow anything you've bought but haven't had time to record in the trust to be automatically included at the time of death.

- *Durable power of attorney.* This allows a person to act on your behalf in all matters if you are mentally or physically unable to make decisions. Think carefully about whom you trust the most to make decisions for you, including choices about your health and finances.

- *People power.* For a will you need an executor. This person will make sure your wishes are followed as detailed in your will. You might also want to name a coexecutor in case something happens to your first choice. This isn't an easy job, so pick people who are good with paperwork and who act responsibly with their own finances.

DON'T FLUNK ESTATE PLANNING 101

So much focus in estate planning is on avoiding taxes and probate court that many people overlook some simple steps that will make sure money from a life-insurance policy or retirement plan ends up with their beneficiary of choice.

Insurance policies and retirement plans are specifically designed to allow an easy transfer of assets to dependents and survivors, says Thomas D. Murphy, Jr., a probate lawyer and senior partner at Murphy, McCoubrey & Auth in Massachusetts. Yet simple mistakes often thwart the best of intentions, he says. "In more than twenty years of practice, I've seen recurring mistakes in naming beneficiaries," said Murphy, the founder of FamilyFiles, an Internet company that helps people store their vital personal records online. Many of those mistakes are made by people whose disbursement of assets should be relatively simple.

"Assigning beneficiaries is something [people] often do their first day on the job when they are going over benefits with a new employer and they don't realize the importance of their choices," he said.

Here are, according to Murphy, several common pitfalls in designating beneficiaries:

- *Naming your estate as the beneficiary.* This can undo certain policy or retirement-plan advantages. For example, insurance benefits are generally not subject to claims from creditors, but an estate is. If your estate is the beneficiary, your insurance benefits may no longer be exempt. Also, naming an estate as beneficiary will result in the liquidation of an individual retirement account upon your death, with taxes becoming due immediately. This can deprive a surviving spouse of continued tax-free growth of that money. Check with a tax expert or lawyer before naming your estate as a beneficiary.

- *Failure to name a secondary beneficiary.* If your primary beneficiary dies before you, or at the same time, and you have not named a secondary beneficiary, your insurance policy or retirement plan will bounce back to your estate. In that event the money will be distributed according to your will or, if you have no will, according to your state's laws.

- *Naming minor children as beneficiaries.* Generally, insurance companies, pension plans, and retirement accounts will not pay death benefits to minors. Benefits are held until a court-approved guardian or trustee is appointed. If you want to provide for minors, name a trustee or establish a trust. Failure to do so will mean the court will name one for you.

- *Overlooking tax ramifications.* Many people have misconceptions about what is and isn't taxed. Life-insurance benefits are generally free from federal income tax. As for tax-deferred accounts, "in general, spouses are the only party that can continue to defer taxes in tax-deferred accounts, and in my experience this is usually done by rolling [the account] into another tax-deferred account of similar type," Murphy noted. Consult a tax professional to find out the tax ramifications when naming beneficiaries.

- *Failing to update records.* People often neglect to change their insurance policies or retirement accounts when their family situation changes. "I had an instance recently with a second wife and two young children—and the policies still designated the first wife," Murphy said. "Even in instances when a will indicates otherwise, designated beneficiaries in policies and insurance plans usually supersede any other indications. Generally, there is no satisfactory recourse—recent case law has ruled in favor of a first wife in such instances." So make it a habit to review your insurance policies and retirement-plan records. FamilyFiles has a checklist of life events requiring a document update at www.familyfiles.com.

- *Failure to be specific.* Ambiguities can complicate payment and leave a door open for dispute. For example, don't just write on the line for beneficiary "my wife" or "my child," Murphy cautions. That wording may not be sufficient, particularly in instances of multiple marriages. In designating beneficiaries, use full names.

- *Assuming your will "has you covered."* Generally, beneficiaries named in insurance policies and retirement plans trump any instructions you leave in your will. Make sure you have specified beneficiaries in your policies and plans. Many bank and investing accounts have mechanisms for naming beneficiaries so those assets can avoid probate. Check your bank and credit-union accounts, CDs, equities, and mutual funds to see if "payable on death" or "transferable on death" options are available.

- *Not leaving instructions as to where your will, insurance papers, and other important records are kept.* "All the financial and tax advice in the world is useless if people can't find your documents or don't know of their existence," Murphy says. Make sure your family is familiar with your most important records and where they are kept. Store important records in a secure file, vault, or online file, and inform your family of their location.

Do your loved ones a favor. Check your records so you can avoid these estate mistakes.

WHERE DID I PUT THAT?

It wasn't until my husband and I decided to hire a financial planner that we discovered how disorganized our records really were.

Of course, we waited until the last minute to pull together all the documents the planner had requested. Just hours before her arrival we were rummaging through our files, running up and down the stairs trying to assemble the information.

"Honey, where is the will-and-trust binder?" my husband asked from the den.

"I don't know," I said in frustration. "Maybe it's in the basement. I think that was the last place I put it. I'll go look."

"I can't find the home owner's insurance policy," my husband called out. "Do you know where it is?"

"Isn't it in the file cabinet?"

"If it were in the cabinet, honey, I wouldn't be asking you."

We tried to remain civil while hunting down our last paychecks, bank statements, employee benefits information, and 401(k) and savings-account statements. But clearly we were getting on each other's nerves.

Stop and think about how many "essential" documents go along with our lives: a will, bank statements, insurance policies, retirement information, guardianship instructions, advance medical directives, revocable powers of attorney, and checking account, stock portfolio, or mutual-fund statements. We're all like little corporations now. It's a pain. Yet if something does happen to you, the last thing your family wants to do is have to piece together your financial life.

Legal experts say the best way to get organized is to prepare what is called a "letter of instruction," a kind of Cliff Notes to your financial world. It's basically a list of all your important financial information—location and amounts of bank accounts, 401(k) plan, Social Security card, insurance policy, home owner's policy, and anything else the executor of your will might need to settle your estate.

I know. It's maddening to think that the best way to organize your documents is to prepare yet another document. But a letter of instruction would be kind of a master list, detailing where you keep your financial documents. For example, write down that your insurance policies are kept in the blue folder under the desk next to the window.

Kenneth Vercammen & Associates (www.njlaws.com—click on "Letters of Instruction") recommends that the letter include:

- Location of your safe-deposit box and its key.

- Location of your will and estate-planning documents.

- Medical coverage and location of the policies.

- Social Security or Veterans Administration records; identify current or potential benefits.

- Life-insurance policies. Indicate where policies are stored and what steps should be taken to collect the proceeds.

- Location and explanation of title documents and other records relating to your assets. Include deeds, stocks, bonds, bank accounts and deposits, retirement plans, and vehicle titles.

- A list of obligations involving periodic payments, such as your home mortgage, car loans, and other debts. Include the amount of the debts, and identify where payments are to be sent.

- The names of your lawyers and any professional advisers, including your accountant, broker, trust officer, and insurance agent.

- If you operate a business, a list of key employees and business friends who will keep it operating until it is sold.

When I complained to a friend about how frustrating it was to assemble all this paperwork, he said he wouldn't bother. "It's impossible to think that individuals should be expected to be so organized," he said. "It's just not possible. Besides, if I die, I'll be dead. What do I care if everything isn't in perfect order?"

You aren't doing this for yourself. Your heirs will be relieved that you did it for them.

What you put in your letter of instruction will depend on your situation. If you write the letter on a computer, remember to print a hard copy in case your computer can't be accessed. And for goodness sake, try to keep it updated. Otherwise you'll have to prepare another letter of instruction to tell everyone where the first one is located.

THE GOSPEL OF GOODWILL

Every so often, the pastor of my church explains why he preaches to the choir. He reminds the congregation that even the choir needs to steadily hear the message of salvation.

I feel the same way about personal finance.

You have to prepare your family for a financial crisis. My child's life-threatening illness reminded me how quickly things can go wrong in our lives. This is one of the reasons I always preach the gospel of good money management. But I've also discovered during our ordeal the importance of building goodwill.

When I talk about good money management, I worry about preaching to the choir. I worry that those who aren't financially prudent will just roll their eyes and see my sermonizing as nagging. I wonder, is it worth repeating over and over how important it is to save and live within your means?

But then I remember why my pastor stands in the pulpit every Sunday and preaches as hard as he does. The truth is that most of us know what we need to do—yet we still don't do it. We talk a good game, but our actions often don't reflect our rhetoric.

For example, you know that you should pay yourself first. But do you? Every payday, before you pay other bills, put some money aside. If you pay yourself first, you have less left over to squander on things you don't need.

If you saved $20 per week for ten years, you would end up with $10,400. If you invested that money and earned a 4 percent annual rate of return, the total would increase to $12,762, as calculated by the American Savings Education Council. It is further proof that even a small sum saved regularly can add up to a considerable amount, thanks to compound interest.

Is it worth saying again that you should be paying off your credit cards every month? You say you can't afford to throw away money, yet every time you pay interest to a credit card company that is exactly what you are doing.

And here's something else many of us also fail to take into account: the value of building up goodwill. In the world of accounting, goodwill is that intangible asset that exists when a business is valued at more than its fair market value, usually because of its strategic location, reputation, or good customer relations.

While you're putting money in the bank, take time to build up the savings in your life bank. Strive to be the kind of relative, friend, employee, or coworker who makes people want to do whatever they can to help you out in a crisis, financial or otherwise.

So, what kind of employee are you? Are you a slacker or a stellar performer?

What kind of coworker are you? Are you surly or sweet?

What kind of person are you? Are you quick to help or criticize?

Being a good person doesn't guarantee your boss won't be an ogre, or that you will get the time off you need to take care of a sick child. Having a nice personality won't pay the bills if a crisis hits. But it can't hurt. In fact, you may be surprised by how it can help.

My husband and I couldn't have gotten through our daughter's illness without the assistance of our family, friends, and coworkers. Their help was priceless. People prepared meals for us. They helped watch our two younger children, saving us the cost of having to hire babysitters. Friends, family, and readers sent gifts to our little girl, and those gifts helped brighten days filled with painful procedures and nasty-tasting medication. Coworkers sent cards wishing our family well. Readers e-mailed me asking for updates on Olivia. They clearly cared.

Thankfully, Olivia is recovering well. In a way, I appreciate what I learned from her traumatic experience. As Karl Kraus, an Austrian satirist, said: "Experiences are savings which a miser puts aside. Wisdom is an inheritance which a wastrel cannot exhaust."

15

THERE'S A SWINDLER BORN EVERY MINUTE

If you never invest a dime in the stock market, you can find financial security and serenity by doing two things. The first is to live within your means. Just by cutting back on your expenses you can begin to build wealth. The second way to build up your assets is to avoid the swindlers in the world.

Every year thousands of people from all income levels and educational backgrounds lose hundreds of millions of dollars of their hard-earned money because of misleading marketing pitches, unscrupulous contractors, and fraudulent investment schemes. People are being bamboozled into everything from buying expensive credit card insurance to paying inflated interest rates for their new or used car.

I don't think a fool and his money are soon parted. I think people are separated from their money because they are too trusting.

My late brother Mitchell was such a trusting soul. He foolishly believed that people meant what they said. I can't count the number of times he called me about some sweepstakes promotion he had received announcing that he had won a car, a sun-filled vacation trip, a big-screen television, or a motorboat. He would get so excited and want me to either drive him somewhere to pick up his winnings or take him to the bank to cash an official-looking check he had received in the mail that proclaimed him a millionaire. But they were all lies. Damnable lies.

I stopped him countless times from sending money to collect his so-called free prizes. Half the time I had to read and reread a letter to find the slick phrases that would prove to him that he hadn't really won a doggone thing. Mitchell would come to me with a sweepstakes letter or postcard in his hand hopeful that he had won money that could help supplement his disability check. I hated to tell him he hadn't won. It hurt me to my heart to see how dejected he would become.

One of the most bodacious cons I've seen is one in which consumers are offered credit card protection or credit card insurance. It works this way: You get a call from someone who may claim some or all of the following:

- That you're liable for unauthorized charges on your credit card account.

- That you need loss protection because computer hackers can access your card number and charge thousands of dollars to your account for which you will be responsible.

- That they're from the "security department" of the credit card company and they want to activate the protection feature on your credit card.

What makes this scam so outrageous is that current law already gives consumers protection from unauthorized charges on their credit cards. Consumers are not liable for fraudulent charges of more than $50, and most card companies won't bill you even if the unauthorized charges are for less than $50.

If you are going to protect yourself from scams, you have to know the games people play. Like cockroaches, some scams never go away. Here are what the Federal Trade Commission calls its dirty-dozen list of scams:

- *Business-opportunity scams.* Most of these scams promise a big return for a small investment of time and money. Some are actually old-fashioned pyramid schemes camouflaged to look like something else. In pyramid schemes investors are sold the right to become a sales representative or member, with the right to sell the same privilege to others. The sale of a product may be involved but that is always secondary to the recruitment of new participants.

- *Chain e-mails.* These electronic versions of the old-fashioned chain letters usually arrive with claims like, "Follow the simple instructions exactly, and in about three months, you should receive more than $800,000 in COLD, HARD CASH!!!" A chain e-mail, which is a subset of a pyramid scheme, promises that if you participate, your mailbox will soon be stuffed full of cash. These chain e-mails promise future riches that are mathematically impossible for almost all who receive them. Don't be fooled if the e-mail is used to sell inexpensive reports, mailing lists, or other such items. That doesn't make an otherwise illegal e-mail legal even if there is a pretense of selling something.

- *Making money by sending bulk e-mails.* These schemes claim that you can make money sending your own solicitations via bulk e-mail. They offer to sell you lists of e-mail addresses or software to allow you to make the mailings. What they don't mention is that the lists are of poor quality; sending bulk e-mail violates the terms of service of most Internet-service providers; virtually no legitimate businesses engage in bulk e-mailings; and several states have laws regulating the sending of bulk e-mail.

- *Work-at-home schemes.* I know you've seen the signs around your neighborhoods proclaiming, "Work at home and earn thousands." Insert a healthy dose of skepticism here. One woman in Maryland conned one thousand people out of a total of $50,000 by offering to send them materials so they could stuff envelopes at home. The unsuspecting entrepreneurs were promised they could make $1 per envelope. They paid anywhere from $35 to $90 for the promised materials. The con artist insisted her operation was legitimate because she was a member of the Better Business Bureau. She wasn't. People got nothing for their money. Two popular versions pitch envelope stuffing and craft assembly. But nobody will really pay you for stuffing envelopes, and craft-assembly promoters usually refuse to buy the crafts, claiming the work does not meet their quality standards. Check out all claims before sending anyone money. With just one telephone call, consumers would have found out that the Maryland woman wasn't a member of the BBB. Hopefully, that would have been a big red flag for them.

- *Health and diet scams.* These offer "scientific breakthroughs," "miraculous cures," "exclusive products," "secret formulas," and "ancient ingredients." Some come with testimonials from "cured" consumers or endorsements from "famous medical experts" no one's ever heard of.

- *Easy money.* Offers such as "Learn how to make $4,000 in one day," or "Make unlimited profits exchanging money on world currency markets" appeal to the desire to get rich quick. If making money was that easy, we'd all be millionaires.

- *Get something free.* The lure of valuable, free items—like computers or long-distance phone cards—gets consumers to pay membership fees to sign up with these scams. However, after paying a fee, consumers learn that they don't qualify for the free gift until they recruit other members.

- *Investment opportunities.* These scams may tout outrageously high rates of return with no risk. Glib, resourceful promoters suggest they have high-level financial connections; that they're privy to inside information; or that they guarantee the investment. To close the deal, they may serve up phony statistics, misrepresent the significance of a current event, or stress the unique quality of their offering. But they are not unique. They're just like the other scams.

- *Cable-descrambler kits.* For a small initial investment you can buy a cable-descrambler kit so you can receive cable without paying the subscription fees. First, they're illegal. Second, a lot of them don't even work.

- *Guaranteed loans or credit cards.* Some offer home-equity loans, even if you don't have any equity in your home. Others offer guaranteed, unsecured credit cards, regardless of your credit history. The "loans" turn out to be lists of lending institutions, and the credit cards never arrive. Some con artists will promise people with bad credit a chance to get a credit card. There's just one catch: You have to pay a fee in advance, which they say they'll use to help pay for the paperwork or "to get you preapproved" or some such line. However, once you've paid the fee, you won't hear from them again. The main target of advance-fee scammers are people who are desperate for a credit card—in other words, people who can least afford to lose money.

- *Credit-repair scams.* These scams target consumers with poor credit records. For an up-front fee, they offer to clear up a bad credit record—or give you a completely clean credit slate by showing you how to get an employer identification number. Basically, you're paying for a service you can do for yourself. By the way, getting an EIN when you're not an employer is illegal.

- *Vacation-prize promotions.* These "prize promotions" tell consumers they've been selected to receive a "luxury" vacation at a bargain-basement price. But the accommodations are rarely deluxe. I can see how you can fall for this. The travel industry has created an environment that encourages consumers to believe that no discount is too deep to be unbelievable. Travel scams are on the rise as more people try to take advantage of cut-rate deals on vacation packages, according to the American Society of Travel Agents (ASTA). According to the National Consumers League, travel fraud is the largest consumer rip-off after sweepstakes promotions, with annual losses totaling $12 billion.

To avoid becoming a victim of fraud, develop a set of house rules. Here are some I recommend:

- Don't accept unsolicited telephone calls. It's too hard to determine who is calling. If a charity calls, ask to receive information through the mail. Legitimate nonprofits will have no problem with this. While many legitimate charities raise money by phone, you have no way of determining who is on the other end of the line.

- Under no circumstances should you give out credit card or bank-account numbers to someone you don't know. If you called a catalogue company to place an order, it's okay. But never give out your credit card number if you didn't initiate the call, even if it sounds authentic or it's a charity to which you regularly contribute.

- Before paying for a service, make a call or two to consumer-advocacy groups or your state's consumer-protection office.

- Never, ever, pay any fees to get a "free prize."

- Don't invest with someone who calls you unsolicited on the phone. Lots of crooks are eager to offer you phony investment opportunities. It takes a skilled investor to sort through legitimate deals, so why, as a novice, would you invest in some real estate deal, cellular-telephone company, or frozen cow embryos? (Seriously, this last scheme was a phony offer used to milk investors.)

- Don't be too polite to hang up the telephone. Just remember someone on the other end is trying to separate you from your hard-earned money.

- Make sure everyone at home—especially your children—understands the house rules. More and more children are using the Internet, becoming susceptible to scam artists. Teach them not to give out any personal or financial information about themselves or you. Post a list of dos and don'ts next to the computer. Don't disclose salary information. Apart from a loan application or tax forms, I can think of few occasions when you need to provide such information. Don't even give out a salary range.

- Learn to say, "It's none of your business." My grandmother always demanded to know why someone needed personal information. If the answer wasn't good enough, she just said, "It's none of your business." Treat your personal and financial information like a wallet full of money. How often have you given out your telephone number? When you fill out surveys, do you readily provide facts about your family, salary range, and other information? Don't.

THINK YOU'RE TOO CLEVER TO BE CONNED?

I've told you how to protect yourself against cons, now let me tell you how I was conned.

As a personal-finance columnist, I've interviewed dozens of experts about how to protect yourself against crooks and schemers. I thought I was too smart to be conned. I was wrong.

Some creep smashed my car window and stole my purse. But that was just the beginning. After that he stole something else—my smugness.

Minutes after snatching my purse, the scoundrel who broke into my car called me at the community center where I was working out. He pretended to be a bank manager. He said they had caught the man who stole my belongings. He said the guy had confessed to stealing my purse. That, said the "bank manager," was how he knew where to find me.

He heard my sobs. He said I should take a few minutes to calm down. He was oh, so smooth. He sounded like a bank manager would sound—professional, assuring, and compassionate. He had the jargon down to a T.

He said he would immediately cancel my bank card even though they had the thief in custody, just to be on the safe side. He said that I shouldn't worry, that this happens all the time and the bank would re-imburse me if any money had been stolen.

He said he was happy for me because now I wouldn't have to re-place all the identification cards I had jammed in my wallet.

He told a tale of how he captured the crook. He described how he noticed broken glass in my purse as the guy tried to use my ATM card at the bank. He said he chased him down and held him until the po-lice arrived.

I thanked him. I thanked God.

But you're not going to believe what happened next. You're especially not going to believe how foolish I was.

The "bank manager" began to gather information. He said he wanted me to verify the contents of my purse and some financial in-formation. How much money did I have in my purse? What branch did I use? How many accounts did I have? Finally, he asked me for my personal identification number so he could cancel it.

Without hesitation, I answered each and every question.

Minutes after the purported bank manager hung up, I later learned, he took six hundred dollars out of my bank account. He would have gotten more had it not been for the quick actions of the police officer who responded to my 911 call.

I gave the officer the number the caller had given me to reach him at the bank. Thankfully, the officer had the foresight to call it right away. It was a phony number.

In that instant, I realized what had happened. I'd been had. The crook had methodically chipped away at my normal skepticism by seducing me with his kindness.

I wasn't prepared for the cleverness of this criminal. I wasn't prepared for how he would use my hysteria to override my common sense.

I spent the entire night of the theft second-guessing myself, unable to sleep. If only I had kept my cool. I now understand why so many victims, especially victims of financial crimes, don't come forward. They feel too embarrassed. They feel stupid. I felt stupid.

But as a friend pointed out to me, these guys make a living out of deceiving. They work at honing the craft of stealing good people's money.

If every experience has a lesson, I'd say this one taught me to be even more careful about divulging any financial information over the phone unless I initiate the contact. I'll especially remember not to reveal passwords or PINs. The legitimate generator of that information *never* needs to ask for it.

I also learned the hard way about lugging along so much personal information. My husband was always getting after me for overloading my purse with so many personal papers and identification cards. That has stopped. I routinely leave my checkbook at home unless I know that I'm going to use it.

I do know this: I'll have more compassion for people preyed upon by con artists. Now I know how easy it is to let your guard down.

IDENTITY THEFT: YOUR MONEY AND YOUR LIFE

Identity theft is rising at an alarming rate, according to the Federal Trade Commission and law-enforcement officials. Thieves use your stolen Social Security number, credit card account numbers, or other personal identifying information to open new accounts or change the mailing address on your existing accounts.

Identity theft is one of those crimes that might not seem so harmful until it happens to you. But from the moment I walked up and saw my car window smashed, I was less worried about my cash than what might happen if the crook stole my good credit name. "A stolen wallet or piece of mail can lead to hardships for hundreds of thousands of consumers every year," said Betsy Broder, assistant director of planning and information in the Federal Trade Commission's Bureau of Consumer Protection.

For 2002, the number of complaints filed for identity theft was 161,819, up from 86,198 in 2001. Identity theft accounted for 43 percent of complaints filed to the FTC in 2002, up from 39 percent in 2001.

Just think about what you carry around with you every day— credit cards, medical cards, a driver's license, and all the other bits and pieces of personal information that can be culled to allow a thief to apply for credit by pretending to be you.

I thought I had been careful not to carry around my Social Security card. As I began to go through the process of replacing the various cards that were in my stolen purse, however, I realized that one company was using my Social Security number as an ID number. I had paid little attention to what identifying numbers were on that card.

The most common method by which a criminal gets personal information is by the loss of a wallet or purse (47 percent), followed by mail theft or fraudulent address change (23 percent), according to the FTC.

The FTC reports that when your information is stolen, the following are the most common problem areas:

- *Credit cards.* More than half of consumers filing complaints reported that a credit card was opened in their name or that unauthorized charges were placed on their existing credit cards.

- *Phone or utility services.* Twenty-seven percent of complainants reported that the identity thief established some type of new service, such as a cellular-phone account, or gained access to existing accounts using the victim's name.

- *Banking.* Seventeen percent of victims reported that a new bank account had been opened in their name, fraudulent checks had been written, or unauthorized withdrawals had been made from their account.

- *Loans.* Eleven percent of complainants reported that the identity thief had obtained a loan (personal, business, auto, real estate, etc.) in their name.

The key to preventing or minimizing identity theft is to act quickly. If your purse or wallet is stolen, file a police report and get a copy of it. You might need it to prove that your personal information was stolen. Cancel all lost or stolen credit cards. If your bank card (especially your debit card) or checkbook is stolen, report it to the bank immediately.

In my case, I created a new secret password in addition to my personal information number. I just contacted the bank, and in my file they inserted a password that I have to use. This way, whenever I try to cash a check or do any banking activity related to checking or savings, the bank knows it's me and not the thief who stole my purse.

Order copies of your credit report from the three major credit bureaus (see page 80). Also have each bureau place a "fraud security alert" notice on your report. Creditors are supposed to contact you to verify that you are in fact applying for credit. However, you may still have to check your report every few months because some creditors aren't as careful as they should be and may not notice the fraud alert. Still, it's best to have the alert put in place. However, it may prevent you from applying for credit quickly. For example, you may not be able to take advantage of instant credit card offers (which is just as well, because you probably have too many credit cards anyway).

Just keep an eye out for fraudulent credit accounts.

Be sure to keep a log of all the calls and people you talk to during your ordeal so that, if necessary, you can demonstrate a good-faith effort to counteract fraud committed in your name.

You may also try the FTC's identity-theft hot line at (877) 438-4338. This service can help those who fear they may become victims, or simply want more information on how best to minimize their exposure to ID theft. You can also visit the agency's website devoted to ID theft at www.consumer.gov/idtheft. There you will find links to the three major credit bureaus, state laws, and an online complaint form.

Also useful is the FTC's consumer guide, *ID Theft: When Bad Things Happen to Your Good Name.*

16

BUILDING A NEST EGG? START WITH ONE TWIG AT A TIME

An architect wouldn't build a house without a blueprint. So why do so many of us try to build our financial house without a plan?

If you want to accumulate wealth and not debt, think of your finances as a pyramid. You have to start with a basic foundation.

The foundation of your financial pyramid should include an emergency fund of three to six months of living expenses. Next, make sure you have enough life, health, and disability insurance. Before building that pyramid any higher, pay off your high-interest consumer debt, such as your credit card bills.

Once you've got a handle on your debts, the rest of your pyramid should be investment-oriented. At the top, plan for short-, medium-, and long-term goals, such as saving for a car, a house, college education for your children, or your retirement.

An important way to achieve your goals is to take advantage of tax-deferred savings plans offered by your employer. According to a survey by Northwestern Mutual, only 6 percent of employees contribute enough to their 401(k) plan to qualify for their company's entire match.

If your company provides a matching contribution to your retirement savings plan, do what you have to do to qualify for all that money (eat in, skip a couple of movies, cancel cable). If you don't, look at what you could lose.

Let's say you earn $50,000 and your company will match contributions to your 401(k) plan, dollar for dollar, up to 6 percent of your total income. Beginning in 2004, the maximum amount that can be contributed on a pretax basis to a 401(k) or 403(b) plan is $13,000.

But you decide to contribute only $500 a year to your plan. The company matches your contribution, giving you another $500. Had you contributed the maximum 6 percent, however, you could have gotten an additional $2,500. Now consider the power of compounding. That $2,500 at 8 percent (compounded annually) could grow to $39,114 over ten years, or $123,557 in twenty years—all tax-deferred.

Think about it. You are leaving some serious money on the table.

As you build your pyramid, include a promise to become better informed. To that end, check out the following websites for information on mutual funds, stocks and bonds, finding a financial planner, and common investment scams.

- The Alliance for Investor Education (www.investoreducation. org). This site provides a number of useful tools and information on getting started.

- "Building Wealth: A Beginner's Guide to Securing Your Financial Future," Federal Reserve Bank of Dallas (www.dallasfed. org/htm/wealth/index.html). At this site you will find a useful budget calculator.

- "Get the Facts: Twenty Questions About Mutual Funds" from the Investment Company Institute (www.ici.org/quiz/get_the_ facts_quiz.html). Test your knowledge of mutual funds. There are several links here for more information on every right and wrong answer.

- "Invest Wisely: Advice from Your Securities Industry Regulators," Securities and Exchange Commission (www.sec.gov/investor/ pubs/inws.htm). This link provides tips on how to select a broker.

GET READY, SET, GO

For many people the risk of losing any of their money is an important factor in deciding how to invest. Ultimately, you have to decide for yourself how much risk you can tolerate.

If you just can't stand the turbulence of the stock market, consider a certificate of deposit or CD, which is insured by the federal government. CDs are purchased for a fixed length of time. Generally, the longer the maturity—the time before you get your money back—the higher the interest rate you earn. But if you cash in a CD before the maturity date, you will have to pay a stiff penalty. You also could consider an annuity, which insurance companies sell. Annuities guarantee fixed or variable future payments, usually upon retirement. Your earnings are tax-deferred within the annuity until you start receiving income from it. To boost the earnings, some companies offer annuities that are tied to certain market indexes, such as Standard & Poor 500 stock index, a measure of the performance of five hundred large stocks.

Another alternative is a money-market account, which usually carries a little higher rate than a regular savings account. The federal government does not insure money-market mutual-fund accounts, but some accounts invest only in U.S. Treasury bills and short-term government bonds, which makes them just as safe. Many funds allow clients to write checks against money-market accounts.

If you want to beat inflation, you may have to venture past your risk comfort zone just a bit. Remember that once you enter the world of investments, the word *guarantee* disappears.

For beginners with a modest amount of money to invest, a mutual fund is a good way to invest in stocks because it holds shares of many companies in several industries, which helps reduce the risk. The experts advise new investors to look for funds that have had consistent returns for at least the last five years. While past growth doesn't guarantee future performance, it is a useful guide to how well a fund is managed.

Novice investors might want to stay away from the latest and greatest mutual funds. Look for funds that have a record of above-average returns, consistency of management, and low volatility.

If you're in a higher tax bracket with fewer tax-deferred options, check out funds that invest in government securities or municipal bonds, which have an added tax-free benefit. For example, a Maryland resident who invests in municipal-bond funds issued by that state doesn't have to pay state, local, or federal taxes on the income. So while such a fund might offer only a 6 percent return, the tax-free equivalent yield could be more than 8 percent.

Before investing, do some homework. Several publications, books, and information are available on the Internet to help you find a suitable mutual fund. Your library should have publications of research firms, such as Value Line and Morningstar, that could help in your search for a fund.

The most important thing about trying to build wealth is to start early and invest regularly, even if you have to begin with small amounts.

If you can get past your investment jitters, here are some ways to get started:

- I can't say this enough: Build up a cash reserve before plunging into the stock market. If you can't manage to save six to twelve months' worth of living expenses, just try to put something away. This will give you the emergency money you'll need to take care of unexpected expenses, such as a large car-repair bill. By doing this, you won't be tempted to dip into your retirement fund or your kid's college money when an emergency strikes.

- Determine your own risk tolerance. You have to be comfortable with your investment strategy. A simple first step is to invest in mutual funds. Start out slow, with perhaps $25 a month.

- Decide on an investment approach for stocks that reflects your risk tolerance. For instance, you could employ a strategy referred to as "dollar-cost averaging," in which you invest a regular amount on a monthly basis. Using this method means you end up with fewer shares when the market is high and more when it's low. The latter is like going to Nordstrom's when the department store is having an after-Christmas sale.

- Take full advantage of retirement plans offered at work, especially those where employers will match some or all of your contribution. To me, participating in such programs is like getting free money—and there's no risk in that.

- Diversify. Are you overexposed in one stock or a single sector? We can all learn from what happened to the Enron employees, many of whom lost much if not all of their retirement savings because it was all tied up in Enron stock. You are not diversified if you own shares in three different small-cap funds (mutual funds specializing in the stocks of companies whose market value is less than $1 billion). Small-cap company stocks are generally more volatile than the stocks of midcap or large-cap companies. Choose to diversify because to do otherwise is to gamble big-time. Don't count on a single stock or sector if you can't afford the losses. If you are a new investor, consider investing in a balanced fund (a fund that provides some combination of growth, income, and conservation of capital by investing in a mix of stocks, bonds, and/or money-market instruments).

MUTUAL ATTRACTION

A friend once told me that investing in mutual funds is boring. "Where's the excitement?" asked my friend, who prefers to get pumped up by picking his own stocks. "I like the thrill of finding a stock that hasn't taken off yet."

I like the thrill of sleep.

Excitement for me is when my kids don't spill their drinks on my clean kitchen floor at dinnertime. As a working mother with three small children, a husband, and household to take care of, I don't want to be bothered with doing the research necessary to pick the latest, greatest, hottest, most high-flying stocks.

I knew my friend was teasing me, but I do get the feeling that some investors, those who can't stop watching CNBC or checking their stock portfolios every day, look down on those of us who have chosen mutual funds as our means of investing. It's as if we are investing wimps.

Frankly, I'm proud to be a wimp. I don't own a single share of stock outside a mutual fund. Why? It's easier on my life to let a professional pick for me. For me the choices come down to mutual funds or a savings account, and that's no contest. Bank interest rates are pathetic.

Mutual funds continue to be the investment choice for the masses. They are the best choice if you want to spend as little time as possible researching individual stocks.

What is a mutual fund?

Mutual funds pool money from thousands and even millions of investors to buy investments such as stocks, bonds, and other securities and mixtures of securities. For that stock-picking service, mutual-fund shareholders pay a range of fees, including a management fee to the fund managers who decide which investments to buy.

The three basic types of mutual funds are:

- *Money-market funds.* Money-market funds invest in short-term money-market instruments, such as U.S. Treasury bills, commercial paper, and certificates of deposit. The fund is managed with the goal of maintaining a net asset value per share of $1. Such funds are not federally insured, although the portfolio may consist of guaranteed securities and/or the fund may have private insurance protection.

- *Stock funds.* Mutual funds whose holdings consist mainly of stocks.

- *Bond funds.* Mutual funds whose holdings consist mainly of bonds. A bond is basically an IOU issued by a company, municipality, or government agency. The company or government promises to repay the loan amount on a specified maturity date with interest.

Picking a mutual fund can be as exciting as you want it to be. There are thousands of funds with different investment strategies and vastly different rates of return. How do you go about picking a mutual fund? The following are some questions investors should consider, according to "Questions You Should Ask Before You Invest in a Mutual Fund" by the Investment Company Institute, which can be found on the institute's website (www.ici.org).

- What is the fund's goal? The fund's goal—whether for growth, income, or a regular flow of earnings—should match your own.

- What is the fund's investment strategy? The prospectus describes the range of securities the fund may purchase, how it selects them, the types of securities it emphasizes, and the investment practices the fund may use.

- What are the main risks of investing in the fund? Understanding risk is critical to being an informed investor. Markets can go up and down, and you can make or lose money in any investment.

- What are the fund's fees and expenses? All funds must fully disclose their fees and expenses in a table in the front of the prospectus. You must decide if the cost of owning a particular fund is acceptable to you.

- Who manages the fund? What firm serves as the fund's investment adviser, and who manages the fund's portfolio? The adviser/management company is the firm responsible for deciding how, where, and when to invest the fund's assets.

- How do I buy the fund's shares? Some mutual funds offer their shares through investment professionals who provide investment advice, such as brokers, bank representatives, and financial planners. Other funds offer shares directly to investors—through the mail, by telephone, over the Internet, or at their own retail offices. Funds may also be offered through employer retirement plans. No matter how or where you invest, mutual funds, unlike bank deposits, are not insured or guaranteed by the federal government.

- How do I sell the fund's shares? By law, the fund must stand ready to buy back your shares on any business day. Depending on their value at the time you redeem, you may receive more or less than you paid for them. Redemptions may be made by contacting the fund company directly or through your investment professional.

- How are the fund's distributions made and taxed? Fund distributions—your earnings—include dividends earned on the investments the fund holds, and any capital gains made when the fund sells investments for more than it paid for them. Funds must make distributions at least once each year. Many shareholders elect to have their distributions reinvested in the purchase of additional shares of the fund, rather than taking them out as cash. It may also be important to you to determine when distributions are made and how they're taxed.

- What services are available from the fund? You should decide what fund services are important to you—such as automated information and transaction options, electronic transfers, check writing—and check to make sure the fund offers them.

For a list of mutual funds that let you start for $50 or less, go to www.mfea.com/NewsCommentary/Fundsfor50.asp.

IN A BEAR OR BULL MARKET, IGNORANCE ISN'T BLISS

Year after year, surveys show that investors get a failing grade when quizzed about their basic knowledge of personal finance, especially mutual funds.

In one survey, the Vanguard Group and *Money* magazine contacted one thousand randomly selected investors in eighteen states and asked them to complete a twenty-question financial literacy test, which included questions on the fundamentals of mutual funds. For example, investors were asked: Does the federal government back mutual funds?

Some of you may think this is an easy question, but only 45 percent of investors quizzed by Vanguard answered that correctly. Unlike federally insured bank accounts, mutual funds are not insured or guaranteed by the government.

Another thing you should understand is how the companies that operate mutual funds make money. One of the ways is to pass each fund's operating expenses on to the investors, expressed as an "expense ratio," or a percentage of the fund's average net assets during the year. This annual expense ratio typically ranges from a low of about 0.2 percent (or $2 per $1,000 in assets) to 2 percent ($20 per $1,000 in assets), according to Vanguard. Just remember this: Even small differences in a fund's expense ratio can make a large difference in your return over time.

Now that you know what an expense ratio is, ask yourself another question from the Vanguard test: If two mutual funds hold the same securities but one has higher operating expenses than the other, which of the following statements is true?

a. The fund with the higher expenses will have a higher return.

b. The fund with the lower expenses will have a higher return.

c. You can't say which fund would have a higher return, because expenses have no effect on returns.

You should have answered b. Sixty-four percent of investors who took the Vanguard test got this wrong. Operating expenses do matter. All mutual funds have expenses, but some cost significantly more to own than others. "Because expenses that you pay directly reduce your investment returns (they're deducted before you get your return), it pays to do your homework on a fund's expenses and fees before you invest," Vanguard points out.

On average, the investors got 40 percent of the questions right. I'm not going to rant about how uninformed people are when it comes to their investments. The truth is that this stuff can be complicated and confusing at times. I stay in the study mode because I can't trust that anyone else will look out for my best financial interests. Even a little bit of knowledge will help you make better choices about how to invest your money.

Many people (myself included), would rather put their money in a savings account or federally insured certificates of deposit because they are easy to understand. You give the bank your money and they give it back with interest. Simple.

But that simple way of saving money won't ensure that today's dollars pay for tomorrow's tuition bill or retirement expenses.

Today about 50 percent of households own mutual funds. In 1980 the number was only 5.7 percent, according to the Investment Company Institute.

The problem is that the 1990s made it easy to be ignorant. It wasn't hard to make money in the bull market. It seemed as though all you had to do was show up with your investment dollars and whether you put them in a mutual fund or bought individual stocks you got a good return.

I don't have to tell you, that is not the case anymore.

The reality is whether we are going through a bear market (a long period in which stock prices generally decline) or a bull market (a period when stock prices are on the rise), you'd better know the basics.

For example, many people know they get a tax benefit from investing in an individual retirement account. But they don't understand that an IRA is just an account designation. You still have to choose an investment to go into the account, such as a stock fund or a bond fund.

So start studying now. To begin your tutorial, go to Mutual Fund Investor's Education Alliance's website at www.mfea.com. This group is the not-for-profit trade association of the no-load mutual fund industry.

When it comes to investing in mutual funds, ignorance is not bliss. It can leave you broke.

DON'T DELAY, MAX OUT YOUR 401(K)

Millions of us contribute to a 401(k) retirement plan through our place of work. What many of us don't do is contribute the maximum allowed by law.

If this is you, you're missing out on a great benefit. Even if your 401(k) investments have declined during this time of economic uncertainty, the program is designed for the long haul. Putting as much in as possible will still leave you in better shape for the future. I understand there are several reasons you haven't gotten around to upping your 401(k) contributions—money is tight, you're too busy to bother, you hate filling out paperwork. I've heard them enough that I decided to make up a list of some of the most common excuses for not maxing out and reasons that you should.

Excuse: I don't need to max out.

Commonsense Truth: It's true that experts advise employees to contribute at least enough to their 401(k) plan to qualify for the company match, if there is one. Under the most common matching provisions, workers get fifty cents for every dollar they put in, up to 6 percent of their salary. That's a good start. But don't stop there. "You can't go back and get that tax benefit," said Gary Schatsky, a fee-only financial planner. "It's a case of use it or lose it."

Excuse: I can't afford to put in the maximum.

Commonsense Truth: Okay, you have me there. It's possible that you can't contribute the maximum right now. The average family does owe close to $9,000 on credit cards alone. But keep this in mind as you put other expenditures ahead of saving for your retirement: I challenge you to look at where you are spending your money. Even an extra $20 a week put into your retirement plan can make a big difference. That's two large pizzas with two toppings. If you invest $20 a week ($1,040 a year) for twenty-five years, assuming a 5 percent return, you end up with $50,000. That will buy a lot of rounds of golf.

"Close to 50 percent of the people who contribute to a 401(k) plan could afford to contribute the maximum," estimates Dallas Salisbury, president of the Employee Benefit Research Institute. "But that might involve other sacrifices. That might mean not buying that new car or that new television set. You have to make the conscious decision that spending less now will allow you to live better tomorrow."

Excuse: I don't want to live my life saving and scrimping to the point where I can't enjoy myself. What if I die tomorrow?

Commonsense Truth: Chances are you're going to live to a ripe old age. Life expectancy for the U.S. population reached a record high of 77.2 years in 2001, according to the Centers for Disease Control and Prevention. Thanks to medical progress, Americans are living longer than ever before. You could end up dependent on your retirement savings for ten, twenty, or even thirty years. Therefore, you had better save enough money for your retirement, unless you want to live in the guest room of a relative's house with the smaller TV and no cable.

Excuse: I don't want to put any extra money in my 401(k) plan when the stock market is doing so poorly.

Commonsense Truth: Sure, the market may be down. But you don't have to put all your money in stocks. Many plans give you options to put funds in a variety of investment vehicles. The important thing is to have a balance in your portfolio.

Excuse: What if I lose my job? I would then have to pay a penalty to pull the money out if I needed it.

Commonsense Truth: Yes, there are restrictions on taking money out of your retirement plan before age fifty-nine and a half. You have to pay regular income tax on the money plus a 10 percent penalty. To hedge against having to dip into your retirement account, try to save in a regular savings account at least enough to cover three to six months of living expenses. "That's your insurance policy against having to take money out of your 401(k) plan," Salisbury said. If you have to, put off contributing the maximum to your retirement plan until you build a cash reserve.

Excuse: I'll get around to increasing my contributions after the stock market starts to go up again.

Commonsense Truth: Ever hear of dollar-cost averaging? The market downturn is an opportunity to get more shares for your money. By investing on a regular basis now, you can buy more shares for less money.

Now if you're finished with the excuses, go straight to your company's benefits office. Time is money. And if your employer doesn't offer a 401(k), you still have no excuse. Open an individual retirement account at a bank or a brokerage and contribute the max. Why? Reread all of the above!

FUND HYPE

It's been said before, but it's worth repeating: Don't believe the hype. In the case of a mutual fund's performance, don't assume that the spectacular returns of the past will be repeated in the future. That's the message the Securities and Exchange Commission wants to get out.

You have mutual funds trumpeting these gigantic returns with huge type, and then they have the disclaimer in microscopic letters that say something such as "Chasing fund performance is often the quickest way to hurt your mutual-fund returns." What you should do is comparison-shop for funds that best match your long-term financial goals and tolerance for risk. Also be aware that investors who switch in and out of funds typically experience significantly lower returns than those realized by "buy and hold" investors.

I'll be honest. When I began investing, I focused primarily on past performance. Looking at the fund performance or return was something I could understand. It's easy math. I figured a fund with a 28 percent gain over five years was better than one with a 15 percent return for the same period.

I believe that many of the people marketing mutual funds prefer investors who concentrate just on returns. They want us to look at performance and forget about anything else. While past performance is something you should consider, you also have to look at other factors, such as a fund's expenses and fees. You have to factor in whether a fund has a front-end load (commissions paid in to buy a fund), back-end load (fees paid for redeeming shares), or no load at all.

Remember that funds have expenses, which you pay even if they don't have a load.

In addition to reviewing past performance, the SEC recommends that when looking at a mutual fund, investors do the following:

- Scrutinize the fund's sales charges, fees, and expenses.

- Know how the fund may affect your tax bill.

- Consider the age and size of the fund.

- Think about the volatility of the fund.

- Factor in the risks the fund takes to achieve its returns.

- Ask about recent changes in the fund's operations.

- Check the types of services offered by the fund.

- Assess how the fund will affect a portfolio's diversification.

Take the issue of expenses, for example. Over time, expenses and fees can really add up. On an investment held for twenty years, an annual fee of 1 percent will reduce the ending account balance by 18 percent. If you want to compare the long-term effect of fund sales charges, fees, and expenses, check out the SEC's Mutual Fund Cost Calculator on its website (www.sec.gov). Go to the "Investor Assistance" page. All you have to do is plug in a few numbers and you can see—in dollars and cents—how costs really add up over time. You can use the calculator to compare the fees of different funds.

I've learned my lesson. I'm not a performance chaser anymore. Oh, I want some evidence of good returns, but now I consider the other factors.

YOUR RETIREMENT PLAN: LET IT BE

There is a Chinese proverb that says: "If small money does not go out, big money will not come in." When applied to investing, that proverb is right on. Investing even small amounts of money over time has the potential to bring in big bucks.

But that wise old saying does not apply if you're talking about small amounts of money sitting in a tax-deferred retirement account that you're considering cashing out when you change jobs. In that case, it's more like, "If small money goes out, big money will not come in."

If you have just a few thousand dollars in your retirement account when you leave one job for another, it's tempting to take the cash rather than roll it over into another retirement account. But it may not be a prudent move, experts say. A $5,000 balance in a tax-deferred plan could grow to more than $50,000 in thirty years, at an 8 percent rate of return.

"People think they can do more good with the money by buying a car or using it for something else . . . but by the time you pay taxes on the money—both state and federal—it's nearly half gone," said Dee Lee, a certified financial planner and author of *The Complete Idiot's Guide to Retiring Early.*

If you're planning to get a new job this year and you have a balance in an employer-sponsored retirement plan, you generally have four options. Here are some of the pros and cons of each one, according to Lee:

- *Leave the money with your former employer.* This option makes sense if you're happy with the investment options in the old plan. It's also a good choice if you're not sure what to do with the money and you need more time to research your options. Just so you know, if the amount in your account is over $5,000, your former employer can't force you to cash out. If you stay in that plan, you'll still be able to direct where the money is invested, but you won't be able to borrow from your account.

- *Roll it into your new employer's plan.* Tax-law changes in 2001 allow portability between retirement plans, so it's now possible to roll money from your retirement account into a new employer's plan, even if it's not the same type of plan. For example, workers switching from a government agency to a public school might roll over their 457 retirement-plan assets to a 403(b) annuity. If you choose to roll the money into a plan offered by your new employer, you retain the ability to borrow from the account.

  Rolling it into your new employer's plan may be an easy choice, but it can also be tricky. Many employers make you wait up to a year before you can enroll in their 401(k) plan. While waiting, you can either leave the money with your former employer or roll it into an individual retirement account. If you choose to roll the money into an IRA temporarily, make sure the 401(k) money is not commingled with any other IRA funds. If it is, Lee said, it may be difficult to then roll it to your new employer's plan.

- *Roll the money into your own IRA.* No matter how much is in the account, you can roll it over into an IRA. For most people, this is the best option because you control how your money is invested. You are not limited to the investment options in an employer plan. For example, you could buy individual stocks and bonds. But be careful. "I've seen people lose their retirement money because they were day-trading or trying to time the market," Lee said.

  If you choose to roll the money over into an IRA, do a direct transfer. If your employer makes the check payable to you, the company has to withhold 20 percent of the money for payment to the IRS. To transfer funds directly, all you have to do is fill out an application for a rollover IRA and send it to the financial institution of your choice. The new IRA custodian will process the transfer for you.

- *Take a cash distribution.* This is a costly option. First, your former employer is required to withhold 20 percent of the money. Any part of the money you don't roll into a tax-deferred retirement account is subject to federal tax. If you live where there is a state income tax, add that too. Then, if you cash out before age fifty-nine and a half, you could be penalized another 10 percent. By now you have to be asking yourself if it's worth it.

  If you're not, consider the most costly feature of this option: You miss the opportunity to allow your money to grow over time, tax-deferred.

SAVE FOR COLLEGE TO AVOID SADDLING CHILDREN WITH DEBT

There is hardly any question that a college education, even if you have to borrow to pay for it, is worth the investment. But many students and their families have to ask themselves: When does the borrowing become too burdensome?

An estimated 39 percent of student borrowers are graduating with unmanageable levels of student-loan debt, according to *The Burden of Borrowing,* a report by the Higher Education Project of the State Public Interest Research Groups. Unmanageable student-loan debt is defined as monthly payments exceeding 8 percent of a borrower's monthly income.

The average federal-loan debt among student borrowers has nearly doubled in eight years, to $16,928, according to 1999–2000 data from the National Postsecondary Student Aid Study conducted by the Department of Education. Yet the average income of eighteen-to-twenty-four-year-olds with bachelor's degrees working full-time and year-round in 2000 was $32,101, according to the U.S. Census Bureau.

Taken together, the data suggest that people coming out of college are having to devote too much of their income to repaying higher-education loans. "Too often debt burden becomes a ball and chain for student borrowers after graduation," said Tracey King, the research group's higher-education associate, in announcing the report.

For example, 71 percent of low-income students (from families with incomes of $20,000 or less) graduate with debt, compared with 44 percent of students from families with incomes of $100,000 or more. In 1999–2000, 64 percent of students graduated with loan debt, compared with 42 percent in 1992–1993. In addition, the number of seniors who graduate with more than $20,000 in debt increased from 5 percent in 1992–1993 to 33 percent in 1999–2000.

But here's what I found most interesting in the report: There has been a rapid increase in the percentage of wealthy students who borrow. The percentage of dependent students from families with incomes of $100,000 or more who took out loans quadrupled from 1992–1993 to 1999–2000 (11 to 44 percent). The percentage of those student borrowers whose families had incomes between $80,000 and $99,999 more than doubled (24 to 58 percent) over the same time.

The report found that low-income students on average needed to borrow $8,351 to attend college. On the other hand, wealthy students needed an average of only $2,520. But the latter group ended up borrowing on average $4,321 a year—or nearly $2,000 more than they needed.

Many middle- and upper-income parents complain that they make too much to qualify for grants or subsidized loans. Without such help, they protest, they can't afford to pay college costs. Some students and their families really do need to borrow, and affordable loans and grant money should be available.

But ask yourself: Does your child have to take on so much debt because you can't afford to pay or because you failed to manage your finances?

I'm not talking about the families who face various financial crises or don't earn enough to meet their basic needs. I'm talking about people with good incomes who choose not to save for their child's college education.

And it is a choice.

After a house, the next most expensive purchase for many families is a car. The average cost of a new car is about $20,000. The average cost of attending a four-year public institution including tuition, fees, and room and board was about $9,000 during the 2001–2002 academic year, according to the College Board. Don't tell me you can't afford to pay for college if you bought a new car instead of a used one, or if your credit cards are near the maximum limit.

And you can find educational bargains. More than 40 percent of students attending four-year schools pay less than $3,700 a year for tuition and fees. The annual tuition at two-year public institutions averages less than $2,000, or under $200 per month. How much money did you send off last month to pay your Visa or MasterCard bill?

Read the study at www.pirg.org/highered/. Maybe it will be the wake-up call you need to stop buying a new car every few years. Maybe you will curb your spending on clothes, entertainment, and eating out when you realize your lack of savings could saddle your child with burdensome college debt.

When it comes to personal-finance issues, I understand things can get very personal indeed. It would be arrogant of me to suggest that someone is a bad parent if he doesn't pay for his kid to go to college.

Personally, however, I've always wanted to do all I can to help pay for the education of my children. If I'm lucky and I get this parenting thing right, they'll appreciate the effort.

I think you owe it to yourself and your family to make a conscious decision about how you spend your money. If you decide you don't want to fund your child's college education, that's your prerogative. Many parents extol the virtues of student loans. The cost is low, they say. Some of it is tax-deductible, they point out. It's "good debt," they argue.

Many of their points are valid. But the fact is, when your children have to borrow to finance their education, they are piling up debt. Debt eliminates some of their options. Several college graduates have written to me to say they appreciated their parents' paying for college because it allowed them to choose a career in public service, such as teaching, and not have to pay back big student loans on a relatively small salary.

Perhaps most parents can't realistically save enough to pay the entire college bill, especially for a brand-name school. But you've got eighteen years from the time a child is in diapers. If you do think it's part of your parental responsibility to pay for your child's college education, put away what you can because whatever you manage to save will help.

Ultimately, I think this parent feels the way I do. He wrote: "We use the money we've saved to help give our kids freedom of choice. The money we've saved becomes the floor rather than the ceiling. Could we have saved more? By definition everyone can save more. But I resent financial salesmen who scare me with tales about how college costs are spiraling out of control so I had better ransom my soul to afford it. In the end, we did what most people other than the very affluent do—we saved what we could."

A COLLEGE-SAVINGS PLAN TAKES HOMEWORK

If you decide that you do want to fully or partially fund your child's college education, one of the best ways is investing through a 529 plan. Yet although many financial planners and personal-finance writers make it sound as though investing in a Section 529 college-savings plan is a no-brainer, I have some reservations about this vehicle.

The marketing of 529s, named after the tax-code provision that created them, has been stepped up lately because of the more favorable tax treatment they now get.

Earnings in state-sponsored 529 plans are tax-free. Previously, earnings grew tax-deferred. When the money was withdrawn, it usually was taxed at a child's income tax rate of 15 percent. In some plans, you can invest up to $250,000 per child regardless of your income level.

There are two types of 529s: a college-savings plan and a prepaid tuition plan. Investing in a college savings plan is like investing in a mutual fund. Your money is combined with money from others and invested by the plan manager. The alternative, the prepaid plan, lets parents, grandparents, and other interested parties lock in today's tuition rates, and the program will pay out future college tuition at any of a state's eligible colleges or universities (or an equal payment to private and out-of-state institutions).

There are numerous websites that will give you a good tutorial on these plans. One of the most useful is www.savingforcollege.com. This site provides a comprehensive look at all available 529 plans. Look for the link to the site's 529 evaluator. You might also try www.collegesavings.org, which is run by the College Savings Plans Network, an affiliate of the National Association of State Treasurers.

Here are some of the basics of 529 plans:

- You can invest in installments or in a lump sum.

- 529 savings plans don't exclude anyone from contributing, even those with high income.

- At this point (the tax law could change after 2010), earnings are not federally taxed as long as the money is used for qualified educational expenses. Graduate, professional, and technical-school expenses qualify.

- You can open an account for any child—yours, a relative's, or someone else's.

- The money in any state plan can be used at any accredited college or university, including seven hundred international schools. All fifty states and the District of Columbia have college-savings plans, and twenty-three states offer prepaid tuition plans to their residents, according to the College Savings Plans Network.

- Most states allow nonresidents to open an account. Many states offer their own residents a tax deduction for contributions made to their state-sponsored 529 plan. Mississippi is particularly generous with its deduction. Residents can deduct up to $10,000 per year ($20,000 for married couples filing jointly). Rhode Island is one of the stingiest, with a $500 deduction

($1,000 for a couple). In Maryland it's $2,500 per account, and in Virginia it's $2,000.

Just so you know, college-savings plans are treated as an asset of the account holder, not the student, according to Mark Kantrowitz, publisher of FinAid.org. Prepaid-tuition plans are treated as a resource, meaning that they reduce financial-aid packages dollar for dollar, but only when money from the plans is actually used, and only for the amount used, Kantrowitz said.

You might be a little too jittery to invest in a 529 plan because of the tumultuous stock market. I can't blame you. But there are precautions you can take to minimize losses.

Many 529 plans have age-based portfolios that automatically become more conservative the closer the child is to college age. Like any investment, there is no guarantee. But the sooner you start, the better the chance that you'll have money to cover college expenses.

Money invested in a 529 plan has to be used for qualified higher-education expenses—tuition, books, and room and board. If you need the money for something else or your child doesn't go to college, there is a 10 percent penalty, on top of the ordinary income tax, that would be triggered when funds are withdrawn for another purpose. Some states may even impose an additional penalty. Of course, there are some exceptions (if your child gets a scholarship, for example), but mostly you are stuck with using the money for college.

As with any investment, you should weigh the touted benefits against your own investment style. And be realistic about your ability to tie up your money. Don't just listen to the hype. Do a lot of homework. For example, some plans have expensive fees, which can reduce your earnings.

As with any financial decision, it always helps me to make a list of the pros and cons. On one side, you can list the disadvantages of a 529 plan: a penalty if the money isn't used for qualified college expenses; little control over your money; and, unless Congress extends it, the tax advantages expire on January 1, 2011.

Now add up the benefits: earnings are free from federal taxes, and some states offer additional tax benefits; and it's a great investment vehicle for parents with high incomes.

Contrary to what some experts say, it takes a lot of brains to figure out whether a 529 plan works for your family.

Personally, I'm a control freak. I want to keep my options open because life has a funny way of interrupting the best-laid plans. I want the maximum flexibility to withdraw any money I save for college expenses or anything else when I want—with few, if any, restrictions, penalties, or hassles.

However, in the end my husband and I couldn't ignore the tax benefits from investing in a 529 plan. So we are putting some of our children's college money in our state-sponsored plan (that way we enjoy the state tax deduction), and we are investing in a non-tax-deferred mutual fund, which gives us complete control of how the money is used.

PUTTING YOUR PRINCIPLES TO WORK

If you're looking to make a difference with your money, you might want to check out socially responsible investment funds. You'll find that you don't have to sacrifice performance to follow your principles.

"Socially responsible funds provide a choice for investors that want to put their money to work to reflect who they are and what they are concerned about," said Steve Schueth, president of the Social Investment Forum, a nonprofit group that promotes social investing.

Socially responsible funds, with three-year records tracked by Morningstar, have consistently earned four- and five-star rankings, according to Catherine Hickey, an analyst for the research firm. (Funds that fall in the top 10 percent of a broad group—domestic stock, international stock, taxable bond, and municipal bond—earn five stars from Morningstar. Funds with results that land them in the bottom 10 percent get one star.)

Social investing, which is thirty years old, allows investors to put their money into stocks and bonds that reflect their values. For example, you can invest in funds that screen out companies that pollute, or sell tobacco or alcohol, or fail to promote equity in the workplace. Most recently, some funds have kept from their portfolios the stocks of companies that sell goods made in overseas sweatshops.

More than $2 trillion in U.S. assets is invested in socially screened investment portfolios, according to the Social Investment Forum. The fastest-growing category of socially responsible investing is in funds that buy stocks and bonds in companies, government entities, and financial institutions that make it possible for local organizations to create affordable housing and jobs, provide services to low-income individuals, and supply capital for small businesses. Individual and institutional assets flowing into community-investing organizations grew by 41 percent between 1999 and 2001, increasing from $5.4 billion to $7.6 billion, according to the investment forum's report.

"In general, people are thinking more about how they live their life and how they can get more meaning out of their life," said David Wieder, chief executive of Domini Social Investments, one of the country's largest socially responsible fund companies. "One way to do that is to make sure your investments are more meaningful."

If this type of investing interests you, start by checking out a couple of useful websites—www.socialinvest.org and www.socialfunds.com. For an independent assessment and rating of funds, try Morningstar (www.morningstar.com) and Lipper (www.lipperleaders.com).

Picking a socially responsible fund is much like purchasing a car. You have to shop around for price, performance, and style, in this case the investment style of the portfolio.

As with any mutual fund, don't ignore costs. Some funds can be expensive, Hickey said, while others, such as the TIAA-CREF Social Choice Equity Fund and Vanguard Calvert Social Index Fund, boast low expenses. A good benchmark to look for is an expense ratio of about 1.6 percent or lower. If the fund's expense ratio is higher, she said, ask for a justification. A fund may charge more because it's smaller and can't spread costs among as many investors or its screening criteria require extensive research.

In many cases your returns will depend on what's being screened in or out of the fund, according to Tom Roseen, a research analyst for Lipper. "If you invest in a fund that screens out what some call the 'sin' stocks, such as companies that sell alcohol or tobacco, when those stocks do well your fund obviously won't benefit from the surge," Roseen said. The tanking of the technology industry has tripped up a lot of screened funds, which favored tech stocks because those companies were seen as being environmentally and workplace-friendly.

Social investing isn't for everyone, but if you feel strongly about some social criteria, with some good research, such as looking at the portfolio manager and the fund's investment style, you can find good-performing funds.

JUST ANOTHER BOWL OF ALPHABET SOUP

It seems to me everybody and their mama is calling themselves a "financial planner" these days. Bankers, brokers, insurance agents, and accountants all claim they can help us manage our money. In fact, anybody can call herself a financial planner without any qualifications to speak of.

Financial planners see themselves as the money doctors of our times. Come in and get treated, they beckon, because we have the skills to make you financially healthy.

But do they?

I know what makes a good doctor or dentist. My doctor listens to my complaints, then fixes what ails me. My dentist fills my cavities and tries not to put me through too much pain in the process (although I've fondly nicknamed him "Dr. No"). At the very least, medical professionals have the credentials that make me feel comfortable putting my health in their hands. Mostly, you feel confident that they are working in your best interest. But you can't always be so sure about financial planners. It is a title now used by too many financial professionals, many of whom are really salespeople with a particular set of products they want to sell.

I want someone who will look at my financial situation and create a plan that fits my needs. I don't want to worry whether their goal is selling me an investment product that will yield them the highest commission. And I don't want to be sold a one-size-fits-all plan.

Many financial planners are doing right by their customers, I'm sure. The problem is there's no one government-sanctioned standard for the planning profession.

The government does oversee the actions of people trying to sell us stocks, bonds, and mutual funds. But there is no government-recognized set of criteria for the planners who dish out advice on such issues as tax or estate planning, buying insurance, budgeting, or retirement planning.

WHEN IS IT TIME TO HIRE A FINANCIAL PLANNER?

If you need to ask that question, it's probably time.

My husband and I found ourselves asking whether we needed to hire an expert to pore over every facet of our finances. We were unsure whether we had enough life insurance once our third child was born. We were setting aside money for our kids' college education, but was it enough? All indications suggested that we were on track with our retirement savings, but we worried that we hadn't put that money into the right mix of investment funds to meet our goal of retiring by the time we both are fifty-five.

Honestly, I wasn't thrilled about paying someone money to tell me what to do with my money. My grandmother wouldn't have approved of engaging the services of a financial planner. "Why pay somebody good money to do what you can do yourself?" Big Mama would have said.

How true that might have been in her day. But now most families are faced with a cornucopia of financial choices.

Think about it. We are told to get life insurance. But how much is the right amount? Should you get term or a cash-value policy? Should you get long-term-disability insurance? When do you need long-term-care insurance?

Got credit card bills? Should you pay them off with the cash in your savings account or with the money in your 401(k) plans?

Speaking of 401(k) plans, how should you invest the tax-deferred money? Do you know how much you will need in retirement? If you want to retire earlier than fifty-nine and a half, how can you make withdrawals from your qualified retirement plans without triggering a penalty? An individual retirement account or a Roth IRA—which is better for you?

Once you're saving for retirement, what's the best way to save for your kids' college education?

See what I mean?

Big Mama didn't have to worry about so many decisions. Her employer of twenty-five years provided her with a pension plan. She depended on her Social Security income to supplement her pension and whatever she had managed to save from her tiny salary. She had basic life-insurance policies to cover the cost of putting her in the ground. That was pretty much it.

I know it's possible to navigate all the financial choices out there on your own. But it might be time to call in a professional. It's like when your child gets an ear infection. By now I know all the signs— tugging at the ear, crankiness, slight fever. All I need is that pink medicine, and in a week or two my child will be fine. But parents can't prescribe the antibiotics that clear up ear infections. You have to take your child to see the doctor, which is as it should be. There could be something else wrong. You need to get an experienced, professional opinion, just in case.

It's the same with your finances. You may have an idea of what to do, but sometimes it's best to get a second, expert opinion. You don't want to find out that you can't retire at sixty-five because of uninformed or bad decisions made decades earlier.

So it might be time to hire a planner. According to the Certified Financial Planner Board of Standards, you might decide to seek help from a professional financial planner if

- You need expertise you don't possess in certain areas of your finances. For example, a planner can help you evaluate the level of risk in your investment portfolio or adjust your retirement plan as family circumstances change.

- You want a professional opinion about the financial plan you developed for yourself.

- You don't feel you have the time to do your own financial planning.

- You have an immediate need such as a birth or an unexpected event such as an inheritance or a lump-sum cash payment coming your way.

- You feel that a professional adviser could help you improve on how you are currently managing your finances.

- You know that you need to improve your current financial situation but don't know where to start.

Most important, if you decide to hire a planner, don't expect miracles. Financial planners aren't prophets. They can't predict the future. They can't and shouldn't guarantee that their advice will make you the millionaire next-door. What you should expect is someone who can help you achieve your financial goals.

PICKING A FINANCIAL PLANNER TAKES SOME, WELL, PLANNING

When searching for a financial planner, start by getting a referral from friends or family members, experts recommend.

That didn't help me much. In my family, the bank teller was the closest anybody ever got to a professional financial adviser. But even if you do know someone who can give a recommendation, that tip shouldn't mean bypassing your own fact checking. A planner who works well with a friend or a relative still might not be right for you. When my husband and I decided to hire a financial planner, we went with one from a well-known firm. We selected her large financial-services company for a couple of reasons. First, the firm has a lot of resources. For example, my planner works with a team of professionals, including a tax expert.

Second, the company subjects its planners to a thorough background check. Last, I felt that if the planner did anything illegal or unscrupulous, I had some recourse for legal action. It's not likely this financially healthy Fortune 500 company is going to go out of business.

Certainly, that doesn't mean you should opt for a brand-name firm. There are plenty of competent financial planners who are independent or who work for small companies.

Here are a couple of routes you can take to narrow your search for a financial planner:

- A number of financial companies and banks have added or expanded their financial-advisory services. Check your local telephone listings. But remember, big is not necessarily better. Just because planners have connections with a brand-name business doesn't mean they will give you first-class service. Investigate planners at large companies just as you would anybody else.

- Check with financial-planning organizations for referrals. Start with the Financial Planning Association, which steers people to planners that have obtained the certified financial planner (CFP) designation. The association can be reached at (800) 282-7526 or on the web at www.fpanet.org. Check with the National Association of Personal Financial Advisors at www.napfa.org or (800) 366-2732 for fee-only planners. Other groups to try: the National Association of Insurance and Financial Advisors, www.naifa.org, (877) 866-2432; the Coalition of Black Investors at www.cobinvest.com (but the coalition's list of referrals is limited); the International Association of Registered Financial Consultants, www.iarfc.org, (800) 532-9060; and the International Association of Qualified Planners, www.iaqf.org, (310) 277-3141.

- Look for credentials. The best known for the planning industry is the CFP stamp. Planners with that designation must meet specific educational and employment requirements and must agree to abide by a code of ethics. If your planner doesn't have that credential, it doesn't mean he or she isn't qualified. (My planner isn't a CFP.) The CFP designation is just another way to begin your search. Visit www.cfp-board.org or call (888) CFP-MARK to find out more about CFPs. Other credentials to look for: chartered financial consultant (ChFC) and certified public accountant (CPA) with a specialty designation as a personal financial specialist (PFS). Financial planners may have a variety of credentials. Some other common financial planning designations are:

CFP: Certified financial planner

CFS: Certified fund specialist

CLU: Chartered life underwriter

CMFC: Chartered mutual fund counselor

RFC: Registered financial consultant.

Note: All these designations are awarded by private organizations. While they can suggest that a planner has a certain amount of experience or training, none are required by any federal or state government or regulatory agency.

Most important, trust your gut. I did. A big part of my decision to hire my planner was the feeling I got when she sat down with my husband and me for that first, free consultation. We just clicked. She listened to us—for hours—talk about our family, our fears, and our financial and career goals. She laughed at my jokes. She was willing to come to my home for our meetings. She never got offended when I challenged her opinion about certain financial products. She was responsive and timely in sending any materials I asked for. And she wasn't afraid to admit when she didn't know something or was unsure.

For many of you, as it was for me, putting your faith and financial business in the hands of a professional planner can be a bit scary. In many respects you won't know how good a planner is until you begin to implement a recommended plan. That's why it's important to do your homework. Don't settle for the first planner you meet. Interview a few before making your choice. Come to the interview equipped with a long list of questions.

A good financial planner should help you get a clear picture of your financial situation and lay the foundation for future investment, tax, estate-planning, and insurance decisions.

"Of the people you talked to, ask yourself who explained the best what financial planning is all about," advised Guy Cumbie, national president of the Financial Planning Association. "Financial planning is very much about goal setting."

In that first meeting, the best financial advisers will focus on the planning process and not on a specific plan or product. Find a person who does that, and you will get your money's worth.

BIG MAMA'S FINAL WORDS OF WISDOM

Would you like a surefire way to have more money? Save. Then save some more.

Throughout this book I keep referring to my grandmother because her simple wisdom on how to achieve financial security started and ended with living within her means. Big Mama never even had a checking account. In her opinion, the only safe investment was a passbook savings account. Up to the day she died, she still carried a tattered red savings passbook held together by a rubber band.

"My money is good right here in the bank," Big Mama said. In fact, when my brother received an insurance settlement after a truck hit him when he was ten years old, Big Mama parked the money in a low-interest savings account. She never touched a penny of it until it was turned over to me to help take care of him more than seventeen years later. I never expected her to invest the money in the stock market, but even putting it in a CD or Treasury bill would have significantly increased the value of the settlement over the years.

I know better than anyone how hard it is to move beyond the conservative financial advice preached by my grandmother's generation. And don't get me wrong. I think you should and can. But your best investment plan should start with a savings plan. That is how you will thrive, not just survive, financially.

I wrote this book because I think a lot of people could use a Big Mama. Warren Buffett may be the grandfather and guru of investing, but my Big Mama was the grandmother of saving.

Big Mama paid off her home and her car notes early and saved enough money to live comfortably in retirement without ever buying a single share of stock or investing in a bond or real estate trust. Her savings rescued us from many financial disasters. In situations like the one I grew up in, the children usually become spendthrifts or savers. I chose the life of an ardent saver because I hated that my grandfather's drinking caused my grandmother—and me—to worry so much about money. When you're little and you watch the adults around you struggling financially, it can have a lifelong impact. I remember my grandmother sitting at our kitchen table counting out pennies to pay the phone bill. I remember having to reuse tea bags to make iced tea for my lunch to the point that it was just sugar water. I recall being teased for wearing "fish-head" sneakers because the toes of my discount athletic shoes had this rubber shape that looked like a fish head. I remember putting up the same silver artificial Christmas tree year after year. No matter how shabby it looked or how many branches became bare, Big Mama wouldn't spend the money to replace that tired-looking tree. But I understand why now. It wasn't a priority.

Look, this is much like the stuff substance-abuse counselors teach in any Twelve Step program. You need to get help, but you also have to stop immediately whatever you are doing that is causing your financial life to spin out of control. You can't say you want to save and invest and continue to pile debt onto your credit cards. You can't say you want to save for your child's college education and in the next breath say you can't possibly cancel cable or give up your cell phone. Just as alcoholics have to stop drinking the moment they realize they have a problem, you, too, have to stop your spendthrift ways.

At some point (preferably before you file for bankruptcy) you will have to take responsibility for the mismanagement of your money. You have to stop worrying about your debt and create wealth.

So, when will you stop making excuses for not saving or investing enough? I'll tell you.

Today.

Right now.

Stop spending and start saving.

Repeat to yourself: "If it's on your ass, it's not an asset."

"Is this a need or is it a want?"

"Sweat the small stuff."

"Cash is better than credit."

"Keep it simple."

"Priorities lead to prosperity."

"Enough is enough."

Through my grandmother's lessons about money, my fussing about your finances, and the seven money mantras, I hope I've inspired you to reevaluate your values and financial goals so you can have the life you want with the money you have.

Acknowledgments

—

Not long after I arrived at *The Washington Post,* the business section got a new assistant managing editor, David Ignatius. One day, David called me into his office to talk about my writing.

"You're a good reporter, but you need to find your voice," David said.

I didn't have a clue what this man was talking about. I thought he was insulting the way I spoke. My southern-born grandmother, Big Mama, raised me, so at times I did sound a little country.

Find my voice? Big Mama warned me about people who hear voices.

It wasn't until I wrote my first "Color of Money" column in 1997 that I understood what David meant.

He meant I needed to find a distinct and personal way to communicate with readers. Be your sassy self, he said. Tell them the same stories you amuse us with in the newsroom. Tell them about Big Mama, he urged.

I followed his advice. And I found my voice.

So, thank you, David, for creating the column that has given me a forum to dispense the commonsense lessons about money that I learned from Big Mama. Thank you for opening up a door that has led to so many wonderful opportunities for me.

Wiley Hall, former executive editor of the Afro-American Newspapers, you are the columnist I hope to become someday. When I sat down to write that first column, it was you who told me to TTT (Tell The Truth). I've been doing that ever since, and what do you know—

folks like it when you speak to them through your writing as if you were chatting with them at their kitchen table! You are such a dear and special friend, and your input and advice on the book, my career, and my columns have been priceless. I really couldn't have completed the book without your help.

In fact, I want to thank all the many people who have helped me in my journalism career. Thanks to the folks at the Baltimore Sunpapers, who created the full academic scholarship that allowed me to attend college and study journalism. Thanks to all my former *Evening Sun* colleagues, especially Liz Atwood, Larry Carson, Michael Fletcher, William Hawkins, Jack Lemon, Patricia Fanning, Jon Morgan, James Keat, and Wayne Hardin. The *Evening Sun* was an incredibly supportive place to work, and I always felt as though the entire staff was rooting for my success from the moment I stepped into the newsroom at age seventeen.

David Vise and Peter Behr, thank you for hiring me at *The Washington Post*. I also want to thank the many editors, reporters, copy editors, researchers, computer technicians, and support staff at the *Post* (current and former) who have encouraged me, helped me, constructively criticized me, and caught errors that would have otherwise made me look like a fool. There has not been one day that I've regretted coming to the *Post,* and it's because of you.

Jill Dutt, thanks for letting me create my "Color of Money" media franchise. It's not often one finds a boss who allows the kind of freedom you have given me. I appreciate your advice and supervision.

To Shirley Carswell, the *Post*'s assistant managing editor for planning and administration. Your friendship and professional backing has meant a great deal to me. And thanks to my career godfather, Milton Coleman, deputy managing editor at the *Post*. You showed me how to go after what I want. Fred Barbash, you taught me to strive for excellence and relax while I was doing it. Thanks also to Jody Schneider, Nancy McKeon, Jim Hill, Alan Shearer, Chris White, and Karen Green. All of you have helped me become a better columnist.

Raymond Lee, you are a gem. Your assistance has been so incredible.

And what's an author without a good agent? A writer with a book idea and no deal, that's what. So, thank you so very much, Richard Abate, my literary agent at International Creative Management. You believed that I could write this book even before I did.

To Katie Hall, my former editor at Random House. Thanks for your initial input and suggestions.

When I found out that my new editor would be Jonathan Karp, vice president and editorial director at Random House, I was both elated and scared to death. After all, the man edited Mario Puzo. How could I measure up to the caliber of writers he has edited? But Jonathan, you have made me feel as though I were the Godmother of Personal Finance. Your praise has meant a lot to me.

To my friends, you all keep me "real," and for that I'm eternally grateful. To my best friends, Terri Ames, Stefanie Cargill, Alexa Steele, Cassandra Waldon, Monica Norton, Angela Davis, Andrea Moore, and Venita Crawford. Thanks for celebrating my successes, letting me vent, holding me up when I've wanted to quit, and coming to my rescue when life happens. Thanks, girls, for always having my back.

To Lenore Riley, my mother. I know that you love me and I will always love you.

To my wonderful and supportive siblings and in-laws Monique Reynolds, Michael Singletary, Kim Singletary, Matwia Singletary, April Riley, Ross Riley, Edmond McIntyre, Vernon McIntyre, Ronald McIntyre, Karen McIntyre, Charles McIntyre, Thelma and Roscoe Martin, and my entire extended family. I love and cherish you.

To my church home, First Baptist Church of Glenarden, and my pastor, John K. Jenkins, Sr. You push me to be a better Christian and member of the community. Pastor Jenkins, you continue to make me mindful of what God says about putting Him first. I thank God for your spiritual guidance. I thank God for all that I have.

Godmother Lois Thompson and family, thank you for always being there for me.

To my dear three children, Olivia, Kevin, and Jillian, thank you for being so sweet and loving. All that I do, I do for you and so that you can have a wonderful life (without debt). Thank you for allowing Mommy to spend weekends and evenings away from you so that I could write this book.

And for all those who have helped me but whom I forgot to mention, please forgive me. Consider it a mistake of my head, not my heart.

Finally, I want to give honor to my husband, Kevin McIntyre. Baby, you have been the rock that has made my life secure. You taught me how to be happy. You let me know that it was okay to enjoy the money I make and not be afraid to spend a little. You have stood back and let me shine, and I am grateful for that. Your patience and kindness have made me all that I am. I thank God for giving me the good sense to marry you. I love you. Big Mama was right when she said, "Girl, you have found a good man. Always treat him right." I hope I have.

Index

———

AARP (American Association of Retired Persons), 199
adjustable life insurance, 184
adjusted balance, 78
adult children:
  of aging parents, 148–50
  returning home, 134, 138–41
advertising, 8–11
  of credit cards, 32, 76
  needs vs. wants, 16
  suggestions for avoiding, 9–11
aging:
  and disability, 145
  and finances, 148–50
  long-term-care insurance, 186–95
agreements, written, 140–41
Alliance for Investor Education, 220
allowance, to children, 163–67
American Bar Association, 87
appreciating assets, 4
APR (annual percentage rate), 77
assets, 3–11
  appreciating, 4
  consuming, 6–11
  debt-to-income ratio, 5–6
  definition, 3
  depreciating, 4–5
  diversification, 222–23
  going into debt to acquire, 71–72
  goodwill, 207
  investment, 4
  liquid, 4
  and net worth, 6, 16
  personal property, 4–5, 6

  protection of, 190
  real property, 4
ATM bank cards, 115–16
ATM fees, 24, 110–13
average daily balance, 78

bankruptcy, 27, 31, 71
  and credit cards, 75–76
  in credit history, 80, 81
  and medical bills, 172
banks:
  ATM fees, 24, 110–13
  bounced-check fees of, 109–10
  CDs, 121–22, 221, 227
  check-clearing practices of, 109–10
  debit cards, 114–16, 217
  financial advisors in, 244
  and identity theft, 217
  information sources, 220
  interchange fees, 114
  joint accounts, 142, 154–55
  money-market deposit accounts, 122, 193, 221
  PINs, 114, 212–13, 214
  savings accounts, 121, 221, 227
bear market, 227
beneficiaries, 202
Big Mama:
  aging, 148, 149
  on cosigning, 94, 95
  and disabled grandchild, 141, 146
  estate of, 199
  funeral arrangements made by, 195–96, 197, 198

Big Mama (*cont.*):
  grown children living with, 130,
    139
  and living expenses, 131
  mortgage debt of, 100
  savings of, ix–xiv, 121, 246–48
birthdays, costs of, 169–70
bond funds, 224
bounced-check fees, 109–10
budgeting, 134, 135–38
  defined, 68
  for disabled sibling, 144, 147
  for holidays, 17–19, 61, 64, 65
  tips, 137–38
  unmarried partners, 155
bulk e-mail scam, 210
bull market, 227
business-opportunity scams, 209–10

cable-descrambler kits (scam), 211
car insurance, 57, 174
car payments, 57, 102–3
cars, 101–8
  budgeting for, 135
  leasing, 104–8
  new, 101–3, 105
  safety recalls on, 104
  trade-ins, 103
  used, 103–5
  websites, 103
cash advances, 77
cash cushion, 99, 100, 219, 222
cash distribution, 233
cash value insurance policy, 181
cash vs. credit, 26–32
CCC (credit card craziness), 26
CDs (certificates of deposit), 121–22,
    221, 227
CFP (certified financial planner),
    244–45
chain e-mails, 210
change, saving, 58
charitable giving, 67–70
  budgeting for, 68, 70
  frauds and, 69
  fund-raising costs and, 68
  guidelines for, 68–69
  school fund-raising, 69

checkbook:
  rounding up amounts in, 55
  stolen, 217
check cards, 114–16
checking accounts, 109–10
ChFC (chartered financial consultant),
    245
children, 161–70
  of aging parents, 148–50
  allowance to, 163–67
  as beneficiaries, 202
  birthday bills of, 169–70
  chores of, 165, 167–69
  disabled, 144–48
  giving away toys, 170
  and life insurance, 179–80
  returning home, 134, 138–41
  savings of, 165
  saying no to, 11
  scams targeted at, 213
  setting an example for, 162–63,
    164–65
  teaching responsibility to, 161–62,
    164
  and wills, 199–201
cleaning house, 11
CMFC (chartered mutual fund consul-
    tant), 245
COBRA (Consolidated Omnibus Bud-
    get Reconciliation Act), 172, 194
collection agencies, 81
college:
  costs of, 23, 24, 235
  529 plans, 236–39
  as priority, 101
  savings for, 40, 165, 233–39
  student-loan debt from, 138, 233–39
college students, credit cards of, 28–31,
    138
compound interest, 124, 206, 220
Consumer Credit Protection Act, 92
consumer-protection office, 213
Consumer Response Center, 87
consuming, 6–11
  advertising and, 8–11
  avoiding temptation and, 8
  credit card debt, 27–28, 72–79
  credit card statements, 9, 19

definition, 7
needs vs. wants, 12–20, 42
personal property and, 6
priorities in, 36–39
reasons why, 9
shopping and, 7–8
spending journal of, 9
time-out from, 9
convertible insurance policies, 182
cosigning, 94–96, 140, 144, 152–53
CPA (certified public accountant), 245
credit:
  available, 77
  and cosigning, 94–96, 140, 152
  cost of, 74–79
  denial of, 81
  establishing, 29
  and FICO scores, 88–94
  home-equity line of, 194
  as other people's money, 32
credit bureaus, 81, 86–87
credit card debt, 27–28, 30, 72–79, 82
credit card premium, 27, 73–74
credit cards, 26–32
  advertising of, 32, 76
  APR on, 77
  available credit, 77
  and bankruptcy, 75–76
  budgeting for, 137–38
  cash advance on, 77
  cold turkey with, 10
  for college students, 28–31, 138
  credit limit on, 77, 94
  in credit reports, 80, 81
  giving out your numbers, 212–13
  grace period, 77
  and identity theft, 216
  interest rates on, 26, 27, 76, 78, 79,
    82, 138
  late-payment charges on, 77, 78–79,
    81, 82, 138
  loans with, 10, 78–79
  minimum payment on, 77, 79, 193
  needs vs. wants, 13, 19–20
  prices for cash vs., 27, 73–74
  putting a hold on, 72–73
  scams, 209, 211–12
  shifting usage of, 13

statements, 9, 19
teens and, 27–31, 138
theft of, 115, 216, 217
unauthorized charges on, 209, 216
for unmarried partners, 152
credit-counseling agencies, 82–85
credit history, 30–31, 79–82
credit limit, 77, 94
credit-repair scams, 212
credit report, 79–82
  annual review of, 82, 87
  consolidated, 81
  correcting, 85–94
  dispute letter, 88
  FICO score, 88–94
  fraudulent information on, 81
  getting a copy of, 80–81
  and identity theft, 217
  reinvestigation of, 87
  removal of information from, 81
  of unmarried partners, 153–56
  updating of, 93–94
credit score, 88–94
croutons, 53–54
currency, scrip, 72

deadbeat, defined, 31, 126
death:
  estate planning, 201–6
  funerals, 195–99
  life insurance, 178–86
  revocable or living trust, 200–201
  wills, 199–201
debit cards, 114–16, 217
debt, 71–108
  bankruptcy, 27, 31, 71, 75–76
  car purchase, 101–8
  consolidation plans, 82–83
  cosigning, 94–96, 140, 144, 152–53
  cost of credit, 74–79
  credit card, 27–28, 30, 72–79, 82
  credit-counseling agencies, 82–85
  credit history, 79–82
  credit report, fixing, 85–94
  good, 71–72
  home purchase, 96–100
  management of, 30, 82–85, 219
  mortgage, 28, 97, 99, 100–101

debt (*cont.*)
  scrip, 72
  student loans, 138, 233–39
  of unmarried partners, 154
Debtors Anonymous, 85
debt-to-income ratio, 5–6
decreasing term insurance, 182
deferred-debit cards, 116
depreciating assets, 4–5
diet and health scams, 211
direct-debit cards, 115
disability, 141–44
  demographics of, 145
  government benefits for, 146
  guidelines for dealing with, 142–43
  housing needs for, 146
  insurance, 173–74
  Internet sites, 147–48
  nonprofit organizations and, 142–43,
    144, 146, 148
  planning for the future with, 144–48
  tips, 144
discretionary income, 8
discretionary spending, 27
disposable income, 38
diversification, 222–23
DMP (debt management plans), 82–85
documents, location of, 203, 204–6
dollar-cost averaging, 230
durable power of attorney, 144, 201

easy-money scams, 211
eating out, cutting down on, 22–23
e-mail scams, 210
emergency fund, 99, 100, 219, 222
engagement ring, 159
enough is enough, 40–44
estate planning, 201–6
  beneficiaries named, 202
  document storage, 203, 204–6
  and insurance, 201–2
  letter of instruction, 204–5
  and taxes, 202–3
  updating records, 203
  wills, 199–201, 203
executor (of will), 201
expense ratio, 226, 240
expenses, cutting, 194–95

Fair Credit Reporting Act, 85
Fair Isaac and Company (FICO), 88–94
family members:
  adult, returning home, 134, 138–41
  budgeting, 134, 135–38
  disabled, 141–44
  extended, living with, 131, 132–33
  loans to, 125–29
Fannie Mae, 100
Federal Reserve Bank of Dallas, 220
Federal Trade Commission:
  credit bureau complaints to, 87
  on funerals, 199
  identity-theft hotline, 217–18
FICO scores, 88–94
55–Alive Mature Driving Course, 57
finance charges, 78–79
financial crisis, preparing for, 206
financial planners, 241–46
  credentials of, 244, 245
  first (free) consultation with, 245–46
  picking, 244–46
  when to hire, 242–44
financial pyramid, 219
financial security, 208, 219
529 plans, 236–39
fixed interest rate, 78
food, money-saving ideas, 50, 57
401(k) contributions, 193, 219, 228–30
fraud security alert, 217
Freddie Mac, 100
free items, scams, 211, 213
fund-raising, school, 69
funeral arrangements, 195–99
  Consumer Reports on, 198
  misconceptions about, 196–97
  prepaying, 197–99

get-out-of-debt plans, 82–85
gifts:
  acceptance of, 62
  birthday, 169–70
  charitable, 67–70
  choosing, 62–64
  criteria for, 62
  defined, 61
  designating, 64
  giving all you can, 64–66

graduation, 63–64
holiday spending, 17–19, 61
  ideas for, 18, 61–62
  loans vs., 128–29
  obligation to give, 63–64, 65–66
  price limits on, 170
  recycling, 48, 60–62
  reusing wrapping paper for, 48
  of toys, 170
  wedding, 63–64, 66–67
good debt, 71–72
goodwill, 206–7
grace period, 77
graduation gifts, 63–64
greeting cards, 24–25, 55
gross pay, 5, 118
Guide to Health Plans (Consumers'
  Checkbook), 176

health and diet scams, 211
health insurance, 171–72, 175–78
  and COBRA, 172, 194
  and HMOs, 176
  and hospitalization, 177
  limitations and exclusions in, 177–78
  long-term-care, 174–75, 186–95
  primary-care physicians, 176–77
  referrals to specialists, 177
  and unemployment, 194
heart currency, 151–60; *see also* relationships
holidays:
  budgeting for, 17–19, 61, 64, 65
  giving all you can for, 64–66
  recycling gifts for, 48, 60–62
  and relationships, 158–59
  spending for, 17–19, 31, 61
  see also gifts
home-equity line of credit, 194
home owner's insurance, 173
home purchase, 96–100
  cash cushion for, 99
  down payment on, 96
  education about, 100
  expenses in, 98
  guidelines, 99–100
  mortgage debt on, 28, 97, 99,
    100–101

rent vs. purchase, 181
  ten-year rule for, 99
hospitalization, 177
housing:
  for aging parents, 150
  in budget, 135
  for disabled persons, 146
  see also home purchase
Hundred-Dollar Holiday, 17–19, 47

identity theft, 215–18
income:
  in budget, 135
  debt-to-income ratio, 5–6
  discretionary, 8
  disposable, 38
  gross pay, 5, 118
  and life insurance, 179–80
  net pay, 118
  paychecks and deductions, 116–18
  real hourly wage, 42–43
  Social Security, 39
  tax refunds, 118–21
  and unemployment, 193
increasing term insurance, 182
inflation, 123–24, 187–88, 227
insurance, 171–95
  for aging parents, 150
  car, 57, 174
  credit card, 209
  deductible of, 173
  and estate planning, 201–2
  health, 171–72, 175–78
  home owner's, 173
  life, 144, 178–86
  long-term care, 174–75, 186–95
  long-term disability, 173–74
  protecting assets with, 190
  rating services, 192
  renter's, 173
interchange fees, 114
interest rates:
  APR, 77
  compounding, 124, 206, 220
  on credit cards, 26, 27, 76, 78, 79,
    82, 138
  FICO scores and, 89–92
investment assets, 4

investments:
  bear and bull markets, 227
  cash distribution of, 233
  CDs, 121–22, 221, 227
  diversification, 222–23
  dollar-cost averaging, 230
  401(k) plans, 228–30
  getting started, 220–23
  inflation and, 123–24
  information sources, 220, 221–22
  IRAs, 233
  money-market deposit accounts,
    122–23, 193, 221
  money-market mutual funds, 123,
    221, 224
  mutual funds, 221, 223–28
  prime-bank scams, 34–35
  rating services, 192
  in retirement plans, 222, 231–33
  risk-free, 121
  risk tolerance, 220–21, 222
  and savings, 121–24
  scams, 211, 213
  SEC, 220, 231
  socially responsible funds, 239–41
  Treasury bonds, 123
IRAs (individual retirement accounts),
    233
IRS (Internal Revenue Service), 119

joint bank accounts, 142, 154–55
journal, spending, 9

land and property, 4
late fees, 77, 78–79, 81, 82, 138
lawyer-referral programs, 87
layoff, 193–95, 229
leasing a car, 104–8
letter of instruction, 204–5
level term insurance, 182
life and death, 171–207
  document storage, 203, 204–6
  estate planning, 201–6
  funerals, 195–99
  goodwill, 206–7
  insurance, 171–95
  wills, 199–201

life expectancy, 145–46, 229
life insurance, 144, 178–86
  on children, 179–80
  convertible, 182
  cutting back, 180
  and dependents, 179–80
  how much to buy, 185
  information sources, 185, 186
  low-load, 186
  for married person, 180
  permanent, 181, 183–86
  questions about, 185–86
  for single person, 179–80
  for stay-at-home parent, 180
  and taxes, 202
  term, 178–79, 181–83
  VUL, 184–85
lifetime limit, 177–78
liquid assets, 4
live-in agreement, 131, 132–33
living trust, 200–201
living will, 201
loans, 125–50
  cosigning, 94–96, 140, 144
  credit card use as, 10, 78–79
  expectations of repayment, 126, 128
  and FICO scores, 88–94
  gifts vs., 128–29
  guaranteed (scam), 211–12
  guidelines, 126
  home-equity line of credit, 194
  and identity theft, 217
  mortgage, 28, 97, 99, 100–101
  sample agreement form, 127–28
  student, 138, 233–39
long-distance calls, cutting, 22
long-term-care insurance, 174–75,
    186–95
  asset protection, 190
  benefit period, 188
  claim payment, 189
  coverage, 187
  elimination period, 188
  inflation protection, 187–88
  portability, 189
  sources, 187
  when not needed, 189

long-term-disability insurance, 173–74
lunch, cutting out, 22

Mantra #1: assets, 3–11
Mantra #2: needs vs. wants, 12–20
Mantra #3: small stuff, 21–25
Mantra #4: cash vs. credit, 26–32
Mantra #5: simplicity, 33–35
Mantra #6: priorities, 36–39
Mantra #7: enough, 40–44
marriage and money, 156–58
Medicaid, 189, 190
Medicare tax, 117
minimum payment, 77, 79, 193
money-market deposit accounts,
    122–23, 193, 221
money-market mutual funds, 123, 221,
    224
mortgage debt, 28, 97, 99, 100–101
mutual funds, 123, 221, 223–28
    analyzing, 231
    buying and selling, 225
    credentials in, 245
    distributions, 225
    expense ratios of, 226, 240
    government backing of, 226
    inflation and, 227
    information sources, 227–28
    marketing of, 230–31
    operating expenses of, 226–27, 231
    performance of, 230–31
    picking, 224–26
    services, 225–26
    types of, 224
    what they are, 223–24
Myvesta, 84–85

National Foundation for Credit Coun-
    seling, 84
National Funeral Directors Association,
    199
needs vs. wants, 12–20, 42, 71
nest egg, 219–48
net pay, 118
net worth, 6, 16
no, saying, 11, 40–44
NSF (nonsufficient funds), 109–10

off-line debit cards, 116
ordinary life insurance, 183

paper, recycling, 48, 51, 52, 55
partners, unmarried, *see* relationships
pay, gross monthly, 5
paychecks, 116–18
penny-pinching, 47–60
    adding water, 50
    appliances, 54
    breast-feeding, 48
    car insurance, 57
    car payments, 57
    cereal, 53
    checkbook, 55
    contest, 49, 59–60
    croutons, 53–54
    doggie bags, 48
    fast food, 57
    gifts, 60–70
    greeting cards, 55
    half-smoked cigars, 50
    Hundred-Dollar Holiday, 47
    lemonade, 54
    long-distance calls, 55
    movies, 53
    overripe fruit, 50
    panty hose, 53
    pay phone, 49
    penny jar, 58
    popcorn packaging, 58
    rationing toothpaste, 52
    recycling, 48, 50–58, 60–62
    saving water, 51
    shower caps, 57–58
    solar cooking, 49–50
    store receipts, 58
    toilet paper, 52–53
    toner cartridges, 57
penny-wise, pound-foolish, 59–60
permanent life insurance, 181, 183–86
personal property, 4–5, 6
photos, recycling, 56
PINs, 114, 212–13, 214
POS (point-of-sale) terminals, 114–15
pour-over will, 201
poverty, and disability, 145

power of attorney, durable, 144, 201
premarital counseling, 153–56
prepaid funeral arrangements, 197–99
price adjustments, 58
primary-care physicians, 176–77
prime-bank scams, 34–35
priorities, 36–39, 44, 154
prize promotion scams, 212
property:
  personal, 4–5, 6
  real, 4
  see also assets
purse, stolen, 215–18

rating services, 192
real hourly wage, 42–43
real property, 4
receipts, keeping, 58
records:
  location of, 203, 204–6
  updating, 203
recycling:
  bread as croutons, 53–54
  calendar photos, 56
  CD-ROMs as coasters, 53
  cereal boxes, 53
  dryer sheets, 56
  envelopes, 51
  gifts, 48, 60–62
  greeting cards, 55
  grocery bags, 54–55
  half-smoked cigars, 50
  kitty litter, 56
  magazines, 56
  overripe fruit as slurpees, 54
  panty hose, 53
  paper, 48, 51, 52
  postage stamps, 50–51
  potholders, 50
  shower caps, 57–58
  shower curtain, 51
  water, 51
regifting, 60–62
relationships, 151–60
  budgeting, 155
  and cosigning, 152–53
  and credit-card charges, 152
  and credit reports, 153–56

different priorities in, 154
engagement rings, 159
equality in, 159
financial goals for, 155
joint accounts, 154–55
legal documents for, 152
marriage and money, 156–58
myths of, 158–60
negotiation in, 156
premarital counseling, 153–56
and retirement, 160
spending limits in, 155–56
unmarried partners, 152
and Valentine's Day, 158–59
renewable term insurance, 182
rent, 130–31, 134, 140, 181
rental form, 131, 132–33
renter's insurance, 173
retirement:
  401(k) plans, 228–30
  investment plans, 222, 231–33
  IRAs, 233
  and life expectancy, 229
  and marriage, 160
  roll-over of, 232–33
  savings for, 39, 59–60, 193, 219–20
  tax-deferred accounts for, 101,
    219–20, 231–33
revocable or living trust, 200–201
RFC (registered financial consultant),
  245
risk, tolerance for, 220–21, 222
robbery, 214–18
roll-overs, of retirement funds, 202–3,
  232–33

savings, 121–24, 206, 219–48
  adding up, 22–23
  bank accounts, 121, 221, 227
  Big Mama's advice on, 246–48
  budgeting for, 134, 135
  cash reserve, 222
  CDs, 121–22, 221, 227
  of children, 165
  for college, 40, 165, 233–39
  dollar a day, 21
  529 plans, 236–39
  for funerals, 199

inflation and, 123–24
and investment, *see* investments
joint accounts, 142, 154–55
mortgage debt and, 99
paying yourself first, 137
for retirement, 39, 59–60, 193, 219–20
sponsor for, 10
tax-deferred plans, 219–20, 231–33
and unemployment, 193
saving sponsor, 10
saying no, 11, 40–44
scams, 208–18
  bulk e-mail, 210
  business opportunity, 209–10
  cable-descrambler kits, 211
  chain e-mail, 210
  children as targets of, 213
  consumer protection, 213
  credit card protection, 209
  credit repair, 212
  easy-money, 211
  free items, 211, 213
  guaranteed loans or credit cards, 211–12
  health and diet, 211
  investment, 211, 213
  prime bank, 34–35
  protecting your numbers, 212–13, 214–15
  theft, 214–18
  unsolicited telephone calls, 212, 213
  vacation prizes, 212
  work-at-home schemes, 210–11
school fund-raising projects, 69
scrip currency, 72
SEC (Securities and Exchange Commission), 220, 231
secret password, 217
service scams, 213
severance benefits, 194
shopping, 7–8
  advertising hype and, 8–11
  ask why, 9
  avoiding temptation, 8
  bargain, 74
  and cleaning house, 11
  with credit cards, 9, 10

journal of, 9
  needs vs. wants, 13–14, 16
  saving sponsor vs., 10
  saying no to, 11
  secondhand, 25
  with spendthrift friends, 10–11
  time-out from, 9
  two-year throw-away rule, 11
  as waste of time, 59
sibling, disabled, 141–44
simplicity, 33–35
smoking, quitting, 23
socially responsible investment funds, 239–41
Social Security, 39, 160
Social Security tax, 118
specialists, referrals to, 177
spending:
  and bankruptcy, 27, 31, 75–76
  budgeting for, 137
  with credit cards vs. cash, 27, 73–74
  discretionary, 27
  examining, 15–16
  holiday, 17–19, 31, 61
  keeping a journal of, 9
  as measure of one's love, 158–59
  needs vs. wants, 15–16
  other people's opinions on, 14
  priorities in, 36–39
  saying no to, 11
  small, 21–25
  thinking first before, 9, 59
  of unmarried partners, 155–56
  see also shopping
spendthrift friends, avoiding, 10–11
stock funds, 224
stock market, 227
student-loan debt, 138, 233–39
Supplemental Security Income (SSI), 147
swindles, *see* scams

tax-deferred accounts, 101, 202–3, 219–20, 231–33
taxes:
  and estate planning, 202–3
  paycheck and, 116–18
tax liens, 81
tax refunds, 118–21

telephone:
  charges for use of, 49
  hanging up, 213
  and identity theft, 216–17
  long-distance calls, 22, 55
  unsolicited calls, 212, 213
temptation, avoiding, 8
ten-year rule, 99
term life insurance, 178–79, 181–83
theft, 115, 214–18
TIAA-CREF Social Choice Equity
  Fund, 240
tiered interest rate, 78
time:
  long-distance calls, 55
  shopping as waste of, 59
  value of, 43, 44
tobacco products, cutting out, 23
travel scams, 212
Treasury bonds, 123
two-cycle average daily balance, 78
two-year throw-away rule, 11

unauthorized charges, 209, 216
unemployment, 193–95, 229
universal life insurance, 184–85
unmarried partners, *see* relationships
unsolicited phone calls, 212, 213
used cars, 103–5
utility services, and identity theft,
  216–17

vacation-prize promotion scams, 212
Valentine's Day, 158–59
values, 36–39, 41–42, 44
Vanguard Calvert Social Index Fund,
  240
variable interest rate, 78
variable life insurance, 184–85
VUL (variable-universal life) insurance,
  184–85

W-4 Employee's Withholding Allowance
  Certificate, 116–18, 119,
  120–21
wage, real hourly, 42–43
wallet, stolen, 215–18
wants vs. needs, 12–20, 71
wealth creation, 6
wedding gifts, 63–64, 66–67
whole life insurance, 181, 183–86
wills, 199–201
  and disabled sibling, 144
  and estate planning, 203
  executor of, 201
  letter of instruction, 204–5
  living, 201
  pour-over, 201
withholding taxes, 116–18, 119,
  120–21, 193
work, layoff from, 193–95, 229
work-at-home schemes, 210–11
written agreements, 140–41

About the Author

—

MICHELLE SINGLETARY's *Washington Post* column, "The Color of Money," is syndicated in more than 120 newspapers across the country. She has appeared on MSNBC, CNBC, NPR, *Nightline, The Oprah Winfrey Show, The View,* and *The Diane Rehm Show.* She has also advised National Football League rookies on personal finance. Singletary is a graduate of the University of Maryland and has a master's of business from the Johns Hopkins University. For more than fifteen years, Singletary has covered business and personal finance, first for the *Baltimore Evening Sun* and then for *The Washington Post.* She lives in Maryland with her husband and three children.

About the Type

—

This book was set in Garamond, a typeface originally designed by the Parisian typecutter Claude Garamond (1480–1561). This version of Garamond was modeled on a 1592 specimen sheet from the Egenolff-Berner foundry, which was produced from types assumed to have been brought to Frankfurt by the punchcutter Jacques Sabon.

Claude Garamond's distinguished romans and italics first appeared in *Opera Ciceronis* in 1543–44. The Garamond types are clear, open, and elegant.